A History of Butô

A History of Butô

Bruce Baird

OXFORD

UNIVERSITY PRESS

OXFORD
UNIVERSITY PRESS

Oxford University Press is a department of the University of Oxford. It furthers
the University's objective of excellence in research, scholarship, and education
by publishing worldwide. Oxford is a registered trade mark of Oxford University
Press in the UK and certain other countries.

Published in the United States of America by Oxford University Press
198 Madison Avenue, New York, NY 10016, United States of America.

Library of Congress Control Number: 2021052046

ISBN 978-0-19-763028-0 (pbk.)
ISBN 978-0-19-763027-3 (hbk.)

DOI: 10.1093/oso/9780197630273.001.0001

1 3 5 7 9 8 6 4 2

Paperback printed by Marquis, Canada
Hardback printed by Bridgeport National Bindery, Inc., United States of America

For Axel, Beckett, and Jeanne

Betsy and Jim Baird

And in memory of Sari Kawana

Contents

Illustrations

Acknowledgments

Most of you will not know many of the people I am acknowledging, so it might make sense for you to skip the acknowledgments, and maybe I should too. But, in a nutshell, the argument of this book is that butô artists reacted in complex ways within and against a world in which a constellation of utility, language, narrowly defined rationalities,* technology, and Westernness threatened to push aside or even obliterate nonlanguage, different rationalities, the body, and non-Western cultures, practices, and histories. Given that broader argument, I *want* to recognize the people, choreographies, other languages, nonlanguages, and non-Westernness that contributed to this book, along with many of the people closer to my own mountain west US upbringing that were also important. And I hope you, the reader, will linger here for a moment as well.

The following dancer/choreographers danced on and off stage, conducted workshops, freely granted interviews, and spent time regaling me with tales over drinks after performances: Kobayashi Saga, Waguri Yukio, Maro Akaji, Murobushi Kô, Kasai Akira, Nakajima Natsu, Seisaku, Nagaoka Yuri, SU-EN, Yoshioka Yumiko, Kaseki Yuko, Shinichi Iova-Koga, Ishimoto Kae, Kawaguchi Takao, Omori Masahide, Tamano Hiroko, Mikami Kayo, Joan Laage, Ximena Garnica, Eugenia Vargas, Aura Gomez Arreola, Teresa Carlos, Natalia Cuellar, Raimundo Estay, Maria Belen Espinosa, and Vangeline. Morishita Takashi and Homma Yu, archivists at Keio University Arts Center, have possibly done more than anybody else to contribute to my scholarship over the years. Critics, scholars, and producers such as Inata Naomi, Kuniyoshi Kazuko, Shiga Nobuo, Takeshige Shinichi, Shinfune Yoko, Mizohata Toshio, Minami Shôkichi, and Nakase Shunsuke talked with me, facilitated interviews, gave me access to archives, arranged for photo permissions, and even comped me an occasional ticket to see a show.

When I started studying butô, there were not so many of us, but over time, we have grown quite a group of scholars. Recently, I coedited a volume of butô criticism and we were delighted to feature fifty-five essays about all aspects of butô (go read the book now!—The essays are fantastic, if I do say so myself), and then I helped co-organize a conference to push the study of butô even further along. That conference featured thirty more presentations. All that scholarship has changed the way I think about butô immensely. I won't list all the contributors here, but I will single out a special group of friends who have formed the nucleus of our studies and been crucial parts of organizing panels and conferences since 2010: Rosemary Candelario, Tanya Calamoneri, Megan Nicely, Michael Sakamoto, Peter Eckersall, Bill Marotti, Zack Fuller, Katherine Mezur, and Christine Greiner. (Some of these folks are also wonderful performers, and I hope they won't be too miffed that I listed them here and not in the performer category.)

Namiko Kunimoto, Anne McKnight, Emily Wilcox, Rosemary Candelario, Bill Marotti, Megan Nicely, SU-EN, and Tanya Calamoneri read drafts of chapters (or the entire manuscript) and made generous comments. At UMass, Amanda Seaman, Kathryn Lachman, Yuki Yoshimura, Steve Forrest, Stephen Miller, Yasuko Shiomi, Reiko Sono, and Mako Koyama have been wonderful colleagues, and always willing to help out with a thorny passage of surrealist Japanese or with a deliciously cooked meal. Mike Foldy of the UMass Digital Scholarship Center cleaned up a lot of the photos and made them presentable. My PhD advisors Linda Chance and Ayako Kano have continued to serve as wonderful mentors long after you would think I did not need such a thing anymore. At Oxford University Press, Norm Hirschy asked for this manuscript right when I was finishing my first book, and he has been a pleasure to deal with at every step of the way. Lauralee Yeary has kept me on track and made sure I jumped through all the hoops. Nirenjena S, Ashita Shah, and Haripriya Ravichandran of Newgen oversaw the production of the book including copy editing. A Fulbright Fellowship funded a year of research for this book in Tokyo, and the College of Humanities and Fine Arts at UMass has funded my research on a yearly basis. Cecile Sakai hosted me at Paris Diderot University (Paris 7—now University of Paris) while I dug into the French reception of butô.

Paradoxically, the end of the acknowledgments usually has the most important thanks. Here as well, massive thanks to Axel, Beckett, and Jeanne for all of the ups, downs, and wonder of daily life. And not to brag too much, but special kudos to Jeanne for getting the Fulbright that took us to Paris, and to the Beckett and Axel for persevering through two new languages in sequence. I like to think they will thank us for it someday if they end up trilingual.

1
Prologue and Introduction

Prologue: We'll Always Have Paris

We begin in the middle. Paris. Late fall 1977. Three Japanese avant-garde dancers, Murobushi Kô, Carlotta Ikeda (Ikeda Sanae), and Hanaoka Mizelle (Yoshioka Yumiko) arrived in Paris, but not to present an avant-garde dance. Rather they aimed to audition a burlesque show at the cabaret Le Jardin Champs-Élysées. If this were a movie, we would show the three approaching the cabaret and then pan to show the nearby Eiffel Tower. Do not be fooled, though. Their goal was to use the cabaret as a foot-in-the-door, with the hope of performing their experimental dance. Alas, their burlesque show did not appeal to the promoters. It was just too strange. They tried the Crazy Horse Saloon and Folies Bergères, but their show was not only too bizarre but also much too small for such venues. At this point, they gave up, their hopes of establishing a foothold in France dashed. Yoshioka reached out to her mother (a high-end cabaret producer in Japan), and she arranged a job for them in Tehran.

Murobushi, Ikeda, and Yoshioka literally went to the airport with all their luggage to fly to Tehran, but no one was there to give them tickets. They eventually found out that the deal had fallen through. For a moment, our story takes on shades of an international espionage thriller. They went back to Paris and burgled their way back into their borrowed apartment through the window.[1] From the account of those strangers in a strange land breaking and entering into their rented apartment after being jilted twice over, one would hardly imagine that forty years later, a Japanese theater expert would proclaim about their brand of avant-garde dance: "Undoubtedly, modern Japanese theater's greatest legacy to the world is *butô*" (Poulton 2014, 320). Fortunately for them and all of us, things turned out differently due to that failed deal and the aborted trip to Tehran.

Perhaps out of pity or out of desperation to get them out of the borrowed pad, their producer, Martine Matyas, proposed that they do an avant-garde show at the Nouveau Carré Silvia Monfort Theater. They spent the rest of December and all of January creating and rehearsing for an original performance. They repurposed choreography from two prior performances and some of the costumes and props from the cabaret show. They had their senior colleague Maro Akaji (of Dairakudakan) send them other props and costumes. The show was titled *The Last Eden: Gate to the Beyond* (Le dernier Eden: Porte de l'au-dela). It premiered on January 27, 1978, at the unlikely time of 10:30 pm after the main events of the day were finished.

A History of Butô. Bruce Baird, Oxford University Press. © Oxford University Press 2022.
DOI: 10.1093/oso/9780197630273.003.0001

Figure 1.1 Bovine-headed figure, possibly Ox-head (*gozu*) or the Minotaur in *Last Eden: Gate to the Beyond*, 1978. Photographer unknown. Courtesy of the Murobushi Kô Archive and Watanabe Kimiko.

What was through that gate to the beyond? A bovine-headed figure (see Figure 1.1). Nearly naked Japanese women with outlandishly large hats and horseshoe bras, one of them sporting an erect knife protruding from her crotch in place of an erect phallus (see Figure 1.2). The same two women in equally oversized, puffy, bag-like costumes, scrunching their faces into anguish or silliness. One of the women wears a kimono backward with a Japanese sword in her hands. She stands over a man encrusted in some kind of thick stringy paste clothed in a paint-splattered gown. The same man caked in plaster and naked, alternately curled up in or reclining on a box.[2] One scene seems to feature the three finding their way in the dark using a Japanese lantern (see Figure 1.3). The program alerts the audience that the soundscape includes "the voice of Mishima" ranting in Japanese.

In their wildest dreams, the three performers could never have predicted the success of this vision into the beyond. To be sure, the first five nights were downright discouraging. Two-thirds of the guests the first night were given complimentary admission, and then attendance nose-dived as people had to pay for themselves. On the fifth night, a paltry 24 people were scattered through the 130-seat hall, and only 12 of those were paying guests.[3] But then word of mouth and favorable reviews by influential critics kicked in, and attendance started climbing. On the last night, a month later, 158 people crammed into the space, ravenous to see the most amazing spectacle that had come to Paris in ages. People seemed shocked by the depth of performance, moved to the core, and sure that they had touched weighty matters of the universe. In particular, people hastily assumed that the anguished expressions and this man

Figure 1.2 Carlotta Ikeda with a knife protruding from her crotch and horseshoe bra in *Last Eden: Gate to the Beyond*, 1978. Courtesy of Fonds Jean-Marie Gourreau—Médiathèque du Centre national de la danse.

with tattered clothes and a thick coat of dried paste on his body were embodied responses to the horrors of the atomic bomb. The performers and press materials called the dance "butoh" and with that dance, butô took its place firmly on the map.

So much that will be important over the course of this history is hinted at in those heady days in 1978: the struggle to be noticed prior to this performance; the close connection of butô to cabaret; the reliance of the butô artists on that same cabaret; the unbelievable reception in Paris by critics and then audiences; the misunderstandings about butô (and the atomic bomb); and the depth of performance. But we are getting ahead of ourselves. These three were not the most important people in the beginning. No one initially used the word "butô" for their experimental dances. Later, these three

Figure 1.3 Finding their way with a lantern in *Last Eden: Gate to the Beyond*, 1978. Courtesy of Fonds Jean-Marie Gourreau—Médiathèque du Centre national de la danse.

dancers were undeniably important, and we will meet two of them again, but they were not even the ones most associated with butô. What is more, the early dances looked almost nothing like *Last Eden*, and much of butô today looks nothing like it either.

Aim of the Book

The coming chapters trace the history of butô up to this point and then expand beyond to cover the most important names in the first and second generation of butô.[4] In the process of relating this history, I have three goals. First, account for the diversity of butô today. Second, show how quirks in the development of butô continue to distort how we understand it. This may sound as if I am mocking audiences. I am not. Audiences work with the information they have. I argue that we can work to a richer appreciation of butô by knowing more about the dances and their contexts.

Some readers may resist this emphasis on context and understanding. There was a broad movement in the world of performing arts away from significance or meaning, and a corresponding assumption that the most important thing that happened in the performance was either inside the body of the performer, or else passed between the performer and the audience in a nonverbal way. Of course, butô artists were aware of that evolution in performance. They consistently resist any attempt to try to pin their performances to any one meaning. Moreover, William Marotti has sought over the course of several articles to highlight the way that butô artists (as well as other

postwar artists) sought to go beyond all the preexisting artistic and political categories in search of new political, artistic, and social possibilities (Marotti 2009, 2013b,
2015, 2018, 2019, 2020). Marotti is right; these artists were looking for something
brand new outside of the simple aim of conveying some meaning. But I want to insist
that they do not fit cleanly into the evolution in the world of western performance. To
try to squeeze them into that mold is to lose some of what makes their dance different
from other kinds of performance.

The richer contextual appreciation is related to my third aim, which is to understand butô as stemming from and responding to some of the most important
questions of our time (and not just, or even primarily, the atomic bomb). This involves exploring the techniques the dancers used. It also involves recognizing that
the artists were desperate to join international conversations and be acknowledged
as belonging to the wider world. So they often used elements that *might* have been
recognizable to the European audiences—those characters might have been intended as Theseus and Ariadne groping in a labyrinth searching for the Minotaur.
But those performers and their counterparts still in Japan had been dancing for their
own fellow-Japanese people for two decades. So another part of that richer understanding entails figuring out what they might have been "suggesting" to an informed
Japanese audience, even if they were adamant that their performances could not be
reduced to one singular meaning. That bovine-headed figure may also have been
the Buddhist gatekeeper to the underworld, Ox-head (*gozu*). They also used a tape-
recording of Mishima ranting in Japanese. That was a specific man with a specific ax
to grind about Japanese society, but although many in the audience likely knew who
Mishima was, his untranslated words were just gibberish to the Parisians.

If we understand more about the performances, we can recognize these performers
and butô in general as linked to the most pressing currents of thought today, rather
than just seeing the performances as exercises in pure affect. In part, the performers
were concerned with Japanese contemporary life, so I touch on that aspect throughout
this book. But the three currents of contemporary life that I deal with most overtly are
the following: technology/new media studies, gender transformations, and cultural
interactions and diasporas. This in no way, however, exhausts the richness of butô. My
wish is that by the end of this book, you come away with the realization that the story
of butô is the story of artists reacting in complex ways within and against a world in
which a constellation of utility, language, technology, and Westernness threatened to
push aside or even obliterate nonlanguage, the body, and non-Western cultures, practices, and histories.

Introduction

In the 1950s, some modern dancers were dissatisfied with dance in Japan. The dance
world included premodern forms, such as kabuki dance and various local festival
dances broadly influenced by the ancient dances *kagura* and *bugaku* (which were in
turn appropriated from Indian and Chinese dance). These coexisted next to recent

imports from Europe and the Americas such as ballet, jazz, tap, flamenco, ballroom, mime, and modern dance, all of which this group had studied. Within modern dance, the three big names, Ishii Baku, Eguchi Takaya, and Miya Misako, had all studied with Mary Wigman. Eguchi and Miya were drawn to the analytical side of Wigman's (and Laban's) attempt to understand the vocabulary of the body and favored abstract dances (Kuniyoshi 2018, 25–26). Ishii Baku also studied with Dalcroze. He was attracted to the side of Wigman focused on the expression of deep emotions, and he championed emotionally expressive dance (Kleeman 2015, 223; Kuniyoshi 2018, 27). German ideas about physical education also entered Japan at the time (Inata 2008, 32). Thus, in the postwar era, modern dance could range from emotionally expressive dance, to abstract dance, to a focus on physical fitness and healthy and powerful bodies (Inata 2008, 33).

Initially, dancers such as Ôno Kazuo, Tsuda Nobutoshi, Oikawa Hironobu, Wakamatsu Miki, Yoneyama Mamako, and Motofuji Akiko led the quest to reinvigorate the world of dance, but they all soon gave way to Hijikata Tatsumi. In 1959, he shocked the Japanese dance world with his *Forbidden Colors* (Kinjiki). In this dance, an older man presents a chicken to a younger man, forces him to kill it, and then intimates having sex with the younger man. The dance kicked up a brouhaha in the world of modern dance, and Hijikata and his collaborators parted ways with the rest of the modern dance world. From then on, the dancers began to experiment with new approaches to movement, with Hijikata always near the center of the action.

Initially many of their dances were story-based, somewhat like Kurt Jooss's *Green Table*. But soon they came in contact with surrealism, Fluxus, neo-Dadaism, and happenings. They also read widely, including Sade, Genet, Bataille, Marcuse, Rimbaud, and Lautréamont. From these sources, they concluded that humans were so completely socialized that they were not free to think and act for themselves. They forsook the story-based dances and branched out, ceaselessly on the prowl for some way around or beyond the power of socialization. Experiments including the following: shocking the audience; depicting new subject matter such as homoerotic elements, people with disabilities, the aged, the infirm and criminals; exploring rigidity and stillness as movement qualities; facing away from the audience to draw attention to the back or other parts of the body; incorporating movements from athletics; using everyday movements in dance; employing mime in dance; and doing many other whacky things such as pumping bellows, shaving the heads of the dancers, and entwining with hoses.

As they toyed with new movements and topics, they also tried out different names for their dances: "dance experience," "terror dance," and then *ankoku buyō* (dark black dance). Finally, they wound their way to *ankoku butō*. The word *butō* is formed of two Chinese characters meaning "dance" and "tread"/"stomp." This word was used at the time for Western-style dances such as flamenco, waltz, and ballet. So *ankoku butō* originally meant something like "dark black waltz." Much later, the compound was abbreviated as *butô*, and then Romanized severally as "butoh" and "buto."

(Incidentally, my background is in Japanese studies, and our convention is to render the doubled vowel sound with a macron, but in quotations, you will encounter "butoh." Same with names. I follow Japanese name order with the surname first, and rather than make Ôno Kazuo look as though he were inadvertently the subject of Munch's *The Scream* by spelling his name "Oh no," I'll use a macron. But in quotations, you will encounter "Ohno" or even "Ono.")

Eventually, Hijikata began a quest to fully understand himself, his own childhood, and the world around him. This was, at the same time, a quest for a new and radically generative method of dance (Uno 1999; 2012, 45–54; 2013, 35). The task was based on three assumptions. The first was that if he could become aware, down to the slightest of details, of everything that had shaped him, it would be easier to free himself from any mental or physical habit or convention. The second was that he could use any and all observations he made about what shaped him (whether from his childhood or from the world around him) as material for new dance movements. The third was that if he successfully rid himself of the physical and mental conventions and habits that were controlling him, he could be all the more sensitive to the wider world and capable of responding to it in increasingly nuanced ways. This would further enable him to generate new movements and dance ideas.

This quest for a radically generative self and dance evolved into a novel method for choreography and dance training. Everything started with detailed observation. Hijikata scrutinized nearly anything in the quest for new material: animals, marginalized people (prostitutes, farmers, criminals, the elderly, disabled people, and the infirm), or even reproductions in magazines of paintings and other art works. From such study, Hijikata took not only poses and suggestions for movements but also hints for qualities and tones. From these he developed new dance steps.

Here we arrive at an important moment in butô history: Hijikata routinely caused strong reactions in his audiences, but during this era he started asking his dancers to move while imagining strange things in order to evoke visceral reactions in his dancers. This was a way of deepening and varying their performances.

Let's make this more concrete. Hijikata might contrive a dance step and then ask the dancers to imagine doing it as a character, such as a young girl or an old woman. Obviously, dancers would perform the step differently as a young girl than as an old woman. Hijikata might alter the background environment. Performing the step while imagining being in water would entail different movements from performing in imagined concrete. Finally, perhaps owing to his background in surrealism, Hijikata would have the dancers visualize or imagine many bizarre things in order to flesh out, or transform a dance step. These images function like surrealist character preparation and include such things as imagining "razor blades on the soles of one's feet," carrying a "water tray on one's head," "suspending joints by a spider's thread," or "affixing a glass eye in your forehead" (Mikami 1993, 100). Interestingly, Hijikata used all five senses in these evocative experiments. In order to produce various bodily reactions, he demanded that the dancers imagine visual images, sounds, smells, tastes, sensations, and feelings while they danced. We can observe that Hijikata developed a veritable database of evocative or imagistic operations. He could have the dancer use any operation on any base step or movement in order to modify that movement, which in turn would yield a vast trove of new and different kinds of movements.

Hijikata would knead these poses and movements into sequences. Apparently, in his own mind, the sequences enacted strange stories, but he did not share those stories with his audiences. Here though, we confront a strange fact: These series of arbitrary steps and poses should have been suitable for any type of narrative, but Hijikata was always drawn to madness, senility, and infirm and socially marginalized peoples, the disabled, and people who were suffering.[5]

One result of Hijikata's focus on his childhood and outsiders in Japan was that he presented characters on stage who wore costumes that were recognizably "Japanese." His self-exploration coincided with a resurgence of Japanese nativism manifest in a tendency to see rural Japan as uncontaminated by modern, increasingly Westernized life. Inata Naomi argues that Hijikata was walking a knife's edge, because he was reacting not only against aspects of Western modern dance and ballet but also against classical Japanese dance, codified Japanese "folk dance," and socialist realist dance, which was supposed to have "socialist content and nationalist form" (Inata 2018). From his notebooks, we can observe that Hijikata was a cultural omnivore drawing most readily on Western artists such as Francis Goya and Jean Fautrier. But he occasionally pulled from Japanese-themed sources, including ones overlooked by the codified Japanese "folk" movement.

In a scrapbook, we see Hijikata borrowing a flower from a Picasso painting to use as the visual source for the creation of a "Japanese" hairstyle, and an Iranian bas relief as the source for a "Japanese-like" stage design in *Quiet House* (1973).[6] Similarly, in *Gibasan* (1972), Hijikata employed Nijinsky's hand movements from *Afternoon of a Faun* (1912). One dancer sports something that looks like premodern "Japanese" courtly headgear concocted with a clog (*geta*) and feather duster pointed backward so the duster hangs in front of the dancer's face, rather than behind (Baird and Candelario 2018, 5–6) It appears that Hijikata was fashioning "Japanese" components from Spanish and Iranian materials, and crafting parodies of high cultural "Japanese" elements from everyday objects. We can see in Hijikata's use of Spanish, Iranian, and everyday elements to create "Japanese" visual vocabulary an intricate and multifaceted intervention in ethnic identity.

However, some people (both conservatives and liberals) thought that Hijikata was exploring fundamental properties of the Japanese body. This has led some observers to neglect important parts of his practice as they sought to pigeonhole him as a representative of Japanese ethnocentrism. On the other hand, many dancers have seen in Hijikata and butô (especially in its focus on marginalized peoples) an invitation to explore their own identities—whether region-, ethnic-, or gender-related. In this way, butô has served as a dancerly form of anticolonialism or as a part of liberation movements.

Hijikata's turn to this imagistic and highly structured choreography caused rumblings of discontent in the small group of dancers. Some dancers preferred the more chaotic happenings-style dances. Others favored improvisations in nature. Eventually, the movement split into various factions. At the same time, dancers began spreading out around the globe taking their view of "butoh" (as it came to be called) with them.

The artist who contributed the most to the worldwide spread of butô was Maro Akaji. He came from the world of theater, where he had performed in the Situation Theater of Kara Juro (1940–) and also met Noguchi Michizô. From 1966 to 1971, he worked with Hijikata. In 1972, he founded Dairakudakan (Great Camel Battle Ship) with several other dancers including Amagatsu Ushio, Murobushi Kô, and Bishop Yamada (Yamada Ippei). He used imagery and evocation techniques from Noguchi and Hijikata and over time developed his own techniques of movement creation. These involved trying to interrupt everyday movements to defamiliarize them and then turn them into dance material. He is, however, most famous for bringing to butô a grand theatrical sense. He and his dancers created monumental scenery and props for magnificent shows featuring a strong dose of shocking and antiestablishment fare. Early dances such as *The Story of the Phallic God* (1973) and *The Emperor's Testicles* (1974) show antiestablishment themes typical of his style. They can be seen to mock, respectively, male-dominated society and the Japanese imperial system. In the mid- to late-1970s, the term *ankoku butô* was shortened to "butô," as this group of dancers struggled to formulate for themselves an understanding of what Hijikata had started. However, even more than Maro's sense of theatrics, his penchant for nurturing other performers laid the grounds for the success of butô. From 1974, Maro's philosophy "One Person, One Troupe," motivated successive performers to start their own dance companies. In 1974, Furukawa Anzu (1952–2001) and Tamura Tetsurō (1950–1991) started Dance Love Machine, Carlotta Ikeda (Ikeda Sanae, 1941–2014) founded the Compagnie Ariadone, and Bishop Yamada established the Hoppo Butô-ha (Northern Butô-Faction). In 1975, Amagatsu Ushio (1949–) instituted Sankai Juku (Mountain-Ocean School). In 1976, Murobushi Kô (1947–2015) established Butô-ha Sebi (Butô-faction Back-Fire), and Ōsuka Isamu (1943–) created Byakkosha (White Tiger Company).

These dancers and companies ranged over Japan, then to Europe and Southeast Asia, and finally over the world spreading their own versions of Maro-inflected butô. This diaspora gets us back to where we started. Ishii Mitsutaka, Eiko & Koma, and an outsider, Miura Issô, had already performed in various places in Europe and used various terms to describe themselves. But two of Maro's collaborators, Carlotta Ikeda and Murobushi Kô, presented the performance *Last Eden* that brought butô to international awareness. Later that same year, Hijikata's dancer Ashikawa Yôko performed *Twelve Phases of the Terpsichore of Darkness: Fourteen Nights for the Louvre Palace* for the Festival d'Automne in connection with the *MA: Space-Time of Japan* exhibition at the Museum of Decorative Arts. The audience was so enraptured with Ashikawa that they demanded that she perform up to five times per day, and she was featured on TV.[7] It was not long before several dancers moved permanently to Europe (Murobushi and Ikeda in 1979, Amagatsu in 1981, and Furukawa Anzu to Berlin in 1989).

To be honest, the artists were not wildly successful during the first two decades in Japan. Before Paris, the dancers had performed once or twice a year on average (and paid the theater owners for that privilege). They had a few champions and were featured in sensationalistic two- to four-page photo essays in the mass media, but they were mainly a curiosity. In France, they were courted by well-connected producers, their shows were reviewed by influential reviewers, and they played to raucous audiences that were also keen to pay for lessons and workshops. In short, butô boomed. And when it boomed, the artists were able to ride the shockwaves through Europe, to North and South America, and eventually back to Japan.

Amagatsu Ushio was the most successful dancer of this wave. Trained in ballet and modern dance, he joined Dairakudakan before founding Sankai Juku in 1975. In 1980, the troupe appeared at the International Theater Festival in Nancy and toured Europe. The following year, Amagatsu relocated to Paris, where he caught the attention of well-placed critics and producers. From 1982 to 2019, the Théâtre de la Ville Paris produced and premiered about one show every other year. In the off years, Sankai Juku toured outlying French cities and they maintain an international touring schedule through Europe, North and South America, and Asia. Sankai Juku is famous for its achingly beautiful performances executed with masterly control and tinctured with shades of the monstrous. This control is based on many of the same imagery techniques developed by Hijikata and Maro, but Amagatsu rarely spoke of such techniques. Instead, he invoked universal themes, casting his dances as meditations on time, space, and gravity. He shared a sense of spectacle with Maro, and his dances always featured high production values, with first-rate music, costumes, and stage design. At the same time, Sankai Juku has been criticized for appealing too much to European audiences and reviled in the rest of the butô community for not really being butô. Whatever the case, Sankai Juku has been the most visible representative of butô outside Japan.

The person who most fully embodied butô for both the general public and within the butô community itself was Ôno Kazuo. Early in his life, he saw Antonia Mercé y Luque (La Argentina) and Harald Kreutzberg perform. He studied modern dance with three of the biggest Japanese pioneers of German modern dance—Ishii Baku (1933–1934), and Eguchi Takaya and Miya Misako (1936–1938), who had all studied with Mary Wigman. Ôno worked as a high school physical education teacher and later as a janitor. His dance career was interrupted for nine years by the war, during which time he worked as a supply soldier, and then was a prisoner of war in New Guinea. He resumed his dance career when he returned home, squarely within, but chafing at the constraints of, modern dance. Hijikata lured him from modern dance in 1960, and Ôno worked with Hijikata until 1968. Then he appeared in a string of experimental movies directed by Nagano Chiaki.

At the age of 71, in 1977, Ôno appeared on stage again in a solo piece, *Admiring La Argentina*. The dance was a retrospective of his prior performance career and an homage to La Argentina. It included a mishmash of quotations from previous dances, scenes from his experimental films, and possibly scenes from his life. Two scenes were a reprise of Hijikata's 1959 revision of *Forbidden Colors*: They depicted scenes from the life of Divine/Culafroy from Genet's *Our Lady of the Flowers*. He restaged the dance at the International Theater Festival at Nancy in 1980 and caught the attention of Western audiences. From dances such as this, Ôno became known for emotional honesty and gender-bending performances.

Ôno employed Hijikata's imagery work in structured improvisations, and he had thirty-eight years of dance training to draw on in his improvisations. However, in public, he never emphasized the imagery techniques that he used. Rather, he spoke of his dances as if they were the purely improvisational expression of his inner being and of his connection to the cosmos. His manner of speaking was often mystifying and likely dovetailed with Orientalist expectations Europeans had about the inscrutable East. In one interview, the translator, Tadashi Endo, confessed to having difficulties in translating Ôno's stream of consciousness ramblings, and the reporter became increasingly frustrated. Endo decided to give his own interpretation of what he thought Ôno meant, rather than what Ôno was saying. Then the reporter went away happy (Geoffroy and Oliveira 2017; Van Hensbergen 2018a, 280). Often observers came away convinced that Ôno's dances (and butô in general) took no skills or training to do, despite his nearly four decades of dance training (D'Orazi 2018, 263–264). Such miscommunications and attitudes still influence how people understand butô today.

Interestingly, a group of Japanese performers mirrored the European audiences. As butô gained prominence, a group of outsiders thought to try their hand at it. They were not trained in imagery work, but they did not think that butô should take any training anyway, or even be passed along in any sort of hierarchical manner. They were starting from much the same place as the original dancers and may have been drawn to the zany happenings side of butô. They all used the term "butô" to describe their works or were understood by critics and producers to be practicing butô even if they did not use the term. Among these were Tanaka Min, Iwana Masaki, Goi Teru, and later Endo Tadashi.

Tanaka (1945–) made a name for himself dancing naked in site-specific dances all over Japan, such as public plazas, construction sites, and even a garbage dump. His work may be fruitfully compared with Judson Dance theater. He appeared at the previously mentioned MA exhibition along with Ashikawa. Consequently, Tanaka was associated with butô even though he did not yet see himself as belonging to that world. To complement this solo work, he created the company Maijuku to focus on similar goals from a group perspective.

Apparently, Tanaka had always held Hijikata in high esteem, so in 1983, Tanaka studied directly with Hijikata, learning Hijikata's techniques and choreography. This resulted in a duo with Ashikawa, *Extremely Quick Respiratory Bromide* (Hijô ni kyûsoku na kyûkisei buromaido), at the 1983 festival *Hook Off 88: One Ton of Hairstyles for the Scenery* and a solo for Tanaka: *Performance to Commemorate the 1501st Solo Dance of Tanaka Min: the Foundation of the Pure Love-Dance School* (1984). In time, Tanaka rejected the "butô" label, although he argues that he is the true heir to Hijikata's original spirit of experimentation. After his Hijikata era, he founded Body Weather Farm to serve as a place for dance training and to provide a source of income. He continued to experiment with the connections between the body and the world and became a leader in fomenting new collaborations and new kinds of improvisations. He was particularly active with free jazz musicians. He is always seeking to increase his sensitivity to the world around him and his control over all parts of his body.

There was one other Japanese dancer at the International Theater Festival at Nancy in 1980: Kasai Akira (1943–). For whatever reason, European audiences did not take to him as they did Sankai Juku and Ôno. He had studied ballet and mime, and then modern dance with Eguchi and Miya. From 1963, for several years, he studied with Ôno and participated in all of Hijikata's dances. Then he struck out on his own, in part, because he felt that Hijikata's wild and crazy dances were taking attention away from discovering some deeper meaning of dance and the world. In 1971 he created his own studio/company, Tenshikan, intended as a place for anarchic nonhierarchical bodily experimentation. In 1979 he shuttered Tenshikan and went to Germany to learn eurythmy and anthroposophy with Rudolf Steiner. Eurythmy is related to other elements of German modern dance in its focus on individual experience and the creation of a universal bodily vocabulary. Considering that butô originated out of German modern dance, it is perhaps not surprising that Kasai interrupted his career to study there. He graduated from the Eurythmeum in 1983. Eventually, he returned to Japan and taught eurythmy. He also choreographed flowing colorful eurythmic performances. In 1994, he rejoined the world of butô with the dance *Séraphîta: My Girl with the Mirror Genitalia*, loosely based on the androgyne of Balzac's novel.

Kasai bases his butô-oriented training on eurythmy. He asks dancers to embody vocalized sounds or move corresponding to music or poetry. He has dancers strive to feel the reverberations of different vowel sounds and let those reverberations transform into movement. Imagine trying to feel the difference between voicing the "e" of "get" and the "a" of "father," and translating the vibrations from the two into different movements. Overtime, the goal is to attune the body-mind to be aware of the differing bodily responses to varying stimuli. Kasai also strives to catalog and systematize various bodily or mental orientations. For example, he maintains that the fundamental "bodily grammar" of existing and moving corresponds to nouns, verbs, and adjectives. He has dancers use the "grammar" as evocative prompts to alter the quality of movements. This might entail moving in a noun way, then trying to do the same movement in a verb way, and then repeating for a third time moving in an adjective way. Then he might mix the categories so that the dancer imagines voicing an "a-sound" while moving in an adjective type way. Much like Hijikata, Kasai created a veritable database of operations he could execute on any movement. To this day, he continues to focus on the connections between words, sounds, and movements, and he persists in his quest to fully categorize all the mental and physical orientations in the world and use them to enable the creation of different kinds of movements. In both his dances and writings, he promotes the idea that butô (and dance in general) should work toward creating unified works that encompass language, body, music, community, and history.

If the reader looked closely at the table of contents, you noticed that there is a gross imbalance between the number of pages devoted to women as opposed to men. I am not the first to have noticed this. In 2010, Sondra Fraleigh wrote, "I think it is time to claim the considerable accomplishments of women in butoh," and devoted her attention to 13 women and 9 men in her reviews of contemporary butô.[8] More recently, Vangeline scathingly critiqued the gender imbalance in butô (Vangeline 2020, xxxiv–xxxviii). She argues that the women were equally talented, but not recognized by the butô establishment, and that the women were not given the same opportunities either by critics, senior dancers, or producers to develop their skills. This was not just the fault of Japan, though. Vangeline notes that French patriarchal society exacerbated the harm that Japanese society had already done. She even graphs the gender imbalance in the number of performances produced in France year by year and highlights the decisive influence of the early "blackout" years when there were no performances by women whatsoever. This was right when butô was booming and women could have benefited from the attention (Vangeline 2020, xxxiv).

This sexism creates a problem that is both real and archival. There is a huge gap between the men and the women in most of the categories we traditionally use to define success: owning one's own studio; attracting funding; forming one's own group; performing frequently (and in high profile venues); being featured in reviews and scholarship; publishing one's own articles and books; appearing in movies and documentaries. To the extent that success breeds success, this disparity grows over time. It should be obvious that the disparity echoes in the resources available to the scholar. There are simply more archival videos to watch, more books and reviews to read, more scholarship to digest for the men than for the women.

That being said, women may have been even more important than men in the worldwide spread of butô. Women have constantly participated at the center of butô. Motofuji Akiko and Nakajima Natsu danced with Hijikata and Ôno from early on. Later, Ashikawa Yôko, Kobayashi Saga, and Tamano Hiroko were integral parts of Hijikata's generative image-based butô. Still later, Eiko Otake (of Eiko & Koma), Ashikawa Yôko, Carlotta Ikeda, Yoshioka Yumiko, Koseki Sumako, Furukawa Anzu, Seki Minako, Kaseki Yuko, and SU-EN were crucial to butô's spread throughout Europe and the rest of the world. Most of them found it impossible to maintain a career in Japan. They had more success abroad as itinerant artists conducting workshops, organizing festivals, and giving performances throughout Europe and the Americas. Rosemary Candelario has proposed seeing the development of butô in terms of diasporas and pilgrimages (Candelario 2018). Women were the main wave of this diaspora, and while some of the butô pilgrims go to Japan to study with men, many pilgrims travel to a metropolitan center or rural art enclave closer to home to study with itinerant women. Audiences may have seen the male performers in the relatively larger venues, and thus the public face of butô may have been Ôno, Sankai Juku, and Tanaka. But these itinerant women did much of the daily labor of teaching butô to non-Japanese dancers. Three of the four women covered in these pages feature teaching predominantly on their webpages, while most of the surviving men do not. The individual contributions of the women to butô are harder to quantify in short summaries, but their value to the worldwide spread of butô is incalculable.

As these second and third generation dancers thrived, butô evolved. This evolution was baked into butô from the beginning. Hijikata had gone through three major evolutions all retroactively seen as "butô." Likewise, Ôno and Kasai had moved into, out of, and into butô again. Everybody had their own ideas about what butô should be. Outsiders such as Tanaka, Iwana, and Goi jumped into butô and made it their own. What is more, some dancers collaborated with or learned from other dancers and artists, such as Kasai with eurhythmy, Tanaka with Anna Halperin, or Tanaka and Ashikawa with free jazz musicians. These interactions changed butô. Moreover, as itinerant artists conducted workshops, they were forced to verbalize aspects of their practice that may have only previously arisen in the context of creating a performance (Calamoneri 2018, 418). Undoubtedly, some of the change to butô happened as artists conformed to Orientalist expectations of what butô or a Japanese art should be (as with Endo making a reporter happy by purposefully refusing to translate Ôno's words and substituting his own understanding).

Today, it is possible to see several different kinds of butô. The differences largely depend on how artists see themselves in relation to the lineage, technique, and stereotypical notions of butô. Some belong to the lineage, and some do not. Some conform to the stereotypes, and some do not. Some use imagery work, and some do not. One group thinks that both the stereotypes and the lineage are irrelevant and instead holds that butô is properly a physical, philosophical, or social orientation. Examples of such physical orientations are contorting, transforming, or articulating and disarticulating the body. Examples of philosophical orientations are anti-aesthetics, self-exploration, exploring and uncovering the mental and physical socializations of the body-mind, challenging and confronting institutional power, and tackling the foundational problems of humankind such as the meaning of life, suffering, and death. The social concerns of butô artists include paying attention to the powerless or marginalized peoples, such as those who are differently abled, diseased, or decrepit, or who do not fit into society for whatever reason. For this reason, it is quite common to hear of an artist or performance that is characterized as being butô-like, even when the artist belongs neither to the lineage nor matches with any of the stereotypes. This overlap extends to other genres as well, so other art forms are often compared to or conflated with butô, such as Grotowski's theater, mime, horror cinema, and clown.

This brings up an important point. Tanya Calamoneri spends considerable labor teasing out various resonances between buto and other art forms including kathakali, kalaripayattu, and certain aspects of traditional Japanese theater (Calamoneri 2012, 2018). Dwayne Lawler builds on this research with an extensive comparison of butô with yoga, tai chi, Lecoq, Feldenkrais method, judo, Stanislavski, Michael Chekhov, Meyerhold biomechanics, and further consideration of Grotowski (Lawler 2021). This is not the place to rehearse all the arguments of Calamoneri and Lawler.

Readers who are interested in this matter should consult their works for more in-depth analysis. Suffice it to say, it appears that there were elements of various non-Western theatrical forms that were relatively unknown to the Western theatrical world but compatible with or inclined toward "psychophysical transformation" and thus attractive to Western theater practitioners looking for a way out of the some of the dead ends of Western performance (Calamoneri 2012, 31). Butô then is a singular synthesis of a particularly powerful movement within the world of performing arts.

Over the top of these various orientations, we can identify some broader dichotomies. Butô stretches from improvisations and site-specific dances (often in natural settings) to carefully choreographed dance (often using imagery exercises). It extends from grand spectacle and audience entertainment to personally authentic and cathartic experience (with marginal concern for the audience). We can also characterize the range of performances by thinking about the movement's relationship to the bodily signifier and signified. Hijikata created a new vocabulary comprising thousands of combinations of bodily positions with imagery exercises. He seems to have assumed that he could arbitrarily use that new vocabulary to convey an underlying narrative. In contrast, artists such as Ôno and Kasai proceeded from the assumption that their movements convey intended emotional states with no gap between the two. They presuppose that all audiences (without regard for language or cultural differences) can understand (or feel) exactly what they intended from the movements of their dances. Today, artists all along these continua and ascribing to these various orientations use the term "butô" to describe themselves. Meanwhile, others (and even those from within the lineage) reject the term. Thus, there are nearly as many ways to practice butô as there are dancers practicing it.

However, despite these differences, there are some overarching correspondences that permit us to think about them as a whole. Consider Tanaka's improvisational response to miniscule changes in the weather with infinitesimal tremors in his body, Hijikata's attempt to imagine the difference between one hundred bugs and one hundred and one bugs stinging himself and let that difference materialize on his body, and Kasai's endeavor to feel the difference between the vibrations of two different vowel sounds and let those vibrations produce two different movements. Obviously, something totally different is going on in the body-mind, but at the same time, something very similar is happening. Among the parallels within the wider butô community is a concentration on and sensitivity to minute detail, subdivision, transformation, and meticulous control of the body as well as an ongoing propensity to shock spectators and agitate systems and societies.

Butô in Japan

We can now consider some of the ways that butô addresses the most fundamental questions of Japan in the 1960s–1980s and in the world today. Butô mirrors successive moments in a Japanese postwar history of the body (Baird 2012, 6, 42, 48, 72).

A starting point is the "nation body" (*kokutai*), an idea promoted as describing the relationship between the Japanese people and the emperor. The common people were to quash their own desires in deference to the emperor, who was the head of the "nation body." When the war ended, Japanese people began to satisfy the urges of their own "carnal bodies" (*nikutai*).[9] A corresponding literary genre was called "carnal body literature" (*nikutai bungaku*). The nudity and (homo)eroticism of early butô echoes this wider tendency to prioritize the carnal body. The obverse side of the carnal body was the athletic body, and there were many allusions to sports and athletics in early butô performances. We can see in these references an analogue with the "Sun Tribe" novels and cinema (which celebrated youthful suntanned bodies sailing, waterskiing, and boxing) and the 1964 Tokyo Olympics. In time, the Japanese economy recovered from the effects of the war, and then entered into what is known as the era of high growth. The buzz words of the era were productivity (*seisansei*) and both physical and mental flexibility. Both ideas were memorably manifest in practices of Toyota-ism and just-in-time production. Hijikata opposed productivity in early essays (such as "To Prison"), in which he said,

> to a production-oriented society, the aimless use of the body, which I call dance, is a deadly enemy which must be taboo. I am able to say that my dance shares a common basis with crime, male homosexuality, festivals, and rituals because it is behavior that explicitly flaunts its aimlessness in the face of a production-oriented society. (Hijikata 1998, 1: 198; trans. Hijikata 2000b, 43–44)

However, considering the way that many butô artists were seeking to use the power of evocation, imagery, and improvisation in their dances, we can see that the artists (each in their own way) were working to realize a generative body-mind that is physically and mentally flexible and sensitive.

Butô in the World

We can extend this history of the body by observing that the body-mind in butô anticipates Japanese conversations about the relationship between the body-mind and technology (both in reality and in popular culture). Increasingly, body-minds come to mimic technology. Three important figures in this regard are the cyborg, the unassisted speedrunners of video game culture, and the *otaku* (pop culture database geeks). Considering these can bring butô scholarship into dialogue with new media studies scholarship in Japan.

All three of these figures in contemporary Japanese discourse are marked by a melding of machinic capabilities with the abilities of the body-mind to extend its abilities beyond that of normal humans. The cyborg (imagine Major Kusanagi Motoko of *Ghost in the Shell*) is endowed with prosthetics that extend its abilities beyond that of normal humans, both physically and mentally. After fusing with the

Puppet Master, Kusanagi has immediate access to the entire Internet, which she processes on the fly, as well as the potential for superhuman strength. It goes without saying that the dancers were not genuine cyborgs. That said, their physical training brought them close to the status of cyborgs because they could endure more tension than ordinary people, twist and contort more than normal people, and be out of balance without falling over, all the while spreading their concentration out to account for more and more areas of (and beyond) their own bodies and striving to be ever more receptive to stimuli.

Early in butô scholarship, this aspect of training led the self-confessed dance-outsider Takeda Ken'ichi to argue that butô was a dance form suited to the age of proliferating information (Takeda 1985, 106–108). We can bring his observation into dialogue with discourses of the cyborg by noting that the cyborg is routinely depicted as having access to all the databases and information of the Internet, which it can process at lightning speed. To the extent that the dancers learn techniques for spreading their concentration ever wider within, on, and around the body, they approximate the cyborg.[10]

However, it is not just butô dancers mirroring machines. Increasingly a subset of (Japanese) people has begun to embody machines even in the absence of express body modification. They are speedrunners: gamers who attempt to finish a game in the fastest possible time. Initially the players' time depended solely on their reflexes. Then gamers developed emulators so that they no longer needed to play the game in an arcade or on a console but could play on their computers. The emulator had the benefit of allowing the players to slow (or freeze) the game and study it in granular detail. Soon, gamers realized that they could program a computer to input keystrokes in set patterns. This led to a split into two different kinds of speedruns (Altice 2015, 312–324). Real time attack runs (RTA) or unassisted speedruns eschew machinic help and depend on reflexes. Tool assisted speedruns (TAS) make use of an emulator to slow the game and study the code to identify faster ways to complete the game. Common techniques include exploiting glitches in the game (such as finding places where the avatar can walk through walls) or finding places in which a humanly impossible set of keystrokes will overcome an obstacle. However, the distinction between the two kinds of speedruns frequently blurs, because RTA runners study the TAS runs and practice mimicking programmed emulator inputs. Some movements remain beyond the ability of any gamer, but unassisted runs increasingly parallel TAS runs as the unassisted gamers study and exploit machinic techniques and then develop their reflexes to be able to approximate the movements previously only available to machines (Altice 2015, 324).

In this, the gamers are like butô dancers, or butô dancers are like gamers. Altice even likens the creation of the TAS runs to choreography (Altice 2015, 322, 319). But he takes this one step further in his discussion of the gamer studying the original game and the inputs of a TAS run in slow motion. He writes that the gamers come to have a "fine-grained level of perception" about the game. This is much like butô dancers coming to have a "fine-grained level of perception" about the effects of weather, the environment, or particular vowel sounds on their body-minds.

We can bring butô into dialogue with one more part of Japanese pop culture: the *otaku* (pop culture database geeks). They have stimulated a considerable amount of debate, but I focus on their treatment by the new media studies scholar Azuma Hiroki. In his *Animalizing Postmodern* (translated as *Otaku: Japan's Database Animals*), Azuma notes that with the invention of the VCR (which they can pause and rewind), otaku became increasingly nuanced viewers of animations. They are able to tell the difference between the styles of different animators even when those animators are drawing the same characters. As character design became a more important part of the otaku universe, otaku began to create databases of character designs from which they could compile their own characters. This leads Azuma to argue that an important attribute of otaku is that they consume databases (rather than narratives). Azuma characterizes the activity of otaku as an "endless movement of slipping sideways" through, across, and over databases (104).[11]

I return to Azuma shortly, but I acknowledge that we do not usually categorize butô dancers and otaku or gamers in the same category. The butô dancer Omori Masahide told me that butô dancers are the anti-otaku, because he saw butô as opposed to the thoroughgoing consumerism of the otaku (Pers. conversation, Sept. 20, 2009). However, if we step back and look at Hijikata or Kasai's choreographic method, we can see that there are some uncanny similarities between otaku and butô dancers. Both Hijikata and Kasai have a matrix or database of operations they can perform on any movement in order to alter the quality, tone, or amplitude of that movement. Their matrices are different. Hijikata's is more thoroughly strange with his imagery parade of stinging bugs, shocking volts of energy, and detail gathered from paintings hither and yon. Kasai's is more systematic with his careful alterations of a movement based on all the options within a given category. It should be obvious that they both create massive mental databases to use in transforming movement. What is more, Tanaka focuses on micromovements and minute responses to subtle changes in the environment and weather. We might conclude that his improvisational brand of butô is just as close to otaku obsession with minutia as anything in Hijikata or Kasai. Therefore, I argue forcefully that butô belongs to and is responding to the same information society that the otaku inhabit.

At this moment, if you come from the world of dance and are used to moving your body, you might be tempted to slit your wrists. If the future lies in the hands of Americans and Japanese who are primarily pop culture consumers, then what hope have we? And if butô is just the dance form of otaku culture, then what? But Azuma argues that otaku have two capabilities beyond their ability to range over databases (which itself is no small thing given that search engines can access billions of web pages). One is the creation of their own (often derivative) works. Otaku are generally not content to merely watch animations or read manga, but insist on creating their own works.[12] Azuma points out that otaku do not create their derivative works with any parodic intent. Parody implies that one finds something unsatisfactory in the original and uses the sting of parody to mock or change something about the original works. Otaku, Azuma thinks, do not engage in parody, but insist on the prerogative of creating their own works. Also, Azuma notes that in the creation of their derivative works, they have the ability to access the underlying code (for example, from database web pages or from visual novel games) in order to reshuffle these elements into new configurations. In this the otaku are similar to the speedrunners who use emulators to understand the underlying mechanics of a game and find ways to go through the game faster.

This is where we can locate an important difference for butô dancers, even when we recognize that they are responding to the same information-laden world as their otaku counterparts. Otaku can access and manipulate databases or the underlying code to produce new arrangements of surface elements. But butô dancers create their own databases as a precondition of creating new works. The value of these butô quasi-cyborgs, these dancing unassisted speedrunners, lies in their ability to understand how our bodies and minds are formed, and then body-mind hack the world.[13]

2
Hijikata Tatsumi

Hijikata Tatsumi was at the center of butô from its beginning until his untimely death in 1986. He was then largely overshadowed outside Japan owing to the circumstances of butô's development, but has more recently begun to receive the attention that he warrants. Here I set the stage for all subsequent developments in butô by charting his path. He started his dance career with narrative vignettes, before switching to neo-Dada happenings and intermedial experiments. He picked up from surrealism the practice of clashing incommensurate items and ideas against each other to see what would come of it. Crucial to his practice was the conviction that one side of a mash-up should not overwhelm and bury the other side, but that both sides of the combination would change. Then Hijikata created his generative butô method, which was both a way to free himself from habitual thinking and acting by extensively exploring himself and also a way to create new kinds of movements. This resulted in the performances and techniques that are increasingly recognized as important contributions to the world of performance. The performances mostly take the form of solos, in which Hijikata himself or Ashikawa Yôko embodies a series of strange characters, interspersed with group dances. The dances invariably convey deep emotions, deal with topical social or political issues, and serve as metacommentary on or experiments with performance practice itself. The techniques are characterized by the ability to direct one's attention to an ever-widening area in, on, and around the body, while at the same time compartmentalizing the body into increasingly smaller units. I see his dance as connected to the wider world not just in the way that he addressed socially current topics and performance and philosophical metatopics but also in its resonance with transformations in the way that society conceives of the relationship between body-minds and technologies.

Hijikata was born Yoneyama Kunio in 1928 and came from a reasonably well-off family from the town of Akita in northern Japan, although he later claimed he came from impoverished circumstances. He wore western clothes and attended an elite grade school and high school (Inata 2008, 13–14). He played rugby and apparently learned taekwondo. He says he saw the Hitler Youth and the modern dance pioneer Ishii Baku (1886–1962).

Sometime in 1946, Hijikata started dancing at the studio of Masumura Katsuko, a student of Eguchi Takaya and Miya Misako. From 1947, he traveled back and forth from Akita to Tokyo, and then in 1952 he moved to Tokyo for good. Inata notes that Hijikata was routinely boorish, a hard drinker, and perpetually irresponsible with money. This made it hard for him to maintain long-term relationships with other

A History of Butô. Bruce Baird, Oxford University Press. © Oxford University Press 2022.
DOI: 10.1093/oso/9780197630273.003.0002

dancers. He bounced around, dancing with Masumura, who had also moved to Tokyo, and then dancing with Andô Mitsuko (who was one of the first dancers in Japan to use jazz music and dance routines in modern dance) (Inata 2008, 39–41). Andô was also working with the ballet dancer Horiuchi Kan, who sought to fuse ballet and modern dance. According to both Andô and Horiuchi, Hijikata was not initially very technically skilled, but Kuniyoshi observes that over time, Hijikata began to appear as a background dancer in movies, on TV, and in the choreography of others (Inata 2008, 20; Kuniyoshi 2002, 179).

In 1954, Hijikata made his Tokyo debut with Andô and met the well-established Ôno Kazuo. Over the next three years, he appeared in combined performances with Andô and Horiuchi and also in a performance with the mime artist Oikawa Hironobu. He also cultivated connections with artists outside the world of dance such as Shinohara Ushio, Kanamori Kaoru, Kawara On, Terayama Shuji, Ikeda Tatsuo, and Yoshida Yoshie. He also came in contact with the American dancer Katherine Dunham when Andô rented her studio to Dunham. Hijikata was apparently captivated by Dunham's vodou-inspired performances, and Inata assumes that Hijikata would have been able to watch Dunham's rehearsals (Inata 2008, 61).[1]

In 1957, according to Andô, Hijikata wanted to stage a performance in which he suspended a chicken from a pole, crawled around on all fours groaning and yelling, and then smothered the chicken, at which point the lighting designer was to flash a red light on stage, and then plunge the stage into darkness (Inata 2008, 49–50). Because the sound and lighting technicians were opposed to the performance, he was not allowed to go through with it.

Next, Hijikata joined the studio of the mime artist Yoneyama Mamako. Yoneyama had been a student of Eguchi and Miya but felt dissatisfied with the abstract nature of their performances and switched to studying mime after seeing Marcel Marceau. She was largely self-taught, because there were no mime teachers in Japan at the time.[2] In 1958, Hijikata appeared in a concert with Yoneyama, but his boorish behavior caused a rift with her. However, he was able to join the All Japan Modern Dance Society, and find a welcome at the studio of Tsuda Nobutoshi and Motofuji Akiko. Tsuda had studied dance with Max Terpis, and was endeavoring to widen the field of dance in various ways, including by choreographing to poetry rather than music (Inata 2008, 59) and by incorporating into dance ugliness and unpleasantness (Kuniyoshi 2002, 173–175). Two of Tsuda's pre-Hijikata dances, "Soliloquy" and "Strong in the Rain" featured abstract movements and dancers reciting poetry or even meaningless syllables (Yoshida 2008, 28–29). Tsuda founded two avant-garde groups: one called Banner of Revolution and the other called 20 Female Avant-Garde. Hijikata participated in them as a producer, dancer, and choreographer.

At some point, he and Motofuji became romantically and artistically involved and Hijikata moved into Motofuji's dance studio, Asbestos Studio. They created two different groups for show dancing in night clubs. One was a duo called Blue Echoes, and another was a team called Dancing Gorgui. Hijikata and Motofuji eventually

managed several night clubs, and in time the night club circuit and burlesque performance became the major sources of funding for butô dancers.

Forbidden Colors (Kinjiki)

Hijikata finally presented his own choreography at a group recital in May 1959. The
title of the piece, *Forbidden Colors* (Kinjiki), was from a novel by Mishima Yukio. The
subject matter is generally taken to draw on the writings of Jean Genet, including *Our
Lady of the Flowers*. As we shall see, societal attitudes toward US GIs may also have
played a role in the creation of this dance.

Hijikata and Ôno Yoshito played the roles of an older and younger man, respectively. Yoshito appeared at the front of a nearly dark stage lit only at the front left side.
He wore tight, lemon-cream-colored shorts and a white scarf, and looked anxious or
despairing. He retreated to the middle of the stage, where a white chicken was passed
to him from behind by Hijikata, who was dressed only in gray pants and had greased
his skin to make himself darker. Yoshito scissored the chicken between his legs while
Hijikata watched. Then squatting to the ground, Yoshito crushed the chicken and
simulated killing it.[3] The lights dropped to near darkness and Yoshito tried to flee,
but Hijikata chased Yoshito down and simulated having sex with him. The older man
could be heard in the dark proclaiming, "Je t'aime." Prerecorded heavy breathing and
sexual moaning accompanied the scuffling in the dark. Eventually, the lights came
up on Yoshito by himself accompanied by the bluesy harmonica music of Yasuda
Shugo.[4]

Considering Forbidden Colors

This was like no other performance in Japan (or the world) at that time. The theater
scholar Kurt Wurmli asserts that we should take care not to squeeze Hijikata's perfor-
mance(s) into our preconceived notions of how a performance should work (Wurmli
2008, 147–148). Keeping that caution in mind, we can observe a few things about the
performance. It was shocking, and in fact, some people left in the middle of the performance. It made the audience work hard as they peered into the dim light trying
to discern what was going on. The dance seems to tell some kind of short story: Man
meets young man, gives young man chicken, young man kills chicken, man has sex
with young man, young man ends up alone. However, the story is not easy to inter-
pret. We have very little information about who or what these two figures are.

In keeping with Wurmli's caution, we might forgo altogether the attempt to inter-
pret the dance and see it primarily as an attempt to elicit strong feelings. However,
the shock comes within the narrative arc of the vignette. It would have been plenty
shocking if Hijikata had just presented homoerotic sex, or just staged the killing of

a chicken. But here, the young man does not just kill a chicken randomly: he kills one that an older man gave him. The two do not just have sex: They have sex after the man has given the boy the chicken. The dance seems to invite curiosity about what it means, even as it resists singular interpretation.

One camp of commentators has viewed the dance as a celebration of male–male sexuality. The dance critic Shiga Nobuo argues that the young man's scarf is an indication that he sought out the sexual encounter and he refers to the young man as a *bishonen* (homoerotic beautiful boy) (Shiga 2005, 74). Doryun Chong echoes this in referring to the dance as "the story of a hedonistic homosexual youth" (Chong 2012, 78). However, these interpretations fail to account for the fleeing, chasing, and despair on the part of the young man. These are disturbing in the era of #metoo, because they signal a murkiness about whether the interaction was consensual.

Another camp has seen Hijikata as having staged an examination of or criticism of society. The dance critic Gôda Nario reads the dance as an examination of social forces and coercion. He sees Hijikata as having enacted a self-proclaimed criminal or outlaw from the world of Genet of Hijikita, who coerces the young man into having sex (Gôda 1987, 40–41). Gôda's interpretation finds an interesting parallel in Kate Millett's interpretation of Genet. She writes:

> Together with the rest of his prose fiction, [*Our Lady of the Flowers* and *Thief's Journal*] constitute a painstaking exegesis of the barbarian vassalage of the sexual orders, the power structure of "masculine" and "feminine" as revealed by a homosexual, criminal world that mimics with brutal frankness the bourgeois heterosexual society.... In this way, the explication of the homosexual code becomes a satire on the heterosexual one. (Millett 2000, 18–19)

If Gôda is right in his interpretation, *Forbidden Colors* was an examination of gender dynamics and unequal power relationships between two men.

Adam Broinowski extends and makes specific Gôda's more general reading. He takes the lack of consent to be a defining feature of the dance and reads *Forbidden Colors* as depicting the rape "of an innocent local man . . . by a foreign soldier/sailor" and, allegorically, the American occupation raping the Japanese populace (Broinowski 2016, 73). However, Broinowski fails to address the older man's usage of French.

Hijikata is not much help, and on one occasion even stated that interpretation is the "right of the viewer" (Nishi 1960, 65). He was also prone to obfuscation, so his writings are not trustworthy. With that caveat, a year later, he wrote that one of his dances (perhaps this one) involved extreme hunger and an initiation into love (Hijikata 1998, 1: 190; trans. Hijikata 2000a, 39). Considering the dance and the essay in light of each other perhaps suggests that the dance portrays a transaction in which a young man trades sex for food. The fact that he is made up and wears a scarf would not be an indication that he eagerly anticipates the encounter. Rather, it would indicate that the young man knew that he could trade his body for resources in the era of postwar poverty, so he knew that he should present his body in its best light.

Arimitsu Michio highlights the grease that Hijikata applied to his body to make his skin darker and calls for scholars to be more attentive to the early issues of race in butô (Arimitsu 2018). It is conceivable that Hijikata intended his character to be a black man. If *Forbidden Colors* was a narrative of a *black* man compelling a hungry young Japanese man to have sex with him, it only compounds the troubling nature of the dance because it puts a racial overtone on the already murky narrative of consent.

Here we should note that Hijikata may have been drawing on or churning through similarly conflicted contemporary accounts of interactions with black men. Genet's depictions of black men in *Our Lady* border on (or cross the line into) racism (Pears 2018, 14–15). In Oe Kenzaburo's 1957 *Prize Stock*, an African American pilot crashes in a small village and is housed there for the summer. The novella is filled with strong homoerotic overtones between the black GI and the young boy who befriends him. The narrator demonstrates some sensitivity toward the black man when he depicts him as able to fix complicated machinery, but other parts of the narrative are downright racist and have not aged well. In one scene, the black GI copulates with a goat while the young narrator admires his large member (Oe 1977, 153). Similarly, Suzuki Seijun depicts a black priest raping a Japanese woman in his *Gates of Flesh*. In this era, Japanese people had very few genuine contacts with black men, and while they clearly identified with the civil rights struggles of black Americans, there was much gross caricature as well.

Forbidden Colors (Revised version)

However we understand this dance today, it set off a ruckus in the modern dance community at the time. Eventually, Hijikata, Tsuda, Ôno, Motofuji, and others left the All Japan Art Dance Association. This was important for the subsequent development of butô, because it meant that the group was cut off from much of the dance world. This left the dancers free to evolve without concern for preconceptions of how dance should look or function.

Hijikata expanded the performance in September 1959. The first scene was "Death of Divine" (the aging transvestite from Genet's *Our Lady*). Ôno Kazuo (dressed in cheap women's cloth) came up on stage from out of the audience and mimicked the tubercular Divine retching blood into a toilet. Some men came on stage and assaulted Ôno with arrows, and she died. Then the men carted her away. In the second scene, "Death of the Young Man" (usually interpreted as a depiction of the young Culafroy), Hijikata reprised the choreography from the first performance (see Figure 2.1). Then he followed it with a section in which four young men in black hoods came on stage and harassed the young man and jerked him around with ropes until he died.

In the second version, the violence toward the two men is striking. Rather than Divine dying of tuberculosis, she is attacked and killed. Then, Culafroy is also attacked and killed right after having sex with an older man. If the first version of the dance was an examination of the power dynamic between two men in a homoerotic relationship (or an allegory of the Occupation), the second was a look at the violence directed toward men who engage in male–male eroticism within a homophobic society.

In the "Second Women Avant-gardists" recital (April 1960), Hijikata participated in a dance titled either *Let's Go to Algeria* or *We Want to Go to Algeria*. According to Yoshito and Gôda, this was a reference to the Algerian Independence movement (Pers. conversation with Yoshito, July 12, 2007; Gôda 1987, 32). Ten dancers made up as black people wrap their heads in white burlap and jump off the stage. Grabbing a large white cloth, they billow it up and down and raise it like a sail. It is possible that these were people intent on setting sail to join the independence movement.[5] The dance gives us another small clue about the dancers' ideas about black people.

We can identify four characteristics of these early dances. The dances treat subjects that were not previously seen on stage. They attempt to engage the audience deeply by shocking them and using other techniques to reach them on a visceral level. They treat social problems or incorporate a critique of society. And finally, the dances are ministories or narratives. Later the narratives became even more fragmented and submerged, although Hijikata continued to inject moments of social critique into his works.

Neo-Dada, Happenings, and Surrealism

Hijikata began to turn away from narrative vignettes to collaborations with visual and plastic artists from neo-Dada, happenings, and surrealism. One collaborator was the neo-Dada artist Yoshimura Masanobu, who designed the costumes for the second "Hijikata Tatsumi DANCE EXPERIENCE Gathering" in September 1961. For the dance *Mid-afternoon Secret Ceremony of a Hermaphrodite*, Yoshimura wrapped Hijikata in gauze and plaster of Paris to make him look like a figure from a George Segal sculpture. When the plaster dried, it cracked as Hijikata moved. Over time, the fissured-mummified look evolved into the use of smooth white face and body paint, which became a signature of butô.

The collaboration with Yoshimura was an early harbinger of change in Hijikata's art. During this period, Hijikata palled around with plastic artists from the worlds of neo-Dadaism, happenings, and anti-art, such as Hi Red Center artists Akasegawa Genpei, Nakanishi Natsuyuki, and Takamatsu Jirô. After the failure of the US-Japan Mutual Security Treaty (ANPO) protests in the 1960s, these artists increasingly sought other means to contest the power of the state, rather than just demonstrations. Eckersall notes that these artists advocated anarchy, direct action, and transformation in their approach to much of the received wisdom of the art world

Figure 2.1a Yoshito in the dark with chicken accompanied by one or two other men. *Forbidden Colors*, revised version, 1959. Photograph by the Kurokawa Shashin Studio. Courtesy of the NPO Dance Archive Network and the Ôno Kazuo Dance Studio.

(Eckersall 2018, 150). Marotti adds that the artists sought "to move beyond presentation, and representation, to an intervention in appearance and perception itself as the necessary first step to transformation" (Marotti 2013a, 201). That is, the artists conceived of reality as not just having to do with the properties of things but also involving how things interact with each other. They thought they should figure out how to see and show the interactions between things, and only then could they work on changing them. They dragged art out of the museum and gallery and onto the street and into the subway; they turned new and found objects into art; they staged

Figure 2.1b Digitally enhanced version of Fig. 2.1a *Forbidden Colors*, revised version, 1959.

performances of their own. Chong describes the era as consisting of "cross-genre or interdisciplinary and intermedia work" and depicts the artists as wanting to find out whether or not "artists and their works can have a truly participatory relationship with reality" (Chong 2012, 46, 34). Hijikata and his peers responded to that broader artistic movement by questioning what kinds of movement and actions could be considered as dance, but also incorporating elements from other spheres and artistic media into their dances.

Two important shows were *Anma* (1963) and *Rose-Colored Dance* (1965).[6] *Anma* (Masseur/Masseuse) featured a stage made of tatami mats set in the middle of the hall with the audience seated both in the back of the auditorium and on stage. Everyday items such as children's toys (*denden daiko*) and codd-neck bottles were visible on the stage. The performers wrestle, sprint back and forth across the stage, ride bicycles, mime throwing baseballs from one side of the universe to the other, wrap up soldiers and carry them off stage, and lean a tatami mat against a performer while he dances with a high-heel shoe on his hand. At one point, a performer grabs grossly oversized testicle-shaped bags suspended between the legs of other performers.

It is not clear whether the dancers intended something specific in all of these elements. Maybe some parts meant nothing at all and are more properly characterized as happenings. But carrying soldiers off the stage was a reference to the homeless soldiers who were gradually disappeared from society in the run-up to the 1964 Olympics (Pers. conversation with Yoshito, July 12, 2007). The athletic movements can also be seen as a reference to the Olympics and the increased importance of athletics in Japanese society in the mid-1960s.

Rose-colored Dance was just as zany as *Anma*, featuring a dancer with a vagina drawn on his back, men and Victor Nipper dogs facing into the backdrop, sports movements, a dancer with a doll, a fake-acupuncture diagram, a rickshaw, and a threesome dancing ballet movements. Two scenes were strongly homoerotic. In one, two men caked in plaster-of-Paris entwine with each other. In the other, Hijikata and Ôno, both in long flowy gowns, perform arabesques and tendu together, lie one atop the other, and Hijikata looks up Ôno's dress. The multimedia or intermedia aspect of this performance is particularly important. In one scene a photographer comes on stage and takes pictures of the performers and the audience. In another, Hijikata poses by a larger-than-life photograph of a shimpa female impersonator. Through this, the audience sees the photographic process from start (taking photos) to finish (developed photo on stage).

Mirroring *Anma* in its citation of homeless veterans being erased from society, *Rose-Colored Dance* contained implicit political themes. A barber shaves heads on stage during the opening. This referred to the military shaving the heads of soldiers. What is more, the photographs of the barber shaving the dancers' heads look strikingly like the photos of the fishermen of the *Lucky Dragon* having the irradiated hair shaved from their heads after being exposed to US atomic testing radiation near the Bikini Atoll (Y. Tanaka 2010). Given Hijikata's fine-tuned attention to daily life and mass media, it seems likely that Hijikata was referring to two different kinds of shaved heads, one a manifestation of the Japanese state exercising power over the bodies of its citizens, and the other a manifestation of the power that the US state exercises over Japanese bodies.

This was a heady era of performances that we can fruitfully compare with Judson Dance Theater in terms of revisiting various kinds of pedestrian movements, and in the intersection of dance with Fluxus, happenings, Dadaism, and surrealism, but contrast with Judson Dance Theater in terms of chance procedures (other than improvisation), which did not interest the Japanese dancers.

"Extravagantly Tragic Comedy: Photo Theater Starring a Japan Dancer and Genius (Hijikata Tatsumi)"

From 1965 to 1968, Hijikata participated in several unrelated photo shoots with the photographer Hosoe Eikô (Hosoe and Hill 1986, unpaginated). One was an abduction scene in the backstreets of Tokyo. In other shoots, Hijikata interacts in dubious ways with other residents of Tokyo, pulling faces at kids and running by concrete, high-density housing projects. A third set of shoots took place either on the outskirts of Tokyo in the fields, or else in a rural northeastern town, where Hijikata's extended family had a summer villa (not shown in any of the photographs). Hijikata cavorts (and appears to defecate) in rice fields, plays a trickster figure with the local villagers, and clowns around with the rural kids. Hosoe collected photos from these shoots into an exhibition, "Extravagantly Tragic Comedy: Photo Theater Starring a Japan Dancer and Genius (Hijikata Tatsumi)" mounted in March and April of 1968. Hosoe then issued a selection of these photos as a photobook, *Kamaitachi* (Hosoe 1969).[7]

Mirroring its varied composition, *Kamaitachi* contains seven distinct narrative strands, including those described already, Hijikata with a bride, and Hijikata possibly dying and being mourned by an old woman. However, most commentators have been unaware of or ignored the original unrelated shoots and the narrative complexity of the photobook, and focused on Hijikata's appearance in rural settings. Commentators have largely assumed that Hijikata's trips to rural Japan led him to explore his rural roots in nature. It is certainly true that Hijikata began to feature ethnically marked costumes in his dances, such as kimono worn sideways or backward, but as we shall see, Hijikata's relationship to rural Japan was considerably more complicated than much of the commentary on *Kamaitachi* would imply. Such interpretations ignore the apparent defecation in the rice field, but they had an outsize influence on the subsequent practice of butô.

Rosemary Candelario notes that the side of butô oriented to nature can largely be traced back to *Kamaitachi* (Candelario, 2021, 212–213). She observes that Hijikata's student and Dairakudakan co-founder Bishop Yamada (Yamada Ippei) was the first person to take seriously the notion that butô should have a connection to nature. He relocated to the foothills of a mountain in the rural area of Tsuruoka "seeking resilience through the power of mountains" (Kosuge 2018, 217, and Candelario, 2021, 223–224). Hijikata was quite sardonic about Yamada's move, humorously encouraging Yamada to "create a community frantically running about to escape from turkeys chasing them" (Kosuge 2018, 220). As it happens, the rural populace did not have much affinity for avant-garde dance, so it was quite difficult for Yamada to succeed, but other dancers were increasingly drawn to rural areas and nature.

Hijikata Tatsumi and Japanese People: Rebellion of the Body

After the 1960s happenings-style performances, *Hijikata Tatsumi and Japanese People: Rebellion of the Body* (1968) was pivotal for Hijikata. He enacted several characters, such as a man being carried atop a cart at the head of a procession, a man dressed in a bride's kimono, a naked man sporting an erect golden phallus, an elegant woman in a ball gown and black gloves, a cancan dancer in a one-piece dress, a sailor, a young girl (shôjo), and a man hoisted into the air as if being vertically crucified. Some scholars have seen the dance as Hijikata's farewell to Western dance before he embarked on his exploration of himself and in the process began to engage with Japanese ethnic identity. Others have seen it as the culmination of the happenings style. I see the dance as continuation of many of the concerns that had already preoccupied Hijikata, but also as the first step in Hijikata's generative butô method.

As William Marotti has observed, the dance is predominantly a collection of Hijikata's prior solos from student recitals. Marotti argues that the best way to ascertain Hijikata's immediate aims is to figure out what he was thinking about in each of these works (Marotti 2019).[8] Lack of space (and the lack of audiovisual recordings) prevents detailed analysis of each dance. But we can get a sense of Hijikata's concerns, because each dance has a set of thematic points that include a literary source work and the concerns of the stage designer, which Hijikata reworks in his choreography.

In July 1967, Hijikata choreographed *Metemotionalphysics* (*Keijijô-gaku*, also translated as "Emotion in Metaphysics") for the recital of his student Takai Tomiko. The title was drawn from a poetry collection by Kato Ikuya (Marotti 2019). The stage designer Nakanishi Natsuyuki painted the insides of a body on Hijikata's back, as if Hijikata's skin had been peeled back to reveal his muscles and skeletal structure. Hijikata entered sitting or standing on a cart borne by stagehands. This was apparently a reference to a procession by the King of Fools or the Roman emperor Heliogabalus.[9] The backdrop (also by Nakanishi) was a blueprint photo of naked men from the back.[10] Takai danced with mirrors on her breasts, perhaps reflecting the male gaze of the audience (Figure 2.2).

In August, Hijikata choreographed *Butô Genet* for Ishii Mitsutaka. Sailors and men in ruffled short dresses appear in the dance, perhaps referencing Shibusawa Tatsuhiko's recent translation of Genet's *Querelle of Brest* (see Figure 2.3). The following June, Hijikata again choreographed a recital for Ishii, *Genetarianne* (*Ojuneshô*; also translated as *My Little Genet*, Marotti 2019). In it, he danced a solo titled "Bride (Cat)" dressed in a dazzling white backward kimono and another solo in a one-piece dress and athletic shoes.

In August, he choreographed the recital of Ashikawa Yôko, with the lengthy title, *To My Friend Violette Nozière Boarding Train D53264 "The Landscape Is Always Already Receding into the Distance" From the Butô Princess Yôko Who Rides the*

Figure 2.2 Mirrors on Takai Tomiko's breasts in *Metemotionalphysics*, 1967, choreog. Hijikata Tatsumi. Photograph by Nakatani Tadao. Courtesy of Nakatani Tadashi, NPO Butoh Laboratory Japan, and the Hijikata Tatsumi Archive at the Keio University Arts Center.

Pacific 231. This mouthful referred to several things. Nozière was a French woman infamously convicted of murdering her father, who was a train driver (Maza 2012). *Pacific 231* refers to the orchestral work composed by Arthur Honegger in 1923. "The landscape is always already receding into the distance" was the title of the Shibusawa essay in Nakamura Hiroshi's photo album *Notice from a Telescope* (Boenkyô kara no kokuji). Nakamura also designed the poster and stage art. His poster featured a train and blue nipples, and separate scenes had a train painted (or projected) on the backdrop. Nakamura's paintings treated trains as symbols of continuity between prewar

Figure 2.3　Sailor and men in ruffled short dresses in *Butô Genet* (1967), choreog. Hijikata Tatsumi. Photographer unknown. Courtesy of the NPO Butoh Laboratory Japan, and the Hijikata Tatsumi Archive at the Keio University Arts Center.

Japanese militarist power and postwar Japanese governmental activities despite the fact that the government claimed to have repudiated the fascist past (Kunimoto 2018, 1–3). Nakamura was also preoccupied with the way that trains served the newly invigorated travel industry in the postwar era. One scene features a hooded figure (likely Ashikawa) greeting a woman in a Hawaiian-flavored floral print dress, perhaps as a reference to the advent of low-cost airfare to Hawaii (see Figure 2.4). Finally, ubiquitous in Nakamura's paintings were the *shôjo*, the young schoolgirls, who were to become more famous as the prepubescent objects of male desire of the manga-anime world, but also as the consumer/producers with disposable income of that same world of manga-anime and the world of domestic and international travel.[11] Nakamura's photo book is an engagement with trains, machinery, and masculinity, and schoolgirls, travel, and femininity. In the dance, Ashikawa enacted either Hijikata's or her own versions of these shôjo.

Just two weeks before *Hijikata Tatsumi and Japanese People*, Hijikata choreographed a second performance for Takai Tomiko, *Mandala Villa*, again based on Kato Ikuya's haiku collection, *Metemotionalphysics*. In it, Hijikata danced a "Corset Dance" solo, and sure enough, the corset turned up during Hijikata's caper as a cancan dancer two weeks later.

I have argued that we should understand the dance as concerning all four parts of the title equally: Hijikata himself, Japanese people, rebellion/revolution, and the body or bodies (Baird 2012, 4). Marotti fleshes out each of these categories. What

Figure 2.4 Woman in floral print dress in *To My Friend Violette Nozière* (1968), choreog. Hijikata Tatsumi. Photograph by Nakatani Tadao. Courtesy of Nakatani Tadashi, NPO Butoh Laboratory Japan, and the Hijikata Tatsumi Archive at the Keio University Arts Center.

was *Hijikata Tatsumi and Japanese People* "about"? Well, it was "about" the ideas that Hijikata was dealing with already; specifically, it was "about" him exploring these issues using Artaud and Heliogabalus, Genet and *Querelle of Brest*, and Shibusawa. It was "about" the way that he himself, and the Japanese people, intersected with crossdressing, gender, masculinity, the figure of the shôjo, mass media, consumerism, domestic and international travel, and technology. Marotti also argues that we should understand the rebellion or revolution in this dance as Hijikata's attempt to explore different kinds of political expression. We can clearly see Hijikata embodying various characters, but also exploring himself and what connections he may have to the

Figure 2.5 Hijikata Tatsumi embodying a character in *Hijikata Tatsumi and Japanese People*, 1968. Photographer unknown. Courtesy of the NPO Butoh Laboratory Japan and the Hijikata Tatsumi Archive at the Keio University Arts Center.

various characters (see Figure 2.5). Given that six of nine scenes are collected from prior performances, if *Hijikata Tatsumi and Japanese People* was a combination of self-exploration and exploration of other characters, it was one that Hijikata had been conducting over the course of several dances spanning more than a year.

Hijikata's Generative Butô Method

As outlined in the introduction, sometime around 1967, Hijikata embarked on a massive project that was to change both his dances and his means of creating dances.

Uno Kuniichi argues that Hijikata's goal was to literally understand everything about himself and what had formed him with the aim of achieving a thoroughly generative body-mind (Uno 2013, section 4). Drawing on Deleuze, Uno calls this the "genesis of an unknown body," that is, a body that has never before been encountered. As noted, there was a widespread assumption that humans are thoroughly socialized and this socialization sets limits on what we can feel and understand about the world. The artists thought it was possible to neutralize the effects of this socialization through various means. One was to use surrealism to bump themselves out of habitual ways of thinking and feeling. Another way to neutralize conventions was to study oneself with the idea of understanding everything that had shaped you so that you could be aware of things that might be blocking you. So Hijikata began to explore himself. He recalled songs he sang as a child, people he met, stories he heard, thoughts he had. Uno refers to this as "an endless recording of all phenomena and sensations that have visited the body" (Uno 2013, section 4).

These surrealist exercises and deep dives into his body-mind freed Hijikata from habitual thinking but constantly had a second function of revealing new poses and movements. Hijikata and his dancers also studied people, animals, objects, art prints, sounds, smells, tastes, sensations, along with philosophies and political ideas. From these they collected thousands of poses, dance steps, and qualities. Many of these are recorded in notebooks, but many more are only stored within the bodies of the dancers. Hijikata could create new movements directly from these observations by taking a pose from a painting or movement from an animal or object (such as a sail flapping in the wind). He could also use these materials indirectly as tools for evoking a transformation in his dancers. By having his dancers imagine a quality from a painting, sensation, sound, or taste while performing dance steps, he could alter their movements.

These alterations could take many forms. They could apply ideas, qualities, or actions to a movement (such as stickiness, melting, granulation, liquification). They might vary the extent of a movement (e.g., let it spread outward beyond the body in clouds, radii, or planes). They could change the bodily organ that performed a movement (make the leg into a hand or imagine the finger as an eye). They could alter the imagined character doing the movement or the imagined background in which a movement was performed (imagine performing the movement as a young girl or an old woman; imagine performing the movement inside of stone). They could imagine different sounds or smells while moving.

Then Hijikata would knit poses and movements together (each with their accompanying imagery work) to create dances. He used these strings of movements to embody stories or characters (which might have been from his past, or might be characters he wanted to become, or might have been strange amalgamations that existed only in his mind). But he did not usually tell the audience what those stories were or who the characters were. Given that the movements and imagery work were somewhat abstracted from the content of those stories, he should have been able to embody any story he liked. In practice, the underlying narratives focused on marginalized people (although there are any number of strange characters flitting through Hijikata's universe).

As Hijikata and his dancers practiced, they became increasingly able to direct their attention to various parts of their bodies, and ever more nuanced about how they could use evocation to alter movements. There was supposed to be a feedback loop in which the more you studied yourself and your surroundings, and the more you created and modified movements, the more you would increase your sensitivity. The more you increased your sensitivity, the more you would be aware of blockages that could be hindering you from seeing yourself and the world more clearly. The more you saw the world clearly, the more successfully you could study yourself and your surroundings, et cetera, et cetera.

To give you an idea of how this worked in practice, here is a sequence of Hijikata's presented at Tamano Hiroko's workshop in 2015 (possibly taken from a *Seaweed* (Gibasa) performance at Kyoto University):

Flower sprouting from torso
Smell good smell
Smell goes up into forehead and sprouts 3rd eye.
Smell blows eyelashes open.
Faust on shoulders (with lots of animals).
Living in forest, spiders, deer, bugs.
Something makes fissures and cracks in your shoulder which crumbles
Waterfall down back (and not imaginary one, but one that actually exists somewhere)
Smell of water coming through your shoulder
Behind belly button is a small pond surrounded by forests with artists living there
Knees are a desert of rolling rocks that is hot and cold, with a small family of pioneers with a new baby living behind your knee
Sky is weighing down on your head
Wind of the universe blowing through you which is like a mother holding a child when it is about to take its first step

At each point, Tamano would layer some new nuance into our movement by having us imagine one of these things and then show us how to execute the movement. If you have not done such dance training, I assure you that it is quite amazing how many new movements and sensations can come out of your body-mind. All these evocation exercises were in turn the basis for what came later. We subsequently got different movements (sailboat contractions and expansions with wind running through our body and talking to the sky with our penis). One dancer misunderstood how the various dance steps should fit together and asked Tamano, "When do we do this?" (the first thirteen prompts) and Tamano replied, "Oh, all the time." That is, in theory, we were supposed to keep doing all these thirteen things while doing the ensuing movements.

A first glimpse into Hijikata's new way of doing things was *Seaweed* (Gibasa— November 3–5, 1970, or January 21, 1972[12]). There are plenty of moments that seem as if they came right out of the previous era. One of the dancers performs behind a plexiglass window (with horseshoes affixed to it) designed in homage to Duchamp's *The Bride Stripped Bare by Her Bachelors, Even (The Large Glass)*. In another scene, one dancer holds a window horizontally in front of her waist, while another dancer (who wears a drum on her chest) pokes her head through a window. In the transformation of Duchamp's window into a dance costume (even to the point of literalizing the drum-like chocolate grinder), Hijikata reworks Duchamp's ideas and brings them into the world of dance. In a third scene (part of the washed-out section), one woman lies on her back holding her window on top of herself with her mouth pressed up against the glass. Meanwhile, the other dancer holds her window horizontally over the first window. Duchamp's window has been turned into a specimen case.

The engagement with rural life or nature is more pronounced in this dance than previous dances. Stalks or reeds cover the floor. In one scene, stagehands covered in stalks carry two dancers around on platforms. During several moments, nearly naked women squat and writhe among the reeds. Many of the movements seem almost animalistic.

Other parts of this dance reflect the different training and a new method of dance composition. A scene in front of brass panels features six dancers clad in form-fitting long dresses moving forward in near-unison in a slow walk. Their bodies are slightly contorted, their arms akimbo. They seem inward-focused. Then the six spread their arms wide but drooping down at the wrists and hang their heads and step slowly from side to side in a way that makes a fascinating sense of planes moving back and forth in relation to each other. Then they use a karate kick to extend their right leg to the front with the knee bent and then swipe their leg in a quarter turn outward and turn and stamp to their right and drop into an animal pose, a hunched 4th position with clenched-wrists and -fists. There is a density to the movements as if they are products of extreme concentration. The dancers have been taught a carefully choreographed sequence.

Scholars and dancers originally came to know about these evocation exercises because dancers published notebooks containing their own records of rehearsals and archivists published facsimiles of Hijikata's notebooks. These records became known as "butoh-fu" or butô-notation, patterned after the Japanese word for musical notation, *gakufu*. However, it should be obvious that while Hijikata's dancers can use the prompts they personally learned to reproduce movements, Hijikata was doing something much bigger than creating a new kind of dance notation. The notebooks were merely an incomplete means of recording something that spanned sounds (and particularly onomatopoeia), smells, sensations, memories, and that is mostly stored inside the dancers' body-minds. Rather than using the term "butoh-fu," I prefer to use the term "Hijikata methods," or to refer to these experiments as something like "generative butô methods."

Origins of the Generative Butô Method

Where did these new methods come from? Disappointingly, I don't know. Previously, I outlined five possible sources for Hijikata. These were surrealism, Stanislavski, Huysmans, Artaud, and Noguchi taisô. From surrealism (via such artists as Takiguchi Shûzô), Hijikata appears to have picked up a general approach to combinations in which one mashes two things together and then sees what results from the combination (Baird 2012, 2–4). Stanislavski's use of various kinds of imagery to change a performance would have been familiar to almost everybody, so it is possible that Hijikata adopted the use of imagery work but gave it a surrealist flare (170–171). Huysmans describes the protagonist of *Au Rebours* (Against the Grain) as using almost alchemical mixtures of various elements and liquors to approximate other sensations (Huysmans 2003, 46–47), so Hijikata possibly drew a hint from Huysmans for mixing various imagery exercises together to produce new dance steps (Baird 2012, 162). Artaud is usually more famous for his idea of a theater of cruelty, but he also advocated cataloging and categorizing all possible movements and noises and then using a broader range of them in his idea of total theater. It is possible to see traces of Artaud in Hijikata's impulse to categorize and catalog a myriad of movements and sensations to be used for creating novel steps and movements (Baird 2012, 134–135). Noguchi Michizô created a movement training system similar to the somatics of Mabel Elsworth Todd, in which one uses imagery work to alter the body-mind complex.

Since the publication of that research (Baird 2012), I have continued to study this puzzle, but only multiplied Hijikata's possible sources. For starters, we can accentuate the case for Artaud. Hijikata's mime teacher, Oikawa Hironobu, studied in France with Etienne Decroux and Jean Louis Barrault (who both had worked extensively with Artaud). Oikawa seems to have returned to Japan with the goal of spreading both the mime of Decroux and his own ideas about Artaud. It is not entirely clear how Oikawa understood Artaud. Yoshida Yukihiko writes that Oikawa took from Artaud a focus on breathing techniques from *tai chi, qigong,* and yoga, but also notes that Oikawa taught Artaud's triads from the essay "Affective Athleticism," and Barrault's discourse on them.[13] In "An Affective Athleticism," Artaud presents nine different kinds of breathing, and states that combinations of these breaths can have color and rhythm, and also says, "an actor can arrive by means of breath at a feeling which he does not have, provided its effects are judiciously combined" (Artaud 1958, 136–137). Therefore, Hijikata might have encountered a specific essay by Artaud or had an indirect connection to Artaud through Barrault.

Vangeline argues that it is equally important that Oikawa was a conduit for Decroux's corporeal mime. She describes the aim of Decroux as "'making the invisible visible' and creating *presence* in the mover." She continues, "corporeal mime relies on genuine sensations and emotions inside the mover, as well as a precise technique sometimes called the 'grammar of the body.'" She describes both butô and corporeal mime as sharing techniques such as "a strong inward concentration, 'waiting' or 'listening' in order to build an internal presence and connection . . . and a condensation of energy and feelings inside the body, which only escapes through movement by following internal impulses" (Vangeline 2020, xxviii). Stephen Barber wrote that Oikawa thought that Hijikata had stolen butô from him (Barber 2005, 28). Perhaps Oikawa's complaint that he had been robbed stems from the similarities between what he taught Hijikata and what Hijikata eventually became famous for.

Another possible source is actually Ôno himself. Kuniyoshi writes of the pre-butô Ôno "borrowing reference images from such literature and art and endeavoring to bring concreteness to his own mental world" (Kuniyoshi 2018, 58–59). She quotes a reviewer who wrote, "Ôno embraced ever further inside himself his own images . . . , it is *fun to follow along with his writhing bountiful images which are whirling around inside him*" (Kuniyoshi 2018, 33, quoting Mitsuyoshi Natsuya from 1959, emphasis mine). Vangeline says that Oikawa argued that Ôno was already doing something like butô in 1960 (Vangeline 2020, xxx). Usually, we think of Ôno as following Hijikata's lead after 1959. We might, however, have cause to reverse the arrow and see Hijikata as learning from Ôno (and Oikawa), although as I explain later there are problems with this thesis.

If corporeal mime was decisive for Hijikata, we may be underestimating the importance of the mime artist Yoneyama Mamako. Yoneyama studied ballet from a young age, and then some time in the mid-1950s saw Marcel Marceau in Japan and began to study mime. Huston's reproduction of Yoneyama's "Internal Monologue" (created after she started teaching in the United States) has the flavor of some of Hijikata's imagery work:

> Where am I?
> Narrow, dark, and wet.
> Am I at the bottom of the pit?
> A little light above me.
> I climb.
> [. . .]
> My hair is caught.
> My neck is tangled.
> [. . .]
> It sticks in my eye. (Huston 1976, 357)

We do not have enough information about Yoneyama's mime to say whether or not her mime of the 1950s was the same as her later "Zen Meditation Mime" in the United States. Consequently, we cannot be sure what Hijikata might have learned from her. But she may have taught the use of mental imagery to Hijikata. Hijikata may have, then, expanded the use of mime imagery work (whether from Oikawa or Yoneyama) in strange and surrealist ways.

Richard Hawkins suggests two other sources. First, he encourages us to tease out what Hijikata might have learned from male prostitutes. Hijikata originally wrote:

> My fierce inclination to the art of imitation arose out of my friendship with the male prostitutes at Ueno Kurumazaka. An unkempt head of hair, size 11 feet, rouge, freezing to death in a public lavatory—with these tools at hand any choreographer, no matter how lazy, must create dance. (Hijikata 1998, 1: 190; translation modified from Hijikata 2000a, 39)

Rather than seeing Hijikata as writing this purely for shock value, Hawkins urges thinking about how prostitutes perform for their respective audiences. He wrote:

> streetwalkers have to maintain a very specific relationship between themselves and the people that pass by. To possible customers they need to . . . give off signals of deniable availability as well as linger but not, in case of cops, seem to loiter. The consciousness of one's own body in correspondence with a divergent spectator-ship and the play between intensities of seductiveness and deniability would seem to be very important things for a dancer to know.

Hawkins further stressed two things: "the peculiar relationship" "of both the deniable and the available" and "the particularities of seeming to walk while standing still" (Pers. correspondence May 25, 2012). In the later imagery work, the performers must simultaneously hold several images in their minds while moving. Perhaps prostitutes have to do something similar—e.g., imagine moving while immobile in order to convey to police officers that they are moving along when in fact they are not. Hijikata may have taken a hint from the prostitutes about imagining contradictory things that could be read differently by different audiences.

Hawkins also suggests the collages of Jean Genet as a source. After rereading Genet's *Our Lady of the Flowers*, Hawkins observes:

> a mere seven paragraphs into *Our Lady of the Flowers*, [. . .] the narrator [. . .] has "managed to get about twenty photographs, and with bits of chewed bread" has "pasted them on the back of the cardboard sheet of regulations that hangs on the wall." Culled from newspapers, magazines and the covers of adventure novels, they are pictures of . . . "a young Mexican half-breed, a gaucho, a Caucasian horseman and . . . [sic] clumsy drawings: profiles of pimps and apaches with a smoking butt, or the outline of a tough with a hard-on."[. . .]
>
> This impoverished prisoner's collage made from handsome cut outs and glued down with spit and cum is the springboard [. . .] from which the entire novel gets launched. If that's not a version [. . .] of how Hijikata's butoh-fu perverted, betrayed and misinterpreted reproductions of deKooning or Dubuffet into new forms of movement in dance, I'm not sure what is. (Hawkins 2015)

As Hawkins noted, Genet describes his imprisoned alter-ego making collages. As I earlier argued, one of the points of Hijikata's collages (both in the scrapbooks and also in one's mind using imagery) was to stimulate some response in his dancer that would lead to a new experience in performance. That is not so different from Genet's alter-ego arousing himself with collages of erotically stimulating cut-outs.

As Hawkins notes, the other point of collage is to pervert the individual elements into something new. Reading further in *Our Lady of the Flowers* reveals Divine doing something very like what Hijikata later did:

> With her head beneath the sheets, [Divine] would devise complicated debauches, involving two, three, or four persons, in which all the partners would arrange to discharge in her, on her, and for her at the same time.... She was willing to be the single goal of all of these lusts, and her mind strained in an effort to be conscious of them simultaneously as they drifted about in a voluptuousness poured in from all sides. Her body would tremble from head to foot. She felt personalities that were strange to her passing through her. (Genet 1963, 125)

And later:

> In the course of a single evening she seemed to be four or five characters at the same time. She thereby acquired the richness of a multiple personality. (133)

And still again:

> It was a simple matter to choose a physique for him, for she possessed in her secret, lonely-girl's imagination, for her nights' pleasure, a stock of thighs, arms, torsos, faces, hair, teeth, necks, and knees, and she knew how to assemble them so as to make of them a live man to whom she loaned a soul—which was always the same one for each of these constructions: the one she would have liked to have herself. (134)

These descriptions of Divine struggling to be conscious of four things at once, feeling as though strange personalities were passing through her, and combining a stock of bodily members to produce a lover sound a lot like the kind of mental exercises Hijikata demanded of his dancers. Thus, Genet is a possible source, not just for Hijikata's earlier works but even for his later experiments in evocation.

The next candidate is the painter Nakanishi Natsuyuki.[14] The poster for Hijikata's 1965 *Rose-Colored Dance* contained a reproduction of the figures in the famous Fontainebleau painting *Gabrielle d'Estrées et une de ses soeurs* (~1594) with their fingers dipped in pink paint. Sometime in 1965 or 1966, Nakanishi borrowed the figures of the d'Estrées sisters (including the fingers dipped in pink paint) and created a collage work of art by combining them with figures from Cezanne's *The Card Players* and Millet's *The Evening Prayer*. Then in 1968, Nakanishi created a photographic collage, in which he restaged the three sets of figures using photographs of people wearing gas masks (Morishita and Yamazaki 1997, 34; and Yanai 2000, 30). Perhaps, Hijikata appropriated his technique of reproducing poses and qualities from paintings in his dances, in part, from Nakanishi's technique of reproducing poses and characters from paintings in his own artworks. Moreover, it is a short step from Nakanishi reproducing figures from paintings using figures in gas masks, to Hijikata creating a dance step out of imaging an artist family living behind one's knee.

In the end, we are probably not going to find a definitive source for Hijikata's generative butô methods. The timing is off for the mime genealogy of Decroux/Oikawa/Yoneyama/Ôno, and for Genet, but perhaps these techniques just needed time to percolate. Art magazines were such a huge source for Hijikata and Ashikawa's evocative experiments that Nakanishi's collages might have been the pivotal point for Hijikata's new techniques, but that is just a guess. It is clear that there were precursors and then later corroborations for what he did. As I noted in the introduction, both Calamoneri and Lawler spend considerable resources pursuing similarities between Hijikata's generative butô methods and many other kinds of theater, so perhaps there were so many things that led to that point that it should not be a surprise that Hijikata ended up there.

Hijikata's Relationship to and Critique of Japan

There was an unintended consequence of Hijikata's turn to exploring himself and his world. As he explored his own past and other Japanese people who might have affected him in some way, he sometimes put characters on stage who wore ethnically marked costumes or moved in ethnically marked ways. His personal trajectory dovetailed with a movement called the "hometown boom," and an advertising campaign called "Discover Japan" to induce urban people to use the train. These movements sought to locate the unsullied core of Japan in rural areas uncontaminated by the modern Western technological world (Ivy 1995, 29–44). This led some chauvinistic Japanese commentators to assume that Hijikata was trying to create a dance suited to the Japanese body, or that he was nostalgic for his hometown area of Tohoku, northeast Japan.

I have argued that in fact Hijikata was critical of his own society (Baird 2012, 151–152, 156). More recently, Sara Jansen has revisited this issue. She archly observes that you can only make the argument that Hijikata was celebrating or nostalgic for Tohoku by ignoring what Hijikata actually said. She also notes that an emphasis on Tohoku makes it seem like the dances just magically appear out of his past. This discounts the genuine labor Hijikata did as a choreographer intentionally assembling movements in sequences (Jansen 2018, 105). According to Jansen, rather than present a nostalgic view of Tohoku, Hijikata,

> associates the countryside he grew up in above all with death, loneliness, and misery. Hijikata underscores the area's marginal position and notes the real poverty and destitution of its inhabitants. In interviews, he contrasts the idyllic image of the rice fields with images of himself as a child, snot and tears running down his

face as he walks along the ridges carrying urns filled with the bones and ashes of his siblings, observing labor so harsh that it made farmers pretend to be working, or experiencing cold so fierce that it makes one's bones snap. (Jansen 2018, 104)

This is Hijikata's Tohoku: "loneliness and misery." Hijikata's fellow dancer Kasai even says that he thinks that Hijikata "did not like Japanese naïve rural culture" (translation modified from Kasai and Ishii 2013).

Jansen and Kasai were preceded in this argument by the poet Tomioka Taeko. She engaged in a dialogue with the theater practitioner Takechi Tetsuji, in which he proposed that Hijikata adapted a form of walking in rice paddies called the *namba*, which he asserts is common to all Japanese performing arts (Takechi and Tomioka 2018, 85, 87).[15] Tomioka interrupts, saying she never heard Hijikata talk about *namba*. Rather, he talked about how a person walks *after* they have stepped out of a rice paddy and are walking on firm ground, but are completely exhausted (Takechi and Tomioka 2018, 87–88). That is, it seems from Tomioka that Hijikata was interested in movements that were not the basis for an art form because they were overlooked by the political and performing arts establishments. To be sure, Hijikata took movements from Tohoku, but they were almost invariably the movements of the most dispossessed and marginalized people, and those movements were passed through a surrealist filter, rendering them almost unrecognizable.

Inata Naomi approaches Hijikata's relationship to Tohoku from a different angle. She argues that he was seeking a place for himself within the Japanese dance landscape, which included kabuki dance (*Nihon buyô*), ballet, modern dance, folk dance, and Soviet socialist ballet (which was supposed to be national in form and socialist in content) (Inata 2018, 59, 62). One might think that he would overlap with "folk" dance. However, she contends that "folk" designated a codified set of performances (60).[16] Instead, she argues that Hijikata was interested in not-yet-commodified local movement. She characterizes this as "all the elements excluded from the two spheres of Japanese dance" and further as "a fusion of Japan and the West, . . . and not simply the given 'traditional folk arts'" (68). Jansen concurs and cites Hijikata's dismissive attitude toward "souvenir dance" (*o-miyage buyô*), precisely the kind of codified dance a tourist might collect on a visit to "discover" rural Japan (Jansen 2018, 104).

Kosuge Hayato takes this logic one step further. Drawing on recent scholarship that theorizes Tohoku as an internal colony of Japan's urban center, he argues that Hijikata's Tohoku functions in just such a way. The urban core sucks the wealth and resources out of rural Japan and displaces to rural outposts all the very real ills of society, such as airports, environmental degradation (and more recently nuclear power) (Kosuge 2018, 214–215).[17] Michelle Dent calls this the "everyday sadomasochism of . . . Japan pimping its marginalized population for economic gains" (Dent 2016, 247). Kurihara notes that Hijikata often observed that "Tohoku's historical past was as a colony which exported soldiers, horses, and women to central Japan" (Kurihara 2000, 21). These people were not untouched by the modern era, but rather connected in bodily ways to the wider world.

The flip side of misunderstanding Hijikata as trying to find the essence of Japanese people has been that many people outside of Japan have seen butô as an invitation to explore their own selves and cultures (Candelario 2021, 210). Even though the circumstances of Hijikata's timing have contributed to cultural chauvinists within Japan seeing him as articulating Japanese uniqueness, butô has become a kind of anticolonial dance practice around the world. I would add a word of caution here. The photographer Kamiyama Teijirô once made the off-hand comment that "for Hijikata there was only himself." Ethnicity only existed for Hijikata insofar as it had affected him, and it was something to be worked through. It was not a fixed category that he had to accept. If you are a dancer thinking about exploring your own origins, remember to spend as much (or more!) time thinking critically about your origins as you do drawing new movements from them.

Twenty-Seven Nights for Four Seasons and Summer Storm

All this research culminated in the October–November 1972 *Twenty-Seven Nights for Four Seasons*, a colossal work featuring five different dances, "Story of Smallpox," "Dissolute Jewel," "Thoughts of an Applicator," "Melting Candy," and "Seaweed Granny." This series of performances is a veritable collection of characters and inventive choreographies, interspersed with Hijikata's solos (see Figure 2.6). Rural prostitutes, courageous prostitutes, shôjo, bulls, felines, Nijinsky, Charlie, Red Mayan, lions. Hijikata's movements are characterized by twisted torsos, hunched backs (accentuated by dancers standing on half point while crouched over), and an almost boneless sinuosity. Borrowing from Artaud (and Deleuze), Uno suggests that Hijikata created a body without organs in a "liquid or atmospheric state, floating and rejecting limit, contour, determined form" (Uno 2013, Section 4). This perhaps overly literalizes Artaud's idea of a body without organs, but the comparison is apt. The dancers are invariably out of balance. They also never lie prone on the ground or stack their bones allowing their skeletal structure to bear all their weight. So, they are never entirely at rest, but at least one major part of their bodies is tense.

Through it all, Hijikata weaves a complex layering of elements into the dances and (indirectly) engages topical and political concerns. In "Story of Smallpox," Hijikata dances covered in wisps of cotton. According to the dance critic Gôda Nario, the title was a creative substitution for the illness of leprosy, and the wisps of cotton serve as the lesions of Hansen's disease. Gôda observes that Hijikata "causes us to confront the suffering of the leper" (Gôda 2004, 148). Even after there was a cure, forced confinement in leprosaria was not outlawed in Japan until 1996 (Kitano 2002, 40, 43), so putting Hansen's disease on stage in 1972 highlights Hijikata's concern with the bodies of marginalized people.

In another solo, Hijikata adopts a reclining posture likely capturing the pathos of Michelangelo's *Pietà*. Hijikata apparently chose the visual vocabulary of the reclining

Figure 2.6 Hijikata Tatsumi in "Dissolute Jewel," *Twenty-Seven Nights for Four Seasons*, 1972. Courtesy of Torii Ryôzen, the NPO Butoh Laboratory Japan, and the Hijikata Tatsumi Archive at the Keio University Arts Center.

figure to superimpose the pathos of the *Pietà* with the environmental scourge, congenital Minamata disease, referencing the famous 1971 W. Eugene Smith and Aileen M. Smith photograph "Tomoko Uemura in Her Bath."[18] The twisted torsos, hunched backs, tension, and imbalance become the bodily vocabulary to convey marginalized characters. Whereas Uno understood Hijikata's body without organs to be a rejection of limits and forms, the tension coupled with the boneless sinuosity further suggests the marginality of the characters—they do not have a place or the wherewithal to stand comfortably or lie down and rest.

Summer Storm (Natsu no Arashi, 1972)[19] features Hijikata again dancing a solo young girl (shôjo). This is nothing like the idealized shôjo from 1968, who bounced around delightedly; rather, Hijikata portrays a middle-aged man playing the role of a young girl without any attempt to hide his age or gender. This shôjo resonates with Ôno's later gender-bending portrayals, which largely eschew sexuality. Another solo deals with leprosy, this time with a bulgy red costume, and fingers clenched at the second knuckle and held close to the body to suggest that the person has lost their fingertips and also the ability to lift their arms out from their body. One scene titled "Three Bellmers" references the surrealist doll maker Hans Bellmer and seems to explore the movements of ball-jointed dolls. In another scene, the dancers change costumes on stage and dance and then change back, questioning the convention that costume changes should take place off stage.

Hakutôbô Performances: *Lady on a Whale-String*

These performances ushered in an immensely productive era for Hijikata. He created a new dance company called Hakutôbô centered around Ashikawa. Space does not permit an examination of all of the approximately thirty-two Hakutôbô dances over the next half decade, and we do not have good records for many of them in any case. Here I will just observe some highlights. Along with the underlying narrative and the myriad of evocation exercises needed to produce all the movements, each dance tends to explore some political or contemporary concern, but also to engage the world of performing arts in some self-reflexive way.

Lady on a Whale-String (1976) features group work interspersed with superlative solos by Ashikawa. The poet Shiraishi Kazuko notes with amazement that Ashikawa seems to be able to shrink herself to half the size of the other dancers on stage without appearing to bend her knees appreciably (quoted in Kurihara 1996, 86). The "whale" of the title is not clear, but in a scrapbook, Hijikata has written a note, "(stomach of whale) inlayed whiteness" (Hijikata 1998, 2: 219). One scene features a tape recording of a German translation of the Latin description of a sea serpent by Olaus Magnus from 1555.[20] This has led Tanaka Kôji to argue that the entire dance takes place inside the stomach of a whale, which is possible, given Hijikata's bizarre imagination (Tanaka Kôji 2011, 32). In one scene, Ashikawa looks like she is covered with fish scales, which may be related to the whale of the title. A closer look reveals that she is covered in dozens of Japanese folding fans. Using fans to create something like fish scales is typical of Hijikata repurposing things. Hijikata and the costume designer use the fan to make something that it has never been used to make before and thereby change our associations with the object. Whatever the case, Tanaka Kôji observes that in the notes for this dance, Hijikata used the word "insert"/"inlay" (hamekomu, but also to trick, deceive) much more than usual in his notebooks (Tanaka Kôji 2011, 33). He concluded that Hijikata was experimenting with the concept of inlaying or insertion during this dance. Ashikawa refers to "the human skin suspended from a metal hook that we did in *Lady on a Whale-String*" (Ashikawa 1978, 97). There is a hook visible in some scenes, but no skin hanging from it. Ashikawa's character dancing under the metal hook seems, however, to have glue or tape disfiguring her face, so perhaps Hijikata and Ashikawa were thinking about how one fits into one's own skin, or what it would be like to be inlayed in your own skin (see Figure 2.7).

Due in part to complaints from neighbors, but also perhaps because Hijikata felt that butô was in danger of being exoticized by Europeans, Hijikata stopped making dances after October 1978. Kuniyoshi reports that he felt that the export of butô was premature—"like buying rice when the field is still green" (Kuniyoshi 2014, 484–485). He was drawn out of silence by Tanaka Min in 1983, and choreographed a duo for Tanaka and Ashikawa called *Extremely Quick Respiratory Bromide*. This dance toyed with the conventions of porn films, and also contained a pun in the title. "Bromide" was the word for a publicity photo (possibly because such photos were originally printed on bromide paper), so it is likely that Hijikata was slyly claiming, "Appearing in my dance is a faster way to fame than appearing in a bromide."

He also sent Ashikawa and Kobayashi on a four-city tour of Europe titled *Breasts of Japan*. This tour received mixed reviews, but it is intriguing to contemplate how *Breasts of Japan* must have looked to Europeans who may have shown up expecting to see what it was that suckled and nurtured Japanese culture, or hoped to see the stereotypical erotic geisha, or were growing accustomed to seeing Japan as a source of high-end technology. Perhaps it is no wonder that the reviews were mixed. From mid-1984 to until his untimely death in January 1986, Hijikata was again prolific. He opened classes to outsiders and choreographed several dances.

Tohoku Kabuki Plan

His final series was called *Tohoku Kabuki Plan*. Jansen observes that while Hijikata certainly toyed with some elements from kabuki, both sides of "Tohoku kabuki" should have the same weight. It was not just supposed to be a Tohoku version of kabuki, but a kabuki version of Tohoku. She writes that Hijikata "employs kabuki as a procedure to spectacularize Tohoku" (Jansen 2018, 104). What is more, Jansen reminds us that kabuki was originally the dance of perversion, stemming from the verb *kabuku* (to slant, to behave oddly, to attire oneself strangely), but also that the word

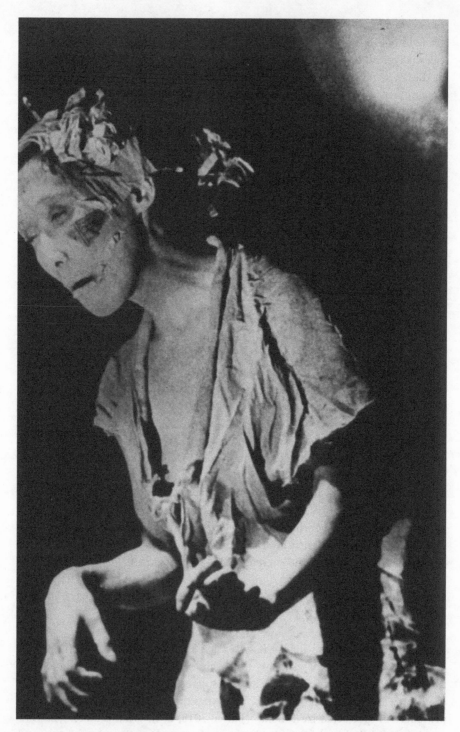

Figure 2.7 Ashikawa Yôko in *Lady on a Whale-String* (1976), photographer unknown. Courtesy of the NPO Butoh Laboratory Japan and the Hijikata Tatsumi Archive at the Keio University Arts Center.

kabuki is currently associated with the red light and gay district in Tokyo, Kabuki-chô (104). So "Tohoku kabuki" should mean the Tohoku version of kabuki, but also the kabuki (perverted/slanted/queer) version of Tohoku.

With Jansen's injunction in mind, let us turn to Hijikata's last dances. They followed a familiar pattern of Ashikawa's star turns interleaved with group dances. In one of the *Tohoku Kabuki Plan* dances, paper serves as the major theme of the dance.[21] The dance takes place against a backdrop of yellowed paper covered with writing, perhaps affirming the essential connection between words and Hijikata's dance. The dancers wear paper shawls, and Ashikawa dances atop a large sheet of paper, gradually crumpling it. Several times she tries to leave the stage, but each time, the paper-covered backdrop prevents her from leaving or slows her exit. Another paper is pulled up with an invisible string so that it becomes a kind of ghost flying across the stage. I read this dance as an affirmation of the ghostly power of paper as potentiality—something that can be used to dance and write on, to wrap with, to make origami out of, or to even make into a kite.

Tohoku Kabuki Plan 4 (December 19–22, 1985) took place on a stage shaped like a cross. The dance is the most obviously ethnically "Japanese" of Hijikata's career. Of course, there is much that is not marked as "Japanese," such as a part of the sound-scape that resembles house music with repetitive short bursts of electric guitar distortion, a segment that sounds like Celtic or American country music, and a segment that sounds like bland 1970s American rumba music. However, both visually and aurally, ethnically marked music, costumes, and props prevailed. Some of the music sounds like *gagaku* music, and in one part, the dancers wear a headpiece that looks like the sunshield of a *haniwa* figurine.[22] Another scene features a character with a zigzag paper streamer like the ones employed in Shinto ceremony. He waves it over the dancers and the audience just as a priest would. Geta clogs figure prominently in the dance, and the dancers use them extensively in their hands as clappers on the stage. One dancer flaps his geta like wings as if to fly. In addition, Ashikawa clatters geta together almost as if the two teeth (*ha*) of the geta are cogs and she is making two cogwheels mesh together.

In another scene, Ashikawa holds a Japanese uchiwa fan. She faces the group and uses the uchiwa like a conductor's baton to signal them to lower and raise their center of gravity in time with the fan. While they are raising and lowering themselves, they seem to be wafted away by the fan and slowly back off the stage. Then she stuffs the handle of the fan down the back of her neck, so it creates a sort of halo for herself. The dance closes with Ashikawa strapped to a huge kite and "flown" by the other dancers, who bear her aloft with one person tugging at the kite string. Her kite-riding character has a huge tongue sticking out. There are any number of kite-flying people in Japanese legends, and several characters in kabuki who stick out their tongues, so perhaps Hijikata was mashing up two of those characters into Ashikawa's character.[23]

The way Hijikata uses the "Japanese" elements is striking. The geta serve as percussion instruments, wings, and cogs. Ashikawa uses the uchiwa fan as a conductor's baton and then literally to fan the dancers off the stage. These are everyday items that we often take for granted. They have a customary use—geta for keeping your tootsies out of the muck, and uchiwa fans for cooling yourself or someone close by. But then Hijikata and Ashikawa repurpose them for something new. In the process, we perceive something about those objects: We do not yet know them fully; they are more versatile than customarily thought. There is the old statement from Maslow: "If all you have is a hammer, everything looks like a nail." But as any mechanic knows, sometimes you need to (or can, just for the hell of it) repurpose a tool for a different use. In that sense, the geta and fans match the paper of the previous dance, which is certainly useful as a surface for writing, but turns out to be as useful for dancing on, or making kites.[24]

I also cannot help but linger over the stage space—the cross in the middle of the audience. Predictably enough, some viewers have seen this as a representation of an *azemichi* (the path between rice paddies) or of the hanamichi of kabuki. And so it might have been. In the vein of a Kabuki-cho version of Tohoku, it is fun to imagine the dancers scandalizing farmers by frolicking on the narrow paths between rice paddies. But the dancers might slip off, get themselves all muddy, and come away changed by the experience as well. However, the interpretation that the stage is an *azemichi* or hanamichi overlooks the similarity the stage has to a fashion runway, and the way in which the dancers appear to be fashion models gone wildly awry. Regardless of whether or not Hijikata was specifically copying the look of a fashion runway (although he might well have been), the fashion runway must owe its aesthetic to the practice of burlesque dancing. In cabaret shows, patrons look up at the dancers but occupy a position of power.[25] The fashion runway allows for a more socially sanctioned version of burlesque dancing: viewers looking at the bodies of models. I argue that the stage structure of *Tohoku Kabuki Plan 4* extends Hijikata's engagement with performance to a consideration of the fashion runway and cabaret performance.

Conclusion

Within a month, Hijikata was gone, taking with him thousands of bits of evocative choreography, but leaving behind a performance form that was to grow and expand, despite his worry that it was not yet ready for export overseas. He may have been right, and in truth, his dances took a circuitous route to the world. But his dances have gradually come to communicate with an increasing number of people about the issues that concern them the most: how to communicate with people using not just language but the entire body, how to stimulate and motivate people, how to think about gender and ethnicity, and how to contest power most effectively in the long term. His techniques have begun to enable dancers and choreographers (and poets, musicians, artists, and fashion designers) to address these same issues.

Those techniques also allow us to bring Hijikata into dialogue with the worlds of contemporary Japan that might seem unrelated to him. The anime aficionado rewinding the VCR repeatedly and studying the differences between two animators drawing the same character is similar to dancers trying to carefully imagine an artist family living behind their knee and then allowing the specifics of the family to subtly alter the movement of their knees. When hackers break into the source code and re-configure a visual novel to their own liking, we are close to reconfiguring images from Bacon, Bellmer, and Bosch into new dance movements and sequences. To reiterate the central thesis of this book, Hijikata and these dancers were the ultimate body-mind hackers. Along the way, they hacked many of the conventions of performance, ethnicity, and gender. They were almost superhuman in their ability to spread their concentration around and compartmentalize their bodies. Performers have recognized these qualities in Hijikata's dances and techniques and increasingly sought to make them their own.

3
Ashikawa Yôko

Ashikawa Yôko occupied a spot near the center of butô from 1967 until sometime in the early 1990s. She directly participated in much of the actual movement creation in the generative butô phase and worked as Hijikata's rehearsal director during that phase. When she reorganized Hakutôbô after Hijikata's death, she quickly moved beyond him in all sorts of creative ways. She trained several highly influential dancers who have carried her legacy forward into the world. This chapter traces her career and legacy.

Ashikawa joined Asbestos Studio in 1967 and quickly participated in the creative ferment. Her first individual recital was titled enigmatically, *To My Friend Violette Nozière Boarding Train D53264 "The Landscape Is Always Already Receding into the Distance" From the Butô Princess Yôko who Rides the Pacific 231* (August 3, 1968). The title referred to the sensationalistic patricide by Nozière in 1933, as well as the paintings of trains and traveling schoolgirls of the stage designer Nakamura Hiroshi. Photos show Ashikawa tromping around the stage in boots, and then lying on the floor with her legs wide apart and a wide smile on her face (Figure 3.1). At one point, Hijikata stands over her spread legs, and at another point, he puts his head under her dress, while she smiles as if she is being tickled. Another shows her with a price tag, as if she is a piece of merchandise. She also appears nearly naked with stage-wide wings attached to her shoulders and sporting a golden phallus. Then she rides on the shoulders of another dancer, making it seem as though the wings have lifted her off from the ground. The dance appears to correspond with the happenings era of performances.

When Hijikata turned to the generative butô methods, Ashikawa remained at the center of the experimentation. Ashikawa and Hijikata locked themselves away for hours to work together (Kurihara, 1996, 80). She was the star of group scenes in the important 1972 performances such as *Twenty-Seven Nights for Four Seasons*, then the soloist for the monthly Asbestos Studio performances from 1974 to 1976. She elevated the skill of adopting successive characters to its pinnacle (see Figures 2.5 and 3.2). SU-EN writes,

> Each solo contains a story of the smallest detail of daily life as well as the most re-
> mote phenomena of the universe. We see layers and layers of questions regarding
> body, culture, as well as absurd stories, silliness, and fantastical ideas.... As a
> being made of dust in a later solo, Ashikawa is paper thin and fragile as a leaf. Her
> breath seems to be the color grey, and there is a smell of old paper—as in an attic
> in an old house. Her flesh has a transparent quality. Her body is light as dust, yet

A History of Butô. Bruce Baird, Oxford University Press. © Oxford University Press 2022.
DOI: 10.1093/oso/9780197630273.003.0003

Figure 3.1 Ashikawa Yôko in *To My Friend Violette Nozière* (1968), choreog. Hijikata Tatsumi. Photograph by Nakatani Tadao. Courtesy of Nakatani Tadashi, NPO Butoh Laboratory Japan, and the Hijikata Tatsumi Archive at the Keio University Arts Center.

shows a being that has lived many decades. In the end, Ashikawa sits on a raised part of the stage, suddenly lighting up an imaginary cigarette, becoming the old lady next door. (SU-EN 2018, 205)

Hijikata sent her to Paris in 1978, and then (with Kobayashi) on a European tour in 1983. In Paris, Ashikawa reprised the choreography from at least three of Hijikata's 1975–1976 Asbestos Studio performances including *Princess Kaguya of Darkness*, *Lady on a Whale String*, and *Human Shape*. She danced four different programs: "Fusa—Dream while Dying," "Night Cherry Princess," "Princess Shirachigo," and "Half Kaguya" (Ashikawa 1978, 97). According to Ashikawa,

"Fusa—Dream While Dying" was the things a person named Fusa saw on the verge of dying . . . such as a crying stump, fruit she wanted to eat, blue rubber boots with an inner glow . . . you might say that she was having rapport with various things and people while on standing at the edge of the abyss of that world. . . . "Night Cherry Princess" started with an old woman who was sold to a foreign country looking at

Figure 3.2 Ashikawa Yôko in *Lady on a Whale-String* (1976), photographer unknown. Courtesy of the NPO Butoh Laboratory Japan, and the Hijikata Tatsumi Archive at the Keio University Arts Center.

the sea and thinking of her hometown and then changing into the costume of a Japanese doll she had once loved and dancing. We did that in *Human Form*. It concluded with "rice cracker granny," who has been abandoned, continuing to dance at the side of the road. (1978, 97)

As is manifest in this list, Ashikawa had a tremendous number of characters at her disposal. Morishita Takashi frequently reminds people that Hijikata used to say to or about Ashikawa that she had one ton of butô movements (*butôfu*) stored inside her.[1]

Given the extent of Ashikawa's involvement, Katherine Mezur proposes that Ashikawa deserves considerable credit for Hijikata's choreographies (Mezur 2020, 262–263, 267–270). I cannot give a tidy confirmation, but here are the contours of the matter: Before joining with Hijikata, Ashikawa was a student at an art university. One aspect of Hijikata's exploration involved scrutiny of paintings. Ashikawa and Hijikata looked for poses and hints for costume and stage art, but also qualities, such as attempting to incorporate the haziness from a Wols painting into a dance move. Hijikata was good at drawing people out, so it seems almost indisputable that when they looked at art magazines, Ashikawa-the-art-student would have pointed things out that he was not aware of, possible poses and potential qualities. When they tried them out ("What happens when we do the bull movement with the Wols atmosphere?"), there must have been exchanges (Ashikawa making some pose: "Like this?" Hijikata: "Yeah, that looks good" or "No, try this."). Longtime Ashikawa student and dancer SU-EN remarks, "Ashikawa . . . provided the resistance for the dance form to develop" (SU-EN 2018, 205).

Mezur expands this line of thinking. Drawing on the work of the dance scholars Judith Hamera and Sally Gardner, Mezur observes that the way we talk about choreography prioritizes the (often male) choreographer and obscures the collective nature of choreography and the skills it takes to embody choreography on stage. To correct this oversight, Mezur sees "Ashikawa's dance making/performing as dancer-interactive collective processes, not 'passive inscription'" (Mezur 2020, 262). SU-EN offers a complementary view. She says there is a difference in choreography between Western dance and butô. The butô dancer already starts out as dancer-choreographer from the beginning even if they are not recognized as a choreographer (email to the author, January 31, 2021). Hijikata's dancers, resist applying the specific word "choreographer" (furitsukeshi) to Ashikawa until after she had her own company, but they acknowledge choreography-*esque* activity. Tamano Hiroko says that Hijikata "poured poetry into Ashikawa's body, and the dance was what was brewed in that ... body" (Hiroko Tamano, email to the author, February 1, 2021). Kobayashi says that during the Hokutôbô era, they would all choreograph movements, and Hijikata would observe them in order to "elicit dance" from them (Kobayashi, pers. conversation, June 27, 2001). Seisaku echoes that in his era (1984–1985), Hijikata would change music at the last second, so the choreography would not match the timing of the music. In these cases, he would tell the dancers to create their own solutions, so all of the dancers had experience in choreographing their own short segments to make the existing choreography fit the timing of the new music. He also notes that Ashikawa choreographed the cabaret shows, which were different from but related to the stage dances (Seisaku, pers. conversation, January 29, 2021).

Mezur hints at another entry point into this question. She observes about a scene in "Story of Smallpox", "Together the women jerk from one phrase sequence to the next, separately and together, catching up to Ashikawa. It is this slight off-balance behindness from the chorus ... " (Mezur 2020, 272). Rosemary Candelario notes that such moments when one dancer is moving more precisely and slightly ahead of the rest are often indications that the dancer was actually the one who choreographed the movements (Pers. conversation, January 27, 2021).

At some point in her career, Ashikawa started serving as the main rehearsal director for Hijikata. At times, Hijikata was in another room (Tanaka 2011, 61), but at times, he was completely absent until just before the show, at which time he would make final adjustments (Seisaku, pers. conversation, January 29, 2021). Since Ashikawa was there with him while he developed his methods and she acted as a rehearsal director for the dancers, she knew more about his later dance experiments than anyone else. One more piece of evidence that she had been playing a major role in the choreography all along is how well she choreographed dances when she was on her own. If she really had been the object of "passive inscription," there is no way that she could have jumped to being able to choreograph such fully developed works. SU-EN concurs and says that Ashikawa could choreograph complicated pieces in an hour (email to the author, January 31, 2021). The difficulty we have sorting out the question of how much choreographic credit Ashikawa deserves is certainly related to how we think about the act of choreography, but again highlights the limitations of archives. Only finished products remain (and precious few of those).[2] Whatever side we come down on—choreography, co-choreography, choreography-esque—SU-EN observes, "The opportunity to create work with an artistic talent such as Ashikawa gave new momentum to [Hijikata's] choreography" (SU-EN 2018, 204). It is almost impossible that Hijikata could have succeeded in the third phase of his career without her.

Despite the recognition Ashikawa gained as Hijikata's principal dancer, life close to the center of the butô world was not uniformly wonderful. Mezur depicts a wider society in which women were eager to join social movements but found themselves in supporting roles (Mezur 2020, 265). She also observes that although not all women fit this pattern, the two main possibilities for women in that era were the virtuous housewife and the prostitute. The men of butô usually treated the women more like prostitutes (Mezur 2020, 267). Yamada Ippei tells of a drinking party in which Hijikata spontaneously decided to recreate the orgy scene from a movie. Hijikata commanded Ashikawa to strip, and then made several men lie on top of her or "assault" her to have (or simulate having) sex with her (Yamada 1992, 92). Mezur reminds us that women often felt trapped by the socially prescribed gender role of Good Wife, Wise Mother, and were in fact excited to break free, so such moments may not have bothered Ashikawa (Mezur 2018, 367). But Yamada reports that the experience made him miserable. So nothing Ashikawa did at the time allayed his worries. Even if she was fine with that moment, she casually reveals that Hijikata pushed her down the stairs when he found out that the 1983 European tour had not been as successful as he had hoped (Ashikawa 2018, Section 5).

After Hijikata died, his wife, Motofuji Akiko, argued that the dances and dance company name Hakutôbô were her intellectual property as the rightful executor of his estate, and that Ashikawa was not allowed to use the company name (Ueno 1992, 20–21; Ashikawa 2018, Section 2). She also forbade Ashikawa from dancing his choreography (Ashikawa 2018, Section 17). Although Ashikawa got the lion's share of the notebooks, she had to leave Asbestos Studio. Having lived on a daily allowance of 500 yen from the burlesque dances, when she left Asbestos Studio, she had no money and nowhere to rehearse. She and several other dancers reorganized Hakutôbô, with her as its head. They bounced around the suburbs of western Tokyo, and finally settled into another communal living space, where they started to make their own dances.

At the 1987 Hijikata Memorial performance, Ashikawa choreographed *Salome of the Construction Zone* (Kôjigenba no sarome). The dance featured a section (or sections) in which the company danced with disabled people (Figure 3.3). As previously noted, Hijikata wrote about disability and observed disabled people, but his dances were predicated on the ability of a nondisabled dancer to approximate the look or movements of a disabled person. As Dind observes, he did not embody disability from the inside (Dind 2019). We do not have much information about this dance,

Figure 3.3 Ashikawa Yôko and disabled dancers in *Salome of the Construction Zone*, 1987, choreog. Ashikawa Yôko. Copyright by and courtesy of Nourit Masson-Sekine.

but we can see that Ashikawa was going a step beyond Hijikata by inviting disabled people to dance with her.

Kuniyoshi Kazuko writes about this era with glee,

> Since the death of Hijikata, Ashikawa has done a splendid job of betraying the expectations of those who considered her no more than Hijikata's leading acolyte, who would inherit his ankoku butoh and spend the rest of her career refining it. Instead, she has staged a series of electrifying performances. (Kuniyoshi 1990, 14)

Kuniyoshi goes on to describe a 1987 series of dances called *Skin Clock for Those Wishing to Become Dogs* (Inu ni naru tame no hifu dokei) as

> a wild scrawl which repudiated any inclusive flow towards completion cutting remorselessly through time yet coming together from the most incongruous direction, and was a fire-bell to the flesh, which if left to itself would immediately show a nostalgic yearning for stability. The violent fragmentation and bold composition of these performances sustained a highly charged atmosphere which spurned whatever discourse attempted to insinuate itself. Though seemingly an outright desertion of butoh, I saw this series as a biting critique of butoh on the part of Ashikawa. (Kuniyoshi 1989, 143; translated in Kuniyoshi 1990, 14–15)

Soon, the company began performing once a month with different dancers as the lead. During this era, SU-EN describes Ashikawa as always training for the next performance, rather than just training in the abstract (SU-EN 2018, 210). SU-EN describes two 1988 shows *Sun Wheel* (Nichi-rin) and *Moon Wheel* (Getsu-rin) as "edgy, funny, and beautiful dance.... The choreography vibrates of art, punk, and color; young and fresh, still with dignity and a serious investigation of butoh" (SU-EN, 2018, 209). These are worlds populated by characters in blindfolds, pointy dunce or wizard caps, and seemingly dead people lying on the stage.

One can see a scene titled "Child in the Mirror" from a similar dance, *Ailing Hidden Butterfly* (Yameru hichô, 1989).[3] The dancer, Mito, wears a costume crafted from and dances on silver mylar sheets. Pounding music is accompanied by blinding light. The light reflects off her mylar costume, and around the stage space, but she jerks and starts as if pulses of light are passing through the mylar and blistering her in spots. It seems as though she will be incinerated by the light (Figure 3.4). As Kuniyoshi notes, Ashikawa was seeking to go beyond Hijikata, to redefine butô, but to continue to defy easy closure. In a letter to the visual artist Yoshida Yoshie in 1992, Ashikawa cautions against the danger of codifying Hijikata's experiments into an "empty shell" and then argues, "It seems to me that inheriting a method is only viable if the person pursuing it stays right in the middle of the creative process. Isn't it the case that form has to be made public and passed along in the middle of creation?"[4]

Another 1988 dance, *Gathering and Bundling the Body: Ashikawa Yôko and Japanese People* (Shûsoku suru shintai: Ashikawa Yôko to Nihonjin), shows her again

Figure 3.4 Mito in "Child in the Mirror," *Ailing Hidden Butterfly*, choreog. Ashikawa Yôko (1989). Screen Capture.

expanding on or speaking back to Hijikata's legacy.[5] We see a ragtag bunch of people gliding through the space crouching on unsteady quivering feet. Two others seem to be unnaturally short, but suddenly their bodies seem to stretch magically, and their height seems to increase by two feet. We realize after the fact that they carefully concealed that they were squatting inside their ankle length-dresses, which have now become knee length dresses as they stand on half-point. In the final, a central woman oozes across the stage leaning forward on her knees as if she is a slug, but with no visible means of propulsion besides the weight of her protruding head.[6] SU-EN describes an Ashikawa solo:

> Her dance reveals the past, present, and future. She slices time and eats space. Her body is surrounded by the space, not swallowed by it and not fighting it. Body and space are one. Through her face, she conveys utmost raw beauty, like a sculpture shaped in rock. This rock has cracks in it. It is made rugged by rain and wind. There is an animal, an old lady, a child. They are all connected through time. (SU-EN 2018, 209)

I have argued that we understand *Hijikata Tatsumi and Japanese People: Rebellion of the Body* as indicating the width of the range of Japanese people. I further argued that we might read his dance as saying that it was going to take more than one kind of Japanese person for a successful rebellion (Baird 2012, 123, 125). Ashikawa one-ups Hijikata by inviting other dancers on stage to embody these varied Japanese people.

SU-EN gives us a related concept for further considering this dance. She writes about the "Butô Body":

> The Butoh Body is an extended body. It is a living artistic organism, in intense in-teraction with the world around it. This body cannot be seen without the space around it, it cannot live without all the other living beings, it cannot move without the tension of different realities. The Butoh Body does not exist without other bodies. (SU-EN 2018, 208)

The Butô Body (butô-tai) is striking because Ashikawa differentiated herself from both the nation-body (*kokutai*) and the carnal-body (the *nikutai*) of Hijikata's dance. It seems as though Ashikawa was advancing a philosophy of the body-mind within a context or environment, but not one specifically identified with the nation. In this dance, clothing serves as a context that changes our perception of the bodies. A body seems to pass over the human-insect barrier. Ashikawa manifests characters, just as did Hijikata, but they are within (and competing against) time and space. At some point, the dance was renamed *Shumu* (or Shiumu), roughly translated as "Thread-Cosmos-Dream." This title relocates the dance in an even wider space-time but loses the sense of Ashikawa trying to articulate who she is in relation to the wider world of Japanese people.

Along with her work as the leader of Hakutôbô, Ashikawa created a second com-pany, Gnome, for younger dancers and Westerners who had come to study butô. The Gnome performers helped make costumes, constructed props, built stage sets, as-sisted with lighting design, and most of all appeared in regular performances (SU-EN 2018b, 285–286). So she was effectively constantly choreographing for two different (but related) dance companies (see Figure 3.5).

As part of their continual investigation, one of these Gnome dancers, SU-EN (who danced with Ashikawa for five years), says that Ashikawa brought art books and phys-ical objects to rehearsals, led tours outside, and bombarded the dancers with words. For example:

> To go on stage is to fall into unknown space.
> We must create an uncertain situation in the body, enter the danger.
> We need to find extreme detail and chaos at the same time.
> [. . .]
> We must look at the real world and find the interesting things.
> Look for the things we cannot see . . . like the layers of paint in a painting.
> [. . .]
> Turn the body upside down/inside out. (SU-EN 2018, 210)

SU-EN observes that in the training she did with Ashikawa, "There was a sense of speed and urgency—no time to intellectualize" (SU-EN 2018, 210). Ashikawa used pieces of Hijikata's choreography but changed them through association with other

Figure 3.5 Seki Yumiko and SU-EN in a Gnome dance, choreog. Ashikawa Yôko, probably 1989. Courtesy of Rob Schwartz.

material and ideas (210). She also designed costumes and the dancers created them together (209).

In 1989, Ashikawa choreographed *Magdalene of the Skin-Cosmos* (Hifu uchu no magudara).[7] SU-EN describes the first scene:

> The main roles are danced by Ashikawa as the Old Tree, dressed in dark brown and Ashikawa Uzumi as the Young Tree, dressed in spring green…. The Young Tree is born out of a seed from the Old Tree. They exist together in the forest surrounded by other living beings. (SU-EN 2018, 211)

These living beings are tiny birds, chickens, and a beast. First birds come on the stage and chirp among the trees. Then chickens take their turn pecking and clucking. Here we see Ashikawa literalizing the chicken-pecking movement from "Story of Smallpox" (Baird 2012, 151). In Hijikata's version, the pecking movement was churned together surrealistically with other images as a source for new movements and in order to create a complex character. Here the chicken is a chicken, and the wobbliness of the dancers' ankles is an effective way to convey the gait of a chicken. Then a beast scares the birds with a growl and then undulates away. This also literalizes choreography from the Hijikata era as well (Morishita et al. 2004, 118). The comparison allows us to observe that in this dance, Ashikawa rejects Hijikata's abstraction for something more concrete.

SU-EN continues:

There is a storm and the Old Tree fractures and falls. The Old Tree has left this life, and now the Young Tree has to live on by herself. The spirit of the Old Tree comes back and dances around the Young Tree. Death is not the end, just the start of another existence. Ashikawa's dance has evolved and aged. She dances on the border between life and death. Her transparent fingertips, the spiral shaped lines through her body, her breath as a black hole, the twisting power through her flesh, the layers of skin around her bones all make me consider my own existence. I am moved to the core of my being. What can we do in this short moment on this planet and in this life? What does it mean to be human? (SU-EN 2018, 211)

Almost as if the old tree giving way to the young tree was symbolic of the evolution of the company as a whole, SU-EN sees these years as a turning point. She reports that in 1990 Ashikawa relinquished her role as lead dancer of the company and then largely quit appearing on stage after 1992 (SU-EN 2018, 212).

The free jazz musician Tomoe Shizune had joined Hijikata's company sometime briefly before Hijikata died. Roughly a year later, he joined Ashikawa's company and first became the music director and stage designer.[8] In time, the company began to incorporate improvisational elements from free jazz into their choreography. In this way, Ashikawa and Tomoe remained forward thinking about butô, rather than continually retreading Hijikata's steps.

At some point, complete artistic control (including choreographic credit)[9] seems to have passed over to Tomoe and the name of the company was changed to Tomoe Shizune and Hakutôbô. Paradoxically, during this transformation, the company began to explore a nonhierarchical organization. For example, they rotated the task of spokesperson and copyeditor. The caveat was that Tomoe was always listed as the artistic director, choreographer, composer, lighting designer, and stage designer, despite the fact that the dancers report that Ashikawa choreographed all dances up until *Renyo* (which was cochoreographed) and was an indispensable part of the costume design. In mid-1989 she wrote, "it is all the same whether one plays the leading role or doesn't" (Kuroki 1990, 165). Apparently, the nonhierarchical model did not extend to Tomoe.

As it happens, the lead role never came back around to her. Maybe she was fine with this. She apparently felt highly ambivalent about the mission thrust on her to continue Hijikata's work, and frequently complained that she would rather quit and do something else.[10] So perhaps her current low profile is her choice, but it also undoubtedly stems from a complex interplay of structural sexism, misogyny, and economic necessities, as well as a genuine desire to explore nonhierarchical organizational modes in a way that other men talked about but never fully put into practice.

Ashikawa is under no obligation to perform just to cater to fans of butô. If her current low profile is her choice, that is fine. More power to her. She has already created a valuable legacy. She trained the current main dancers of Tomoe Shizune and

Hakutôbô, and was massively formative in the training of Hijikata's late-era dancers such as Seisaku and Mikami Kayo, who have gone on to thriving butô careers. Through her Gnome activities, she also trained three influential Western butô performers, Joan Laage, SU-EN, and Jocelyn Monpetit, who have gone on to perform all over the world. A final testimony to Ashikawa's abilities as a teacher and choreographer lies in the dances of these students.

SU-EN is an excellent example. More than any other woman, she has implemented the model that the men in this book followed, with her own studio, her own apprentice and training system, and her own books. It takes nothing away from her incredible work ethic to point out that part of her success was predicated on relocating to her native Sweden and, much like Amagatsu (discussed later), she has benefited from strong institutional support. The result of her tireless work and this support is that she churns out numberless thoughtful and engaging performances. One such is *Headless* (Pula, Croatia, 2001).[11] The program notes say,

> *a head that is looking for a body*
> *a body that is looking for a head*
> *love which is looking for pain*
> *pain which is looking for love*

SU-EN, dressed in red panties and with a red scarf wrapped entirely around her head, curls around a single light on a dark stage. As I watch, I wonder what it means for a headless creature to be drawn to the light almost like a bug. She makes her way slowly across the stage and comes to an upright position with one knee up and one knee down underneath a strange head-like object. She stares (if you can call it that) out forcefully at the audience. Her hands reach out to a nearby crescent of mud, which she slowly slathers on her body. I think to myself, "What does it mean to stare forcefully at someone when you have no head? How should we reconfigure our notion of the gaze? How much does the gaze depend on the posture of the body and not just on the eyes? What does it mean to block the scopophilic gaze at the naked female body by rubbing mud on it?" SU-EN's headless creature traverses the stage sometimes on its knees and elbows, sometimes in a bear-crawl but with clenched knuckles. I see glimpses of Ashikawa/Hijikata animal choreographies, but whereas Hijikata's animals are invariably lithe and romanticized (as if animals could never look clumsy or make a mistake), this creature stumbles and falls off its appendages. After a scene change, SU-EN reappears in a red dress. She takes off the scarf and feels her body. Her motions are halfway between the sensuous manner in which strippers call attention to parts of their bodies and a genuine exploration of the body as if the head is trying now to figure out just what is under it. SU-EN slowly puts her wrist in her mouth. To kiss it? . . . To eat it? She seems to bite off a piece of flesh. Then bite off a piece of forearm. The skin actually pulls away from her arm, and then the limb pops away as if she has bitten through. Her lips are pulled back and her teeth biting together. Then she bites at a piece of bicep. Her fingers go into her mouth, and I feel my gorge heave like I might throw up. SU-EN is clearly exploring the border between pain and pleasure, but there is more than that. After quelling my nausea, I am left wondering about the relationships between body, head, eyes, and onlookers. Can the head eat the body? Does the onlooker consume the dancer?

This is Ashikawa's legacy: She dances on in her students, who, just like herself vis-à-vis Hijikata, continue to make butô their own.

4

Maro Akaji and Dairakudakan

No person has done more for the worldwide spread of butô than Maro Akaji. He developed his own methods of movement and dance creation, ensuring that the dances are always striking. He and his troupe churned out main stage productions and monthly smaller performances for decades. They traveled the world performing to audiences eager for those dances. He became a successful movie actor, using his butô skills to springboard to fame beyond the dance world. More than these obvious markers, Maro has been the best mentor in assisting others in establishing their dance careers. Not all have survived the process, but with his shotgun approach, enough have survived to flood the globe with dancers. In this chapter, I track his remarkable career, touching particularly on his ideas of "expanded interpretation," "one person, one troupe," and his means of creating new dance movements.

Maro started performing as a member of the troupe Budou no Kai, where he met Noguchi Michizô. That very year, Budou no Kai disbanded, and Maro helped found Kara Jûrô's Situation Theater in 1965. He was an integral member of Kara's troupe, participating in the traveling Red Tent performances (Senda 1970, 18–25). The theater critic Senda Akihiko argues that Maro embodied Kara's conception of the "Privileged Body" which was, in short, the idea that the body was more important than the script (Senda 1988, 26). Tomioka Taeko said that Maro had the "body of a rampaging actor, as if he chops his way through the jungle with a hatchet" (quoted in Aihara 2018, 182). Maro's background in theater makes his performances seem more like dance-theater than dance proper. Whatever else Maro may have taken from Kara and the Situation Theater, Maro learned a do-it-yourself sensibility, as the performers routinely created their own performance spaces (Senda 1970, 20). In 1965, Maro met Hijikata when Nakajima Natsu invited him to participate in their cabaret. Maro did not study formally with Hijikata, but lived at Asbestos Studio and participated in some training. Maro recalls Hijikata yelling at him, "Why do you push your left leg forward? Why are you walking on your right leg?" Flummoxed, Maro became unable to walk (Aihara 2018, 182). In time Maro began searching for an art form that was less language-centered than Kara's theater (Maro 2011, 128–129); however, like Hijikata, Maro remained preoccupied with language.[1]

A History of Butô. Bruce Baird, Oxford University Press. © Oxford University Press 2022.
DOI: 10.1093/oso/9780197630273.003.0004

Founding Dairakudakan

In 1972, Maro founded Dairakudakan with several other dancers, including Tanikawa Toshiyuki, Bishop Yamada (Yamada Ippei), Ôsuka Isamu, Amagatsu Ushio, Tamura Tetsurô, Mitani Sankichi, and Murobushi Kô. "Dairakudakan" literally means "Great Camel Battleship." Maro observed that although modern dance is like a thoroughbred horse, butô resembles a camel, noting that camels have endurance and are used on the silk road (Hoffman and Holborn 1987, 76). Holborn interprets the camel as a symbol of cross-cultural communication (Hoffman and Holborn 1987, 13). We might add that in contrast to the thoroughbred, the camel is "lowbrow" and genetically diverse.

In the beginning, the choreography emerged from group exploration spread among the dancers. The main choreographer provided a container (sometimes just an idea) for solos and group pieces and chose the order of the various components (Aihara 2018, 184; Kosuge 2018, 219). In part, this method of composition imparts a unique characteristic to Dairakudakan performances, which is that frequently, there is no single vision unifying the dance. Critic Kate Dobbs Ariall highlights this aspect of Dairakudakan in her review of *Secrets of Mankind* (2008). She observes that the dance contains "different scenes that are a challenge to link mentally but are nonetheless engrossing." She continues, "One doesn't exactly 'make sense' of a Dairakudakan performance," but "Sometimes you get it, sometimes you don't" (Ariall 2008). This is the pleasure of Dairakudakan: the performances are challenging but engrossing. You cannot quite resolve the performances into a tidy whole, but something about them suggests it ought to be possible to at least "get" individual scenes.

"Expanded Interpretation"

Maro uses a technique called "expanded interpretation" (*kakudai kaishaku*) in his own artistic practice that provides a clue for how to negotiate this kind of polyphonic performance. In his own acting and dancing career, he uses "expanded interpretation" as a way of creating a character. Specifically, he "thinks about the background the character is in and tries to give shape to the significance of the character's existence" (Kanazawa 1994, 125). He also uses expanded interpretation on a work as a whole. He describes portraying a cop in Sai Yôichi's movie *An Irresponsible Family in the Heisei Era: Tokyo Deluxe* (1995). The cop is cheated by his wife's "fake family" of his retirement savings. The cop then joins the fake family, becoming a criminal himself. Maro invokes "expanded interpretation" to see this as Japan in the family of nations (Kanazawa 1994, 127). The implication is that Japan, once the object of Western imperialist policies, has now joined the "fake-family" of imperialist nations plundering others.

"Expanded interpretation" assigns a background and significance to individual characters, but then goes a step beyond to consider the geopolitical and historical context for the actions on stage. A dancer can do this to deepen a role. Viewers can use it to highlight the geopolitical context of the dance. Maro justifies this kind of interpretation by noting that it is "increasingly difficult to tell where the boundary lines are" in fields such as "art and politics or the government and economics" (Maro n.d.c). Because no clear boundary line exists between art and politics, viewers should not treat the two as separate, but rather note the connections between them.

In the dances of Dairakudakan, the viewer is provided numerous elements from which to construct their own performance and perform their own "expanded interpretation." These include posters, titles, program notes, costumes, and elements of recognizable choreography (called *miburi* or gestures), as well as other hints about potential connections from interviews, newspaper features, and even other related dances.[2] If the viewer does not know Japan's history of suffering from Western imperialism and then engaging in imperialism themselves, they cannot understand *An Irresponsible Family in the Heisei Era* as a metaphor for Japanese imperialism. The more the viewer knows about Japanese history, the better these historical resonances or indications of authorial intent can deepen their understanding of a dance as they engage in expanded interpretation, but no one interpretation exhausts the possibilities of the dance. Moreover, there may be scene-specific "expanded interpretations" at cross-purposes with the "expanded interpretation" one might make for the dance as a whole.

The Golden Spunk Bird, the Aleutians, and the Eight Span [Crow]

I hope I will not tax the reader's patience overly, but if you have not seen a Dairakudakan performance, to provide insight into just how completely wacky and wonderful they are, here is a synopsis of the dance *The Golden Spunk Bird, the Aleutians, and the Eight Span [Crow]* (AKA *Record of a* Horsehead, May 15 and 16, 1973), which is divided into several different scenes marked by different music, costumes, characters, and movement palettes.[3]

1. A wagon wheel and two swings hang in a dark stage. A man draws a Japanese sword and cuts a thick tube encrusted with vegetal matter (straw, weeds, sticks, etc.). Rice pours onto another man sitting on a small *go* table directly below the tube.
2. Two characters (Tanikawa and Maro) sit fumbling their fingers, then dancing one behind the other. The two come together and embrace in sixty-nine position, appearing to licking each other's anuses. They roll over and over sideways, and one stands and carries the other; they part, and Tanikawa mounts a swing. Maro shoves him, sending him swinging.
3. Three men (later expanding to eight) crouch hopping on one leg with the other leg wrapped on their opposite thighs in cross-legged position, and an arrow

hanging from a rope between their legs. One hand holds their foot up, while the other gesticulates in the air. They lie in the same position and raise their legs, so we see a line of buttocks. They bounce their heads on the floor.

4. Three (or four) dancers stacked like a totem pole walk slowly around the stage. The man on top (Tanikawa) throws feed to crows tethered to the suspended wagon wheel.

5. Two groups. A group of men (including Amagatsu) have lutes on their backs. They dance around in sinewy fashion. On the other side of the stage, Maro reclines in a square pool of mud filled with stuff. He tries to rise, slips to the floor, then rises and scratches his armpits, head, and face.

6. Men (including Ôsuka), holding shiny black parasols, wear lumpy costumes as if covered with pillows. They quiver, fall to the ground, rock backward, and then return to their feet. They sidestep to their right across the stage with their arms crossed in front of their chests. Their left hands extend to the right in palm-out stop pose. Their right hands pass under their left armpits holding their parasols upright.

7. Two groups. Eight men carry Tanikawa on a palanquin. He stands inside a rectangular wooden frame about two feet wide by six feet high. He raises one leg and powder drips off. He stamps his foot and powder shoots everywhere. Meanwhile, a chain of three men seated crotch to butt rock backward in unison to gradually move backward. They stop their backward progress but continue rocking until the front two men are atop the third. The top man's legs and buttocks are pointed into the air and the three move like a giant spider. Tanikawa descends from the platform, approaches the threesome and attempts to burrow into their pile. He grabs a leg as if he wants to take a bite from it. Then he bends over and backs himself into the pile, so his buttocks are rubbing the men. The four finally break apart with Tanikawa climbing back on his platform, while the other three pull themselves onto a structure at the back of the stage. They leap wildly about as the eight men carry the palanquin off the stage.

8. "Luck of the Mountains; Luck of the Seas." Two women escort a man wearing a metal platter on his head to the *go* board, which he sits on. Three women and several men surround him. The women, costumed with artificially large vulvas, then recline in crabwalk fashion facing the audience, and begin to bounce up and down. Because of their recumbent positions, the bouncing suggests sexual thrusting and birthing motions. The men hold their hands above the figure on the *go* board and seemingly brush dust off their hands into the platter on his head. Then the men escort the platter-man off stage and three men kneel in front of the women. They put their heads in the crotches of the women (who are still bouncing/humping wildly) as if to perform cunnilingus. There is a cut, so it is not clear how the dancers change positions, but the women rise onto all fours and the men lie under them facing upward. The women still bounce/hump in the same rhythm, and the men reach their legs up and wrap

them around the backs of the women and put their arms around the necks of the women, so the men are embracing the women from beneath. The women thrust and look like they are penetrating the men. The men finally fall flat, and the women stand on them and tread on their torsos.

9. Three gaunt women recline on stage facing men who are standing in traps with only their heads and one arm (which holds a Japanese fan) visible. It appears as if the men are directing the movements of the women.

10. Three men crawl forward carrying three women who sit side-saddle on them with their hands in a guitar-playing pose.

11. Two groups. The three men with lumpy costumes and parasols stamp their geta sideways across the stage. They proceed to the *go* table and put one foot on it. They hold their closed parasols in their right hands while extending and retracting their left hands almost as if asking for donations. Meanwhile, a man (Murobushi) enters with several rabbits attached to him by cords. He grabs one rabbit and cradles it tenderly, but then humps it, first missionary style, and then rear-entry style. The lights go down, and Murobushi lights a fire on his wrist and dances, illuminating himself with the fire. Then he seemingly dies. A man (Tanikawa) in a thickly padded *dotera* squeezes through the three men standing with one foot each on the *go* table. He proceeds to the dead man and uses a knife to cut the cords, freeing the rabbits.

12. The dance enters into an extended grand finale. Tanikawa swings on a swing and Bishop Yamada swings on a chair with a wagon wheel attached to it. A character in the lumpy pillow costume poses archly. Tanikawa kisses the dead body of Murobushi. They all freeze in a tableau. One man lies atop a woman as if to have sex with her. Two other men lie in sixty-nine position. Another pair of men are in anal sex position. One man holds another muddied man in his lap in a contorted pietà. Tanikawa wanders among the frozen statues with a knife in hand. Will he stab them? He lifts Maro from his position sitting on the go board and drags him off stage. He cuts a mesh of tubers off one of the men. He staggers off stage and then the camera circles around the muddy *go* board.

Considering *The Golden Spunk Bird, the Aleutians, and the Eight Span [Crow]*

There are several things to say about this dance. In the absence of any other overriding movement schema (about which, more in a minute), the movement generally has several characteristics, including sinuous but vigorous athleticism, strong facial expressions, everyday gestures, silly or absurd movements, and sculptural quality. To take each of these in turn, the dancers often move their arms like eels, sometimes while stooped over with their wrists relatively close together in front of them and other times with their arms extended outward to the sides. Unlike Hijikata's wavering boneless sinuousness, Dairakudakan's is more stable. It is seemingly the product of a healthy well-trained body, rather than an indicator of marginality, even though these characters exude nonconformity to social norms. Facial expressions tend toward the imbecilic, orgasmic, or emotionless. Harada notes that they frequently use silly or absurd movements (banging their heads lightly on the ground over and over) as well as daily motions such as drinking from a cup or licking something. The dancers were drawn to movements that function in the space between obvious meaning and full abstraction. We see something that looks like twisting a lid off, but we cannot make any connection to what the dancers might be imagining. Harada also argues that one of the features of Dairakudakan is sculpturality, and this they share with Sankai Juku as well (Harada 2004, 193). It is likely owing to the intermedial nature of the time that the dancers were interested in mixing sculpture with dance.

A main thematic theatrical movement is developed through each scene. One example is from scene seven. Three men initially sit in a chain tightly spooning each other. They rock backward in unison to propel themselves backward as a unit. Then they rock backward in order for the first to slide onto the torso of the second and the second to slide onto the torso of the third, forming a stack of men laying on their backs one atop the other. Once they are stacked up, they exploit the proximity of their legs and arms pointing up in the air to achieve an effect like a giant six-limbed three-headed spider (Figure 4.1). The movement is clever and striking. The

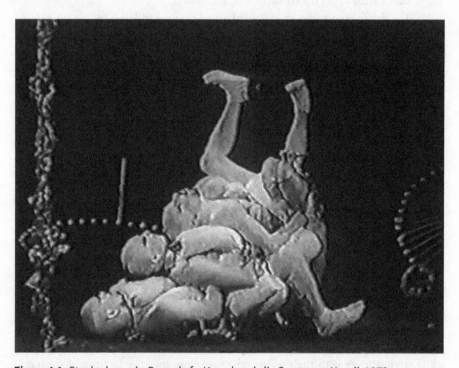

Figure 4.1 Stacked men in *Record of a Horsehead*, dir. Susumura Yasuji, 1973 (Dairakudakan, *The Golden Spunk Bird, the Aleutians, and the Eight Span [Crow]*, Scene Seven). Screen Capture.

movement might mean something to the dancers, but it does not need to "mean" anything for the viewer. There is a homoerotic overtone to the movement, but it is interesting to watch just as it is, because it is so creative, and because the dancers move with such gusto.

The dance also has many elements that invite the viewer to construct an "expanded interpretation." The poster for the dance was designed by Yano Makoto. On a pale pink smudged background, an empty suit of Japanese warrior-era armor is split down the middle. The right half of the armor tilts off kilter as if it may fall over. The type of armor appears to be *niô dô*, in which the cuirass or breastplate is molded to look like the torso of a starving monk or old man. Even before the start of the dance, one might have the sense that the performance concerns war and privation.

The Eight Span Crow of the title would be obvious to any relatively well read Japanese person. It refers to one of two mythical birds who helped the first mythical sovereign of the archipelago, Iwarebiko (known posthumously as Jinmu), as he endeavored to pacify other tribes in the bottom third of the archipelago. There are two extant versions of the myths: the *Kojiki* and the *Nihongi* (which were reworked from prior sources to legitimize the rule of the descendants of Iwarebiko). In these sources, Iwarebiko and his older brother travel from present-day Kyushu to present-day Osaka and there encounter a rival chieftain Nagasunehiko (Long-Legged Man). In the *Kojiki*, Iwarebiko's older brother is killed in battle, and the gods send a gigantic (eight-span) crow (or raven) to help Iwarebiko. The crow relays a message demanding that a local chief submit to Iwarebiko. In the *Nihongi*, Iwarebiko fights Nagasunehiko and things are going badly, but a golden kite lands on Iwarebiko's long bow and blinds the enemy with its brilliance. As a consequence, Iwarebiko is victorious. The golden kite is the "Golden Spunk Bird" of the title. As for the Aleutians, apparently, Maro conceived of Iwarebiko's journey as having passed through the Korean peninsula and the Aleutians (which are also obliquely suggested in scene nine through the folk *enka* song *Aleutian Ballad*).[4]

Yamada Ippei implies that the title is the pretext for a pun. He says, rather enigmatically, "The title has the Chinese character for gold, and centers around golden balls, with other meanings included" (Yamada 1992, 214). Later, Maro apparently suggested the title "Golden Balls" for a subsequent dance to which Yamada replied, "Golden Balls again? ... It's not clever enough," implying that a previous title had cleverly used the phrase "Golden balls" (Yamada 1992, 217). The first word, *kinkondori* (Golden Spunk Bird), contains the word *kinkon* (golden spirit), which appears as if it could also be pronounced *kintama* (usually accompanied by different Chinese characters). This is a vulgar word for "testicles" meaning, "golden balls," hence my translation, which tries to suggest "golden spirit" by playing on two meanings of the word "spunk."

The movie version of the dance is titled *Batôki* (*Record of a Horsehead*). The "Horsehead" refers to a low-ranking demon in Buddhist hell who torments the dead.[5] It is not clear where the film's title came from, but it is hard to imagine that Maro did not have some say in the matter.

With this extra information in mind, we might think about potential expanded interpretations. Little in the dance corresponds to the myths, other than the crows. The *go* board does not have any obvious counterpart, and Iwarebiko certainly did not travel to the Korean peninsula or the Aleutians as he tried to pacify neighboring tribes. As noted, the main choreographer was supposed to provide a structure for various pieces of choreography. Perhaps, the idea of a mythical journey was merely a pretext for combining several chunks of unrelated choreography. Let us though, take Maro at his word, and assume that this is a portrayal of the foundation of Japan. If so, the founding of Japan is depicted as including homoerotic sex, and also sex in which women occupy a relative position of power. Who are these two men who sixty-nine each other? Tanikawa and Maro have extended roles. It is intriguing to imagine them as Iwarebiko and Nagasunehiko trying to solve their problems through mutually pleasuring each other rather than fighting each other (Figure 4.2).

The movie version is titled *Record of a Horsehead*, so maybe the dance portrayed more than one thing. Perhaps these are the activities of a low-ranking functionary in Buddhist hell, and each group of dancers represents different denizens of hell. If that were the case, one would have to conclude that Maro/Susumura's version of hell is not such a bad place.

Figure 4.2 Two characters mutually pleasuring each other in *Record of a Horsehead*, dir. Susumura Yasuji, 1973 (Dairakudakan, *The Golden Spunk Bird, the Aleutians, and the Eight Span [Crow]*, Scene Two). Screen Capture.

What of the three pairs of dancers in scene eight? Yamada identifies the men as "soldiers" and "bandits" and the women as "pregnant women," and says the scene was called "Luck of the Mountains; Luck of the Seas" (Yamada 1992, 215). This layers another mythical reference onto the scene. The title of the scene refers to a myth in which a younger brother lost his older brother's magical fishhook and had to retrieve it at the bottom of the ocean. There he has a son by the daughter of a sea god. The son becomes the father of Iwarebiko. In the dance, the women adopt a birthing posture, but the rhythms and movements suggest female empowerment and enjoyment. Initially, the men seem to orally pleasure the women, who thrust and grind into the interactions. The second half of the scene suggests intercourse, but the position and movements of the women reverse the stereotypical "missionary position" in heterosexual sex. Rather than the men penetrating the women, the women stand above the men. The men have their legs wrapped around the women holding themselves diagonally upside down. Although the women are not wearing dildos, the women thrust and grind as if they are pegging the men (who look like they are enjoying it immensely; Figure 4.3). Finally, the men fall flat as if in postorgasmic exhaustion, and the women literally walk all over them. This could certainly be a male fantasy of female sexuality, but if this is the grandparents of Iwarebiko, it is a reconfiguration of

Figure 4.3 Women pegging the men in *Record of a Horsehead*, dir. Susumura Yasuji, 1973 (Dairakudakan, *The Golden Spunk Bird, the Aleutians, and the Eight Span [Crow]*, Scene Eight, "Luck of the Mountains; Luck of the Seas"). Screen Capture.

the myth that partially transforms the sexuality and gender politics from militarist heterosexist patriarchy to homoerotic and women-centered pleasure.

Let's not overstate this. Many scenes do not contain women, and Bishop Yamada extensively critiques Dairakudakan as a male-centered, militarist, "phallic company" (Yamada 1992, 210–214). Yamada also notes that the women are only given first names in the credits and on posters and fliers, while the full names of the men are listed![6] So, despite the frank display of female sexual pleasure and the depiction of the women as active participants in sex, neither the dance, nor the dance company Dairakudakan, functioned as a gender-equal utopia.

One part of the title seems ambiguous or even troubling: the idea that Iwarebiko's journey passed through Korea and the Aleutians. During World War II, there was the idea (attributed to Iwarebiko by nationalists) of "eight directions under one roof," which meant that the Japanese Empire would expand over the world (Dower 1999, 223). It is troubling if Maro was echoing nationalist sentiments. However, archeologists think that the imperial family in fact came from the Korean peninsula or intermixed with people there.[7] So Maro may have been suggesting not only that there was homoeroticism and (a modicum) of female empowerment in the foundation of Japan but also that the Japanese people intermixed with (or stemmed from) people from the Korean peninsula and the Aleutians. We may be justified in understanding Maro as writing (or restoring) an internationalism and gender fluidity into the foundations of Japan.

Harada notes that the small table is a *go* board. Go is a strategy game in which players try to capture territory from their opponent. Apparently, the idea of the *go* board came from a song with the lyric "The world is a game of go" (Harada 2004, 192). Thus, the *go* board might be an invitation to perform an expanded interpretation that recognizes that these actions (whatever they are) take place within (or symbolize) a wider world of geopolitics. Viewers would be warranted in drawing a further connection between the *go* board and the mention of the Korean peninsula and the Aleutians.

Harada has apparently interviewed Maro, and although she does not clearly distinguish between her own conjectures and attributions to Maro (or some other Dairakudakan dancer), she states that the men dancing on one leg were "intended as an everyday army squad" (Harada 2004, 193). Later, she implies that Maro indicated that the tubers hanging from the men were daily rations for soldiers *as well as* symbolic testicles (Harada 2004, 193). Since the Tanikawa character cuts the tubers from the men, it would seem the soldiers undergo a kind of castration and lose their source of food simultaneously.

Let's review: samurai armor split down the center, *niô dô* breastplate that suggests starvation, tubers as daily rations (or testicles) for the army (which then get chopped off), the quest to unify various tribes that seems to include a homoerotic encounter, one title suggesting that the quest involves Korea and the Aleutian islands, an alternate title evoking Buddhist hell, a *go* board suggesting geopolitical context, heterosexual sex that features women seemingly penetrating and then walking on the men.

It would be a mistake to ascribe one single meaning to the dance. It is obvious that the dance could support several different expanded interpretations. The dance is a complex re-envisioning of gender, sexuality, and Japanese identity, history, and militarism. I suggest that an outer bound for expanded interpretations of this dance must acknowledge that complexity.

The Story of the Phallic God

The Story of the Phallic God (Yôbutsu shintan, October 1973) opens with a thick braid of onions hanging in the middle of the stage.[8] Men process across the stage with strange antennae sprouting along their backs creating almost inverse exoskeletons. Women follow carrying short tables. The women set the tables down and begin to eat gobs of food from them throughout the dance. In a second scene, two men with long golden phalluses lick their own arms over and over. A third scene features men with globes covering their heads. The globes are upside-down or rotated by 90 degrees with Australia clearly visible on top or on its side, and North America visible on the bottom. Meanwhile, Maro, in blue body paint, clutches the onion braid. In a fourth scene a pile of nearly naked men squirm around in a jumble of futons and gradually disappear into a stage trap, and then later make their way squirming back out of the trap. Still clutching the braid of onions, Maro says, "Kill the emperor." The men reappear, spooning each other and writhing while screeching, scolding, and repeating, "I am sorry," "Please forgive me," "Please have patience with me," "Please stick it in me," and "Please give me a break." Finally, Hijikata appears, standing nearly motionless with only fingers moving, and then rotating himself imperceptibly. A man in military uniform with a gun raises out of the floor and aims the gun. Then he sinks back into the floor. Hijikata reappears for a second scene in which he embraces the onion braid. The same young man, now naked, appears out of the floor. Hijikata sits on a dais with the young man lying down at his side, in front of a Duchamp-inspired window. Hijikata lies down atop the young man and French kisses him and then minces off the stage.

The Story of the Phallic God nominally takes its source from a work of the same name by Shibusawa Tatsuhiko, which was in turn based in part on Artaud's *Heliogabalus* (Yamada 1992, 271). Shibusawa's story tells of a young nobleman (who comes from a culture that worships onions) becoming the emperor of a larger empire that worships peacocks (just as Artaud's Heliogabalus was a Syrian-Emesani who came to power in Rome). The young emperor oversees the destruction of the peacock idols and their replacement with idols erected to onions. In the center of these onion-shaped idols, he secretly has a few of his most trusted stonemasons create a "cavity the size of a small fisheye." This cavity, he says, is "emptiness" or "nihility" and is indestructible (Shibusawa 1986, 85–86). The emperor discloses that he has had an operation to give himself a vagina and become a hermaphrodite, thinking that the unification of both sexes in one body will produce the perfect existence (Shibusawa 1986, 82). He leads a decadent existence, and then is killed by mistake by one of the imperial guards when he is wandering outside the palace dressed as a female prostitute during the mayhem of a festival.

As with the previous dance, this one is a strange mix. Take the upside-down or sideways globes covering the heads of the dancers. Most Euro-American, and Asian mapmakers place Europe, North America, and Asia at the top of the map/globe, in what amounts to a Global North bias.[9] So, it is humorously subversive in Dairakudakan style to turn the globe over or on its side and make the tip of Chile and Argentina the top of the world.(Figure 4.4). Characteristically, Dairakudakan's inversion includes their own country in the topsy-turvy upending of the global order.[10]

Maro's "Kill the emperor" and the soldier pointing a gun at Hijikata are intriguing. Harada sees the penultimate scene as an assassination attempt instigated by Maro with Hijikata as the emperor and Yamada as becoming the emperor's lover after a failed assassination attempt (Harada 2004, 198). In Shibusawa's story the emperor is a young man, and there is no plot to kill him. He is killed by accident when he is outside the palace disguised as a female prostitute. The military uniform and gun are completely anachronistic to the time of Shibusawa's story. We are left unsure about which emperor is to be killed, and by whom. However, in 1973 Japan, it was not possible to stage a dance with the command "Kill the emperor" without it sounding like

Figure 4.4 Men with globes on their heads in *The Story of the Phallic God*, dir. Susumura Yasuji, choreog. Dairakudakan, 1973b. Screen Capture.

a reference to the Japanese Emperor system, which was the subject of intense debate throughout the postwar era.

In November 1960, the writer Fukuzawa Shichirô published a story in which a man dreams about a revolution in which the emperor is killed. A right-wing man attempted to assassinate the publisher and Fukuzawa received death threats (Treat 1994). Meanwhile, Oe Kenzaburo published two novellas featuring a right-wing youth modeled after the assassin of Asanuma Inajirô, chairman of the Socialist Party. The youth is erotically attracted to and masturbates to images of the emperor. Like Fukuzawa, Oe received death threats from right-wing fanatics (Napier 1989; Hirata 2005). An expanded interpretation might posit that Maro's exhortation to kill the emperor and the youth (Yamada) in a military uniform aiming a gun at Hijikata (the emperor) and then becoming his lover constitute a creative mash-up of Shibusawa's story with postwar literary treatments of the emperor. These would include Fukuzawa's story of the beheading of the emperor, Oe's sardonic stories of right-wing youth erotically attracted to and masturbating to images of the emperor, and the assassination attempts on Fukuzawa and Oe.

Yamada writes that the dance "had a motif of nothingness, symbolized by onions and the Emperor Heliogabalus" (Yamada 1992, 217). The onions refer to the onion-shaped phallic idols of Shibusawa's story, and Heliogabalus was the model for the young emperor. But it is not clear from Yamada how Dairakudakan understood the issue of nothingness. However, Shibusawa's story is an extended meditation on nothingness or nihility, which is taken to have negative and positive aspects.

In the novel, a subgroup of people including bored upper-class people and slaves are so miserable that want to commit suicide. For these people, nothingness is an attractive escape from unbearable misery. Nothingness is also taken to have its own power. The emperor has his stonemasons insert small cavities in the onion-shaped idols. He characterizes these cavities as "emptiness" or "nihility" and says that they are indestructible (Shibusawa 1986, 85–86). Nothingness is bound up in contradictory ways with sexuality as well. The emperor belongs to a culture that worships the onion as a symbol of the phallus. However, he personally feels that the phallus is incomplete. Just as the emperor introduced tiny fisheyes of emptiness into the phallic idols, he undergoes an operation to give himself a vagina and thereby opens an orifice in himself. It would be too clever (and too dismissive of the corporeality of the vagina) to say that the original (phallic) emptiness was augmented by a second (vaginal) emptiness. However, the emperor certainly feels incomplete (we might call this "gender dysphoria"), and he compensates by modifying his body.

In this light, the scene of the men apologizing and asking for forgiveness is striking. Harada reports that Maro told her that the scene was about everyday complexes (Harada 2004, 198). Possibly, the dancers are manifestations of Shibusawa's young emperor, who secretly feels incomplete in his own body. If this were the case, it would cast light on "Please stick it in me," which is otherwise a strange addition to the line-up of responses to complexes. Perhaps one of the men is an embodiment of the young emperor who desperately wants someone to penetrate him, but also feels uncomfortable in his own skin. It would be in keeping with a broader concern in butô with different and marginalized peoples to recognize that all people have their own complexes. And perhaps that concern doubles up with Shibusawa's ruminations on a person who seems to be the most powerful person in the empire, but feels apologetic about himself, and wants nothing more than to be forgiven.

After considering these two dances, we can observe that the initial dances of Maro and his fellow dancer/choreographers were complex (and possibly contradictory) dance-theater spectacles involving sexuality, ethnicity, and history. Maro had two ideas that led to the proliferation of dancers with this basic orientation to butô. The first was *tenpu tenshiki* (天賦典式), which literally means something like "innate canonical form" but which Maro glosses as "Just being born in this world is a great talent." The idea was that everyone has innate talent. The second idea was "One person, one troupe." In principle each dancer is valuable in their own right, and each had already choreographed individual scenes. With those mottos as an impetus, from 1974, many of the dancers started their own companies either in different places in Japan or in other countries.

Maro's Dance Creation Techniques

Perhaps drawing on shared experience with Noguchi taisô, Maro uses imagery similarly to Hijikata. In a workshop at UCLA May 22, 2011, Maro demonstrated a movement in which one drops to a squat with one leg extended and then bounces back up to standing, while imagining a string pulling up the crown of the head. Maro observed that if you tried to do the exercise with your muscles, you would soon tire, but if you imagined that a string was pulling you up, then you could do it for much longer. In this, Maro follows other butô practitioners (and even other somatics practitioners) who assume that imagery exercises cause a physiological change in how the body-mind moves and enable the body-mind to move more effectively or for a longer period of time (Franklin 1996, 34).

Maro expanded on Noguchi/Hijikata using several interrelated methods through which he discovers and cultivates new dance movements. He describes these methods using a shifting set of terms.[11] One method he calls gathering *miburi* (usually translated as "gestures"), which are opposed to what he calls "actions" (or sometimes "fake actions"). Actions are everyday ways of moving controlled by purposes, such as using a tool. *Miburi* arise from mistakes, and accidents/incidents (*jiken*), which momentarily disrupt everyday movement and open a crack that possibly gives us access to an unconscious realm. Then a movement occurs that is outside of the everyday and purposiveness. Maro writes:

> For example, when you cut yourself with a knife, the initial "ah," before you can say ouch, it's one of those movements. Of course, these kinds of movements

are quickly controlled and restrained by everyday actions, but the presentation of these gestures as temporary fissures is the starting point for our dance.
(Maro n.d.c)

By being attentive to such accidents/incidents, Maro "gathers" or "harvests" movements that are different from customary movements.

Another technique derives from the temporary immobility when one cannot rely
on one's usual movements during these accidents/incidents. At these moments, Maro
thinks that the body instantaneously gains a visually appealing density. Maro says,

> You can feel your density increasing. But really, there is no way to explain what
> kind of density it is. . . . The moment you start moving again, the density is gone. So,
> the question is, what happens if you try not to break off the density, and capture it
> alive, once you stop moving. (Aihara 2018, 187)

Maro tries to "freeze-dry" such moments (he also uses the term "stop-motion") to
preserve that density (Maro n.d.c). Somewhat paradoxically, Maro terms this freeze-
dried moment the *chûtai* (鋳態 also, *igata* 鋳型), the "casting phase" (also translated
as "form condition" and "mold phase"). The idea of casting (as with a bronze statue)
might make this word seem unsuitable to the unpredictability of the *jikken*, but Maro
intends this word to capture the immobility *and* indeterminacy of the moment when
your conscious mind cannot respond to the accident/incident. Moreover, Maro plays
productively with the idea of the "casting phase" as a pre-existing unconscious universal archetype and/or as something that can become a template for the choreographer to use subsequently (Bradley 2017, 89). However, Maro feared the casting phase
might become a fixed pattern. Maro acknowledges that Dairakudakan has repeatable
elements in their choreography, but he says that ideally these are approaches to movement such as "melting or warping" rather than steps such as a pirouette (Maro 2004,
139). But elsewhere Maro acknowledges the danger of falling into a routine and says
that dancers must "shake" or "wave" the casting to understand how it is entrapping
them (Matsuoka et al. 1985, 94). If the casting becomes a set form, "then the task [is]
to smash it" (Maro 2004, 139).

This density is related to three other concepts Maro uses. The first two are the related ideas of *okippuri* (way of holding one's body or the quality of one's stance) and
taidama (body-spirit/energy). *Okippuri* consists of standing motionless. At that
moment, the dancer must rely on *taidama*. The term *taidama* plays on the Japanese
idea of the *kotodama* (word-spirit/energy) or the *kodama* (tree-spirit/energy) (Hara
2001). If the dancers' *okippuri* is good, and they have *taidama*, there will be a " 'diversity of the body' that makes the viewer sense a number of directional possibilities"
(Maro and Konuma 2005).

Maro also relates the "casting phase" to the density of the spinning of a top.
Dairakudakan dancer Vessey writes, "Like a spinning top, the body looks still and

quiet but is dense with movement" (Vessey 2018, 453). Maro writes that when he was young, he wondered why all the colors in a top bled together when it was spun. An adult told him "When it spins, the colors disappear, and when it stops, the colors come back." Reflecting on this glib answer, Maro concludes:

> "When it spins, it erases its Being, and when it stops, it expresses its Being." And more exaggeratedly, "When you are alive, Being disappears, and when you die, you express Being." (Maro 1999, 26)

The implication is that something only has Being (a fixed identity) when it is motionless, but when it is in flux it has no fixed identity. Density and *taidama* are ways to talk about flux and possibility in what might seem like a motionless state. Density involves a person suddenly entering into flux (even if unmoving) because of the incident/accident and coming to seem more interesting to look at.

The body was taken to suddenly acquire immense density during an accident or incident, which Maro sought to capture in a metaphorical casting. Given that, the third technique might seem paradoxical, because it involves considering oneself to be empty, or even imagining that "the contents of the body (blood, bones, organs) work their way out through the pores of the skin and the orifices to the outside making the space around the body dense and full, and the inside hollow and empty" (Bradley 2017, 91). Maro calls this the "space-body" (*chutai*, not to be confused with *chûtai*, "casting phase") or the "universe-body" (*uchutai*). Once the dancer is empty, they can become receptive to what is around them. Maro writes that in this technique,

> We consider our body as an empty being, and the space around us as a substance that has volume and gravity.... The space around us has [a] different power and possibility from what we have with just ourselves. (Maro n.d.a)

Rather than imposing oneself on the world, one endeavors to be as open as possible to the world in all its richness. Maro observes: "There is the saying, 'Thanks to you,' [*okagesama de*] but what would happen if we were to say 'Thanks to you' to everything?" (Maro n.d.c). Maro's "thanks to you" is related to emptying yourself and then becoming open to (and acknowledging) what the world has to offer.

Maro often uses the Japanese term *ma* when he talks about the emptied-self receptive to its surroundings. *Ma* is sometimes romanticized by non-Japanese speakers as something mysterious, but it simply means "interval," with the understanding that an interval can be spatial or temporal. There is *ma* (interval—space) between two pillars in architecture and *ma* (interval—time) in comic timing, or a dramatic pause. Imagine someone saying, "Those pillars are well spaced" or "That comedian has perfect timing." That is *ma*. Gradually, a rich set of connotations have grown up around this word, and connoisseurs and practitioners have come to talk about the quality of artists' intervals (*ma*).

Maro has expanded on this use of "interval" (*ma*) by thinking of the interval as a place for injecting new transformations into movement. Vessey glosses Maro's idea of "flavored ma": "there is an emotion, a situation, an animal, anything imaginable that can influence [. . .] your *ma*" (Vessey, 2018, 454). Maro's "flavored ma" is related to Hijikata's use of imagery techniques to alter some dance steps. Vessey categorizes the various ways that Maro "flavors" ma.

The first tool is time. The dancer is encouraged to study the effects of time. For example, he might study the transformation of a baby into an old woman, a tree blossoming in spring and losing its leaves in the fall, or rust spreading across a fence.... The second tool is the environment. Imagining frigid cold, stifling heat, fierce wind, or gentle breezes exerts influence over movement.... The third tool is occupation. A Japanese rice farmer might display a chronic hunched back from working the rice paddies; a sumo wrestler would be large, aggressive, and powerful; a Japanese businessman might be small, intense, and anxious. Occupation affects body shapes and actions, thereby influencing how a dance might reflect that reality. The fourth tool is emotion, as the dancer's emotional state affects the shape of the body. The fifth tool is an awareness and acknowledgment of physical differences in people, such as a handicapping condition like palsy or the loss of a limb. (Vessey 2018, 454)

These are similar to Hijikata's manipulations such as character type or background medium, but more straightforward.

But Maro goes beyond the idea of emptying the self and becoming receptive to something else or flavoring your interval with some imagery work. Maro says that he "thinks of empty space as a substance" (Maro n.d.c).[12] As noted, Maro also acknowledges that gravity fills space. Perhaps influenced by current scientific theory, Maro seems to use the term "interval" (*ma*) as a shorthand for the properties or generative density of the interval (*ma*). He says,

We . . . make the supposition that the space surrounding [our bodies] has density. Everything is full of something. The thing that fills this space is an interval (*ma*). [. . .] You try to think of yourself as a cavity and live with an influx of this interval (*ma*) into your body, and try to cultivate it. (Maro n.d.c)

Elsewhere, Maro plays with the homophony between the interval (ma) and demon/evil (ma) (Bradley 2017, 92). Thus, the interval (*ma*) is not just the space between two things, but has become a metaphor for the different densities that surround us (or are within us), each having their own generative properties. These densities can pour into our newly emptied selves and generate something within us. Using all these ideas, Maro and his fellow choreographer/dancers discover and shape movements, and then use those movements to enact their strange seminarrative spectacles.

Sea Dappled Horse(s)

Maro used the dance *Sea Dappled Horse(s)* (Kaiin no Uma, 1980) to capitalize on the European butô wave, which was caused primarily by his own colleagues. Dairakudakan performed the dance in 1982 at the American Dance Festival and in 1983 at the Avignon Theater Festival. Aihara says that it tells the story of "Maro encountering numerous monsters" on his way to search for a mythical horse (Aihara 2018, 184).

Scene 1—Those Who Live
A row of near-naked dancers bite a cord held taut by two dancers. They release the cord from their mouths, sink to the floor and move like animals. They come together on their hands and knees as a group, inhaling and exhaling in yoga cat-cow pose (Marjaryasana-Bitilasana). They convulse progressively energetically until they are exploding outward and shrinking in repeatedly.[13] Returning to the line, they take the rope in their mouths and back off stage between the panels.

Scene 2—In and out of the Sliding Doors
The cord-holders play tug of war in front of a tall rickety box made of sliding doors. Eventually the two drag on stage and into the box a woman in a red kimono with yellow ruffles. She caresses a prisoner and then pulls down her shirt to reveal a gigantic silver breast, which she uses to suckle him. They drag her back out of the box, and after much pulling and tugging (in which it appears she may be choked by the rope) the two rope-holders drag her into a similar box on the other side of the stage. A man enters in a white robe that has wire supports inside so the bottom hems turn up like flower petals. He sways and jerks and sometimes reaches out for the rope. He backs up to the original box and discovers the captive. He then seems to bow/convulse in front of a large pan of rice. The two rope-holders fight over the mound of rice and mash their heads into it. While they fight, the captive stirs and stands in the cage.

Scene 3—The Journey
To gentle piano music, a group of women clad in cream-colored dresses clasp their hands and raise and lower them in an inverted U from one side of their waists up their torsos and back down the other side. Meanwhile, they shift their torsos and the direction their heads are pointing to where their hands go. They then stand in a row trembling with their mouths stretched wide open in fish lips. Finally, they retreat behind the panels and poke body parts out, sometimes climbing their hands up the panels, and sometimes on their hands and knees with their buttocks and legs poking out.

Scene 4—Growing Wild
Maro wears a gray kimono and holds two small boxes. He seems to want to make some kind of contact with another dancer in a gray shroud and so reaches out to him.

The two rope-pullers pull on ropes to keep the two apart, and then contrive to hoist Maro up into the air so the two cannot make contact.

Scene 5—Headless Regret
A man lies in front of the rice bowl in a half-sideways pietà position with only his buttocks on the floor and holding the rest of his body off the floor. Two white-clad women dancers wave, sway, and twirl slowly as if to provide a bodily frame for him. They gradually spin more wildly, and grasp and flail their hands above their heads. Then they convulse and rub hands over and over, and fall to sitting, still rubbing their hands. They reach out and rock their bodies to gradually come closer to the man.

Scene 6—A Prayer for a Safe Birth
Seven men with ornate golden crowns that look vaguely inspired by Thai or Indian art hold their hands in front of them as if holding reins, and they bob up and down as if each is on his own horse (somewhat as with the king and knights in Monty Python). Behind each follows a dancer bent double under a folded futon looking like a huge headless sheep and walking like a duck. After much holding of court and processing by the kings and pulsing by the futon-sheep, the dancers under the futons throw them off. The kings quickly whisk the futons away revealing women in pink shifts and red bows.

Scene 7—Sin and Punishment
The characters in pink (including Maro) repeat a kind of two-armed bouncing throwing movement (discussed in more detail later). Meanwhile, a character in a golden kimono comes through the audience and on stage. The women in pink twirl around the stage occasionally running into each other and sometimes encountering the golden-kimono character. They exude imbecilic happiness. Maro separates from the other women and seems like he wants to attract the golden kimono man (Figure 4.5). However, he is left out as the other women bounce around the man. Maro looks unsure of herself while the man basks in the adulation of the pink bouncing women. Eventually pink-girl-Maro screws up her courage and chases Mr. Golden Kimono. Mr. Golden kimono kisses her, dips her ballroom-dance-style, and then sucks her blood vampire style. After dropping Maro on the ground, Mr. Golden Kimono lies atop Maro in sixty-nine position and appears to pleasure him/her.

Scene 8—Nymph and Light—Record of the Back
Three near-naked men have long red narrow capes hanging from the back of their necks. They pose, stamp, and leap so the capes billow. Then they crawl along the ground with capes dragging behind. Three women in pale pink kimono become visible at the back of the stage. A character enters wearing a Japanese warrior kabuto helmet and what appear to be caterpillar tracks or tank treads and sporting a giant golden phallus. He wanders among the women, while Maro stands in the back. Maro is naked and slightly hunched over, with his legs pressed together and his penis tucked

Figure 4.5 Maro by himself in *Ghost Story: Sea Dappled Horse*, 1990. Photograph by Kamiyama Teijirô. Courtesy of Ikeda Hayato and Minami Shôkichi.

behind so that he looks like a woman. He trembles and looks forsaken. The kabuto helmet man and the other dancers never acknowledge him.

Considering *Sea Dappled Horse(s)*

Parts of this dance are fascinating wordless theater: the rope pullers entrapping characters in boxes, the kings with their futon-duck mounts. We have no idea what these scenes mean, but they are engrossing vignettes. Other scenes feature Maro unable to fit into a community and looking like a poor forlorn young woman. In one scene he eventually succeeds in attracting the attention of the object of his affection. In the other it never happens, and Maro ends the piece looking as if the weight of the entire world is on him/her. The scene with the character attired in a kabuto helmet and golden dildo is striking. It may say something about Maro's attitude toward Japanese samurai that Maro is on the outside looking in and never gets invited to the party. And the pairing of a samurai helmet with tank tracks in place of the standard lamellar armor (*kozane*) provides a visual proposition about the nexus between samurai values and modern Japanese militarism.

The Book of the Five Rings

The Book of Five Rings (Gorin no sho) premiered at the Butoh Festival '85. The title was taken from the treatise of same name about swordsmanship written by the celebrated swordsman Miyamoto Musashi (1584–1645) in about 1643.

The Dance

The dance is a typical Dairakudakan adventure. It opens with five women wearing A-line cream-colored dresses with square boxes affixed to the hems of the dresses. They generally lean to one side with their legs crossed and their hands to the other side. They twitch and let the ripples travel through their bodies before bringing them to a stop suddenly. After some time, they form a line and begin to run/glide in a clockwise circle around the stage. They are joined by two men in huge capes (one black and one cream) with long trains dragging behind. The men run/glide in the opposite direction around the stage in an inner circle. After the women leave, the two men continue to circle each other. Eventually they stick their tongues out at each other. They stare each other down as if to win a battle against each other with their tongues. Neither one will give up. They draw closer. Who will win? Their tongues are almost touching each other. Without realizing exactly when something changed, it is not clear whether this is a fight or a mutual seduction. Finally, the tips of their tongues brush for a millisecond and they fall back. Renewing their courage, they approach again. Their tongues graze again and again they fall back, but this time quickly grab for each other so that they fall into each other's arms. They begin to spin with each taking turns spinning the other so that his feet can rise coyly off the ground. Centrifugal force spins them apart and they retreat to their respective sides. They pull out black toy machine guns and begin to fire at each other. Hold on, these are water guns. They are squirting each other. Two men dressed in A-line box dresses come on the stage and seem to egg them on. The white-clad dancer wins and brandishes a Japanese sword, and the two box-dress-men kneel in front of him. The dancer in the black robe returns, and the dancer in the white robe collapses on the stage. They are replaced on stage by five pairs of dancers. One of each pair wears a bonnet and one is wrapped in paper. The bonnet-dancers stand behind the paper-dancers and manipulate them like puppets, and then the paper-dancers turn tables and they manipulate the bonnet dancers. One set of five back their way into the center with their buttocks touching each other, while the other set make their way around the outside slowly walking while reaching their hands out and pulling them in in time with their steps. After a solo by Maro, the entire troupe appears in yellow rags and breastplates. They make their way through the audience, randomly throwing their hands out to the side, up, or behind themselves. Three of the breastplate dancers remain on stage and bounce, glide around, and explode their limbs outward. While they are doing this a dancer dressed in a schoolboy uniform and cap crosses the stage looking like an imbecile and winding his arm constantly like a Pete Townsend guitar solo. He is followed by a red-skirted woman with wire in her skirt to make it stick straight out and a wire in her bouffant hair to make her hair slant out to the side. She screams her way across the stage. The three breastplate dancers seem to take no notice of the two interlopers. They retreat to the back of the stage, and, in extremely low light, take their breastplates and rags off. They reappear in pink minidresses and red caps (just as in *Sea-Dappled Horse*). Standing around a wooden barrel, each puts one leg in the barrel and flirts shamelessly, provocatively showing a little thigh. Maro comes out for a star turn, and almost as if to place itself diegetically before *Sea-Dappled Horse*, the dance ends with the line of dancers connected by a rope through all their mouths.

Considering *The Book of Five Rings*

The author of the original *Book of Five Rings*, Musashi Miyamoto, was a complicated character. For example, you might expect to find in his book grandiose secrets of swordsmanship, but in fact, Musashi advocates slashing the hands and wrists of opponents (Miyamoto 2021, 92). But Musashi was not above tooting his own horn. He bragged that he bested sixty opponents and never lost. The most celebrated of all his duels was with Sasaki Kojirô, and Musashi supposedly won using a wooden oar. He was already the subject of kabuki and puppet theater plays from 1737, and later a novel by Yoshikawa Eiji serialized between 1934 and 1939. In the war years, his image became caught up in militarist discourse, and he "became a kind of poster boy for samurai culture" (Bennet "Introduction," 20, in Musashi 2021).[14] Later, he became a symbol of Japanese business and economics practices during the supercharged Japanese economy of the 1980s (Hurst 1982).

Predictably, Maro refuses to accept this image at face value. In an interview, he said:

> Musashi Miyamoto wrote this book on swordsmanship. Rather than form, it concerns tactics of how to win against others. His book is a symbol of present-day Japan's economic strength. I wanted to put some light onto it and see it negatively. It is about the business technique of winning, but to me it is not too interesting, because even after one wins, one eventually dies. How to use nature and win against

man—those are the principles of Musashi's the *Book of the Five Rings*. It may be interesting in these times for business reasons, but not for me. (Maro n.d.b)

It is not clear whether the white-clad dancer and black-clad dancer are Musashi and Sasaki. But if so, smack dab in the middle of the 1980's cultural and economic climate, Maro treats a duel by the "poster boy" of samurai-wannabes and business-samurai-wannabes as a match to see who can stick out his tongue the most determinedly, or as the prelude to a male–male French kiss. Then, rather than paint Musashi as a courageous warrior who could be an inspiration for modern-day (economic) warriors, Maro depicted him wildly spraying water from a black toy machine gun, and at the end of the scene, it is not clear who wins.[15] The scene is hilarious, and an expanded interpretation might see it as a satire of Japanese military and economic culture.

One Example of Maro's Technique (perhaps)

The whole business of freeze-drying movements, the casting phase, and gestures might seem abstract, but one of the movements from *Sea-Dappled Horse(s)* can perhaps serve to make this more concrete: the throwing-bouncing of the pink-women in scene 7—"Sin and Punishment." The base of the movement is a repeated syncopated hop or double step with the right leg kicking out to the side or slightly back (Figure 4.6). This is accompanied by a repeated double-arm throw and then continuing the arc down, back, and up again. The movement starts small and gradually builds in amplitude. Noguchi taisô emphasized allowing movement to ripple through the body. Here also, the movement ripples through the neck and the head rocks gently side to side and slightly diagonally back and forth. This goes on for several minutes as the dancers spread about the stage. For a brief moment, they vary the arm movement while keeping the leg and torso rhythm, so that the hands snake out front and cross each other and the palms rotate up and down. Then as they line up on the back wall, the movement resolves into an arms-out bouncing movement while rotating the palms up and down with each bounce. The bigger movement holds our attention as the object of interest, but then the smaller movement serves as the backdrop for the entry and activities of the golden-kimono-clad character. The movement changes over time but is dictated by the overall bouncing/throwing pattern.

It is pure conjecture, but perhaps Maro (or another dancer) had an incident/accident in the moment of throwing something. Try "freeze-drying" yourself in the middle of the action of throwing an apple or a rock. Throwing might seem as if it is led by the hand but is actually led by the shoulder and then the elbow with the wrist snapping forward at the end. Once my conjectured "incident" had happened, and Maro was no longer throwing purposively, he would have been able to study the motion carefully. Frozen in the "casting phase," some density would accrue to the movements, and Maro could take them as a "starting point for [a] dance." This is all conjecture, but the next point might have been to wonder: "What happens if I make

Figure 4.6 Line of bouncing throwing women in *Ghost Story: Sea Dappled Horse*, 1990. Photograph by Kamiyama Teijirô. Courtesy of Ikeda Hayato and Minami Shôkichi.

the throwing motion without allowing the elbow and shoulder to ever be in front of the hands and wrists?" Then the choreographer would combine these into the motion as it appears in the dance with the arms rotated out to the side and sort of tossing something forward. The next step would presumably have been exploring or adding reverberations through the body to arrive at the right leg popping out sideways and the neck and head jerking softly to and fro. What is more, we see that Maro "smashes" the "casting phase" in the middle of the scene by letting the hands snake out in front and by adding supination and pronation to the wrists, so as not to let the movement become monotonous.

My conjecture only covers half of the choreography. The other half lies in conceiving a small story arc in which to fit the choreography. In Hijikata's case, these story arcs were almost impossible to recognize from the outside. How would we know that Ashikawa was dancing the role of a prostitute? But in Maro's case, they are easier to grasp. In this case, it would be the story of individual desire vis-à-vis the group. The pink characters are dressed and move alike. One demonstrates an individual desire and the action is concerned with how that will play out. In the beginning it seems that the individual cannot be part of the community, but in the end s/he gets pleasured by the object of her/his desire. Sometimes the palm-flipping-throwing-bouncing movement functions purely abstractly, as when the women flounce around the stage. Sometimes, it turns into the background for the other actions. Sometimes, it seems to take on meaning as an indicator of group belonging. When the movement takes on contextual significance, it makes the scene amenable to Maro's expanded interpretation as we can briefly consider how groups and individuals interact or ought to interact.

Kochûten and the development of young talent

The second phase of Maro's talent incubation was the creation of the monthly Kochûten (Paradise in a Jar) performance series in 2001, which was designed for younger members of the dance troupe to choreograph their own dances. Each dance passes through a "Maro-entire-company check" (Maro sôken) one week before completion (Aihara 2018, 189), in which Maro helps the younger choreographers tighten their choreography. As an example, here are several scenes from Mamiana Zengoro's *Gospel* (*Fuku-in*, 2002):

Scene 1—All Bound Up

A male dancer in a Western suit looking like a corporate worker answers hundreds of cell phones.

Scene 4—Blind Faith and the Badger (*tanuki*)

A male dancer is blinded by a Japanese Rising Sun flag wrapped around his head. A pissing and sniffing badger appears, sporting a Hitler moustache. The badger-Hitler sniffs at the flag-blinded man and then when Japanese man tries to touch him, the badger-Hitler beats the Japanese man. Then the badger-Hitler climbs aboard him and humps and sodomizes him.

Scene 5—In the Countryside

Three Japanese females in worn hakama hold babies. A high-school-aged boy in a black Prussian uniform looks as if he has been crucified on a Rising Sun flag. The women gradually go insane. Facing away from the audience, the women squat and repeatedly fall on their sides and then get back up again. Then they face the audience and dance with their mouths opened grotesquely.

Scene 7—The Portrait of a Family

The businessman with cell phones. The high school boy with black uniform. A TV watcher. The boy strips and poses seductively on a table in front of the TV watcher, but the TV watcher is oblivious. The boy cries out and leaves. Black-clad kuroko stagehands take the TV and table away from the TV watcher. He does not move an inch. They then come and haul him away and he seems unaware that he is being hauled away.

It does not take much expanded interpretation to see this as a dance in which Hitler is able to sodomize a Japanese person whose head is wrapped up patriotically in a Japanese flag. Mothers lament their sons sacrificed to the same flag. A corporate warrior slaves away to his cell phone. A young man is rendered insensate by his solipsism with his TV.

In conclusion, Maro was the first dancer to enter the butô world from outside the direct sphere of Hijikata. He created his own version of butô, which drew on some of Hijikata's techniques. It involved interrupting purposeful ways of moving and thinking, and then using the new movements to create grand seminarrative spectacles. He and his fellow dancers share with Hijikata some of the spirit of the critique of Japanese culture, and a focus on marginalized peoples, but they rely on the audience using "expanded interpretation" to situate the performances within a sociopolitical context. Owing to Maro's ideas of "tenpu tenshiki" and "One person, one troupe," numerous dancers started their own companies and traveled the world spreading variations on his understanding of butô.

5

Kobayashi Saga

Kobayashi Saga stands second only to Ashikawa in the level of immersion in the world of Hijikata's evocative experiments. She participated in all the performances employing his new methods, from the 1970 *Seaweed* (Gibasa) to the 1974 *Siren Salmon*. Then she and fellow company member Tachibana Ryûichi formed their own company, Suisei Club (Comet Club). In 1977, Hijikata choreographed another dance for her, *Bitter Light* (Nigai Hikari), and he chose her to join Ashikawa for the 1983 European tour of *Breasts of Japan*. Tachibana died in 1985. In 1987 Kobayashi started a solo career, and then in 1995 created a new dance company, Kobayashi Saga and Kirin (Strange Giraffe), and then in 1998 renamed it, Kobayashi Saga and Nosuri (Buzzard). This chapter highlights her remarkable career focused on the boundaries between what we can and cannot know, what we can and cannot see, and the ethical breaches that occur when we confuse the categories.

Kobayashi grew up in a rural village, and she attributes some of her views on dance to experiences she had as a child (Kobayashi 2005, 32–34). Her family's miso business failed, so she spent her childhood playing among abandoned miso manufacturing equipment (water tanks and barrels). This gave her a taste for the oddities of life. She studied modern dance after high school; then heard about Hijikata. In 1969, she went to Asbestos Studio to meet him. The very next day she moved in and started training with him.

By then, Hijikata and Ashikawa had already started working on Hijikata's new project, so she was joining midstream. At 2 am on her first day, Hijikata roused her out of bed, and they began training. They practiced walking on all fours like an animal until morning (Kobayashi 2005, 47). Two events that catalyzed her understanding of butô happened when she climbed into bed after that first night of grueling training. Out of the blue, she remembered a moment when she was in elementary school and found herself suddenly unable to stand up. Then she remembered a moment when she was dozing off to sleep as a child, and the middle finger on her right hand suddenly twitched all of its own accord (Kobayashi 2005, 48). She took from these experiences two assumptions: The first is that an enormous part of our past is stored within us, and the right trigger can bring it back to us. The second is that sometimes we can be moved without our conscious mind doing the moving.

At some point, she read the works of Miki Shigeo (Kobayashi 2005, 29),[1] who argues that our DNA encodes the memory of our species. It's a short jump from the idea that we can access our individual past with the right trigger to the idea that we

A History of Butô. Bruce Baird, Oxford University Press. © Oxford University Press 2022.
DOI: 10.1093/oso/9780197630273.003.0005

can access some part of our species' past through the right trigger. And it's a similarly small hop to the idea that we can be moved by something beyond the boundaries of our own self.

These insights led to the notion that the *ankoku* (darkness) of Hijikata's ankoku butô is a way to designate everything we do not understand. It also reminds us that the part we do not understand is much greater than what we understand, and so we should be humble about what we do not understand. She writes, "Hijikata used many words, but wasn't the amount that he couldn't put into words much bigger? I'm always worried about this portion, rather than the portion that he could put into words" (Kobayashi 2005, 38). Her work is based on trying to tap into the vast reservoir of the universe that we do not yet understand, while acknowledging that there are limits on what we can understand.

The 2007 work *Half-Dream: Double Aura* (*Hanbunmu: Daburu aura*) was one of a string of works in which Kobayashi worked through a constellation of ideas related to these larger themes: aura, hysterics, dreams.[2] She enters a dark stage featuring a bowl set on the right side of the stage. She is covered in a white strip of cloth draped over her head and hanging down her front and back just past her waist. She lights a match and with it lights two candles and puts them in the bowl. The flickering of the candles seems strangely like a strobe light. She takes off the covering, facing us naked, dancing behind the basin, but there is not enough light to see her face or much of her upper torso. She comes in front of the candles and dances again but this time all we can see is a silhouette. She retreats to the back of the stage and when she faces front, she has reflectors in front of her eyes. She scowls and makes a coughing sound like a cat and imitates animals such as chickens and apes, but without the facial expression matching the bodily movement. She goes over to the side of the stage and drapes a new piece of fabric over herself. She also carries a paper lantern suspended from a stick. The outer part of the lantern begins to burn, and she becomes much more animated and cycles through faces, passing from one to the next almost instantaneously, including one in which she is grimacing in pain. But my attention is divided between her face and the flickering of the fire. I want to watch both. She douses the paper lantern and, in the process, intentionally spills a bucket of water all over the floor. Then she hooks herself to plastic tubes from the ceiling (Figures 5.1 and 5.2). She is backlit by bright lights and there is so much smoke in the room that it's hard to see anything, but she waves the wet cords, and they shimmer in the light. She repeatedly pulls backward and slingshots forward, sliding across the floor. Flickers of light shoot up and down the wet cords as they expand and contract. She wraps herself in more and more cords, retreats to the back wall, where she looks like she is trying to escape but she is trapped. The lights go down.

Kobayashi is clearly toying with light, visuality, and darkness in the dance. The flickers of the candles are echoed in the streaks of light shooting up and down the wet rubber tubes. In one scene it is too dark to see clearly, and in another it is too light and there is too much smoke to see clearly. Both scenes remind us that there

Figure 5.1 Kobayashi Saga in *Half-Dream: Double Aura*, 2007. Photograph by Kamiyama Teijirô. Courtesy of Ikeda Hayato and Minami Shôkichi.

are limits on what we can know. On a more metaphorical level, when she puts reflectors on her eyes, we cannot see her eyes, those all-important "windows into the soul." Therefore, we do not know everything about her. I also have the feeling that she cannot see me, and that she is signaling that she does not presume to know everything about me.[3]

At a deeper level, the title invites us to think about the aura and half-dream. Does this performance have an aura? Does her naked body have an aura? Does fire have an aura? Do grimaces and pain have an aura? If so, where does each come from? Is the aura enhanced by the light, or does it function better in the dark? Are we in a dream world, or a half-dream world? If a dream world, is she dreaming? Or are we dreaming?

Whatever the answers to these questions may be, the aura of the title also serves as a connection to hysteria and the ideas of philosopher Didi-Huberman. In his book, *Invention of Hysteria*, Didi-Huberman examined the relationship between photography and the "discovery" of hysteria by the neuropsychiatrist Jean-Martin Charcot who worked at a hospital called Salpetrière. Didi-Huberman demonstrated that irregularities and imperfections in the photographic printing process during the early stages of photography in the 1870s were interpreted by doctors as evidence of auras accompanying hysterical attacks. In a section titled "Double Aura" on her webpage, Kobayashi cites a slightly transformed version of Didi-Huberman's analysis in *Invention of Hysteria*:

Figure 5.2 Kobayashi Saga in *Half-Dream: Double Aura*, 2007. Photograph by Kamiyama Teijirô. Courtesy of Ikeda Hayato and Minami Shôkichi.

> An aura is the air that passes over the body. The air of an event which invites pathos, that pressure is as of the fleeting night fog before a storm, it refers to the breath which passes over the body in the instant when the body is just about to fall into suffering or spasm.[4]

Right before this passage, Didi-Huberman has just dropped a bomb on his reader by explaining that the patient Augustine suffers from 1,293 "attacks" per year and that she could not use her right arm. Charcot had called the "aura" that supposedly accompanied her "attacks" *aura hysterica*. One moment later, Didi-Huberman reveals to the reader that Charcot admitted that such aura were "never displayed" because they were "too short . . . and always overwhelmed by the attack itself" (Didi-Huberman 2004, 100). The aura is thus revealed to be Charcot's self-admitted fiction.

Kobayashi does not write enough about the aura and this passage to say for sure how she understood it, but it leaves me with more questions. Here is Didi-Huberman succinctly laying out the argument of his book:

With Charcot we discover the capacity of the hysterical body, which is, in fact, pro-digious. It is prodigious; it surpasses the imagination, surpasses "all hopes," as they say.

Whose imagination? Whose hopes? There's the rub. What the hysterics of the Salpêtrière could exhibit with their bodies betokens an extraordinary complicity between patients and doctors, a relationship of desires, gazes, and knowledge.... A reciprocity of charm was instituted between physicians, with their insatiable de-sire for images of Hysteria, and hysterics, who willingly participated and actually raised the stakes through their increasingly theatricalized bodies. In this way, hys-teria in the clinic became the spectacle, the invention of hysteria. Indeed, hysteria was covertly identified with something like an art, close to theater or painting. (Didi-Huberman 2004, xi)

Was the figure wrapped in plastic tubing a "hysteric" from Salpêtrière? And if so, was Kobayashi impressed with the "capacity of the hysterical body, which is, in fact, pro-digious"? Or with the "insatiable desire [of the doctors] for images of Hysteria, and hysterics"? Or with the acting ability of the "hysterics" themselves "who willingly participated and actually raised the stakes through their increasingly theatricalized bodies"? In short, did the "aura" of the title hint at something beyond our know-ledge that we can only barely sense as if we are peering into darkness or smoke? Or was Kobayashi suggesting that we spectators sat in the same position as the eager at-tendees of Charcot's infamous Tuesday Lectures who came hoping to see a show and were amply rewarded? Did she occupy the same position vis-à-vis us, that the "hys-terics" occupied in the Tuesday Lectures? Was her rejection of visuality a rejection of the scopophilia implied in the standard butô practice of full-frontal nudity? In *Short Night* (Mijikayo, July 19–21, 2013), Kobayashi disrobed to reveal that underneath her dress she had on a thin skin over her skin. Usually, butô artists associate taking off one's clothes with getting to the real person. Was her costume slyly suggesting that we had not yet encountered the real her, because when she took off her clothes, rather than the real Kobayashi, we were confronted with yet another skin?

To give a definitive answer to any of these questions would pin the performances into one thing only, when they were many things at once. *Half-Dream* remains in a su-perposition of indictment of a doctor who thought he knew everything, admiration for patients whose abilities to negotiate terrible conditions were prodigious, indica-tion that there are still things we do not know, and invitation to us to continue to peer into the dark to try to understand more. After a long and storied career, Kobayashi continues to train younger dancers. And she continues to make dances that puzzle us with their hidden depths, plumb the depths of our individual and species memory, remind us of the limits of knowledge and sight, and hint that there are ethical costs to ignoring our limits.

6

Interlude

Butô and Cabaret

Artists cannot make art without support. They need to eat and have a roof over their heads, and they need resources to realize their visions. There might be cases in which the source of artists' money would not be particularly meaningful for understanding their art. However, in the case of butô, the source of funding has far-reaching implications, because for about 30 years, funding for a large percentage of the dancers came from performing in burlesque shows. This chapter explores the function and implications of the cabaret in butô.

Hijikata and Motofuji started performing in the cabaret very early on, and in time came to own or manage as many as six or seven different clubs. Eventually most of the dancers from the Hijikata and Maro lines (roughly 70% of the dancers) used the cabaret to support themselves. Often the dancers covered themselves with gold body paint as a sort of signature look of the butô-derived burlesque performances (Hoffman and Holborn 1987, 84–87; see Figures 6.1 and 6.2)

In the most basic way, the cabaret provided time for the dancers to dance on stage and hone their stagecraft. Several dancers comment on the experience they gleaned of gaining stamina or becoming used to performing nearly naked in front of people (Coker 2018, 414–415). The title of one article about Maro put it this way, he "discovered from the gold body paint show, how to draw someone's attention" (Maro 2018). Rather than presume an attentive silent audience, the cabaret trained the dancers to draw and hold the attention of an audience that is liable to be distracted. Amagatsu noted that the cabaret also gave the performers practice in stringing scenes together in an effective manner (Amagatsu, pers. conversation with the author, May 18, 2014). Maro observed that when the dancers were on tour in remote locations in Japan, there were extra benefits:

> You could kill two birds with one stone. Even if you didn't have a real position in the theater, in the cabaret show, you were a star. And you had a lot of time on your hands. In the winter, while waiting for the show, you would read books, train your body, and also . . . train your mind. (Maro 2011, 164)

Here Maro notes that the cabaret allowed each person to be a star, but he also emphasizes the physical and mental training the dancers could do in their free time. From

A History of Butô. Bruce Baird, Oxford University Press. © Oxford University Press 2022.
DOI: 10.1093/oso/9780197630273.003.0006

Figure 6.1 Promotional photograph for gold-body-paint show. Photographer unknown.

comments such as these we can see that the burlesque shows constituted a specific training regimen for the dancers.

As important as that aspect is, the ability to use the cabaret to raise funds is even more important. A stage with two swings and a structure at the back does not come cheap, even for a dancer used to do-it-yourself. The money has to come from somewhere. In his biography, Maro tells of sending out a team of three dancers in 1970 to Sapporo to dance in a cabaret, but the cabaret owners refused to pay the dancers their contractual three million yen (Maro 2011, 164). Maro and his manager went to collect their money in person, and while there they took the opportunity to watch the show unannounced.

They went to the cabaret and the tout wooed them with the following spiel:

It is mystical and has an eastern magical power to it! It is a fantastically boisterous dance, and in the end, they risk their lives. They are painted in gold paint, and they are pushing themselves to the limits, because in fifteen minutes their breathing is labored, and in thirty minutes, they risk respiratory failure! (Maro 2011, 205)

Once inside, the MC finally announces:

Figure 6.2 Front and back of leaflet for "Gold Paint Package" by the troupe "Kamasutra," featuring Murobushi Kô and others at the Moulin d'Or Club in Shinjuku on Saturday, October 10, 1974. Courtesy of the Murobushi Kô Archive and Watanabe Kimiko.

"And now, the moment you have all been waiting for! Today's show is eastern mysticism glittering in gold. The Gold Dust show by the Golden Trio. Please sit back, relax, and enjoy yourselves." (211)

Maro then describes the show:

The Bolero drum rhythm begins, and the three dancers come on stage quickly and quietly, and pose as Golden Buddhist Statues with the woman Takeda Sanae in the middle. The green and red spotlights melt into gold.

Wow, they really look good don't they! The bustling of the audience dies down in an instant. The costumes are good. The men have shaved heads, and satin loin clothes with red sashes. The woman has a loin cloth with a purple sash, and hair sharpened into a ponytail. They have bells on their hands and feet, and when they stamp their feet, it makes a jangling noise, and when they wave their hands, it makes the air move with jangles. The dance was movements taken from old Egyptian paintings drawn on pots. And matched to the rhythm of Bolero. They were not the least bit unsteady, and their footwork was nicely lined up. The gold body paint is slippery, and there were several difficult adagio variations that were sometimes rough and sometimes calm. In one the woman stiffens herself like a pole and the men hold her up and spin her quickly—what we called the "mambo adagio." (211–212)

Maro exults to his manager:

I will make ten or so teams like this and promote them all over the country. These guys have given me a real dream and power. I'll make an unrivaled peerless dance company and march all over the world. (212)

To understand what so excited Maro, it is just math. Three million yen would equal between $64,000 and $190,000 in current values.[1] For ease of calculation, let's use the low mid-range $100,000. If Maro could get roughly $100,000 dollars for three people for four months, then he could gross roughly $300,000 dollars per year. It is not clear how much Maro was paying his dancers, but elsewhere he says that they adopted a communal lifestyle to save money, and he confesses that he treated his dancers as slaves in order to build his envisioned empire (Maro 2011, 220, 257). Many butô dancers claim to have worked in the cabaret for five hundred yen per day (approximately five dollars).[2] Maro would have had to pay for housing as well, but if the dancers were willing to work for such low wages because they believe in the larger project of butô, then he could have cleared quite a sum. Then if he created ten teams, that is somewhere close to 3 million dollars a year.

An insight into the staggering sums of money involved can be seen in two other anecdotes related by Maro. In one, he tells of a show, the *Emperor's Testicles*, in 1974 on the Tama River in the outskirts of Tokyo during typhoon season. In passing, Maro mentions that each dancer was required to raise five hundred thousand yen ($12,000) in order to put on the show. The locals warned them about the danger of a typhoon, but they did not move their production equipment far enough out of danger and ended up losing eight million yen ($186,000) of equipment including lights, generators, and a truck (Maro 1994).[3]

That is a lot of money to lose because of carelessness, but it pales in comparison to what came next. In 1978, Maro and his cohort amassed enough capital to make a down payment on a four-story building, which they remodeled into a 200-seat theater, rehearsal space, lodging, and cafeteria called Toyotama Garan.[4] For tax purposes, they incorporated into an organization with Maro as president. Maro was entrusted with the seal for their bank account along with a booklet of checks or promissory notes. Not long afterward, his manager (K) asked to borrow the seal and a check. Maro assented with hardly a second thought, and K left with a check for 3 million yen (approximately $45,000). A year later, K came back for another promissory note to the tune of 2 million yen ($30,000). Then 1.5 million yen ($22,500). Then 2.5 million yen ($37,500). Next 4 million yen ($60,000). Then even a blank check. From time to time, Maro asked a few questions, but he did not pay too much attention. One year, Maro estimates that he must have given his manager seven or eight checks. The next year, ten checks.

There is a train wreck at the end of this story. In 1981, Maro noticed strange people poking around the theater, and then one of the shifty-looking folks mentioned in passing that Maro ought to be more careful with his promissory notes. Eventually it all came spilling out, and Maro realized that his manager had taken the company's promissory notes to loan sharks and the mafia and in the end blew through roughly 200 million yen (2.6 million dollars). Maro was the person of last resort on the notes, so when his manager could not repay them, the bill collectors came to him.

Let's consider Maro's attitude toward his finances. If a friend asked you for 20 or even 100 dollars/euros/pounds, you might well give them the money without a second thought. But what if a friend asked you for a couple thousand dollars eight or ten times a year for four years? You might ask more probing questions, or you might just refuse. Keep in mind that Maro was being asked for promissory notes worth roughly 40 thousand dollars a pop, and he hardly batted an eyelash. Only if you think you have the potential to get a lot of money fast, do you let 40 thousand dollars slide by easily. Maro tells this story to demonstrate how preoccupied he was with creating dances. Certainly, there are legions of artists who are financially clueless or present themselves as unconcerned with the mundane world of finances, but we get a glimpse into the financial world of Maro and other butô artists through this vignette. You might think that losing nearly 200 thousand dollars of equipment in a typhoon would serve as a lesson to be more careful. But the burlesque shows were such a cash cow that Maro could afford to be careless. In one article, he off-handedly remarks that the "fastest way to make money" is through burlesque shows (Maro 2018).

Maro arranged to have all the creditors and mafia come to his studio. He penitently apologized for the checks having been used without his knowledge. One of the mafia men scolded him and asked, 'What the hell are you saying? Just who do you think is letting you eat your fill?" (Maro 2011, 239). Suddenly a woman who had been hiding behind a screen door burst out and yelled, "We have been eating by means of my body!" (240). Her outburst did not matter. They were still kicked out of their theater-home, but they just started over and bought a new one. But from the anecdote, we see a woman who knows exactly how they have purchased the swings, lights, trucks, building, how they have been eating their fill. It was by means of her body.

Just to be clear: From the 1960s through early 1990s, the capital that sustained a large majority of butô artists came from dancers presenting their nearly naked bodies in cabaret shows. We need not have any moralizing impulse about nude cabaret dancing. Many dancers say they enjoyed it. But this situation may occasion discomfort because it borders on (partially gendered) exploitation.[5] If the dancers left the company, they could not sell their share of the company to someone else or back to the company. Their labor never resulted in them owning a share in the first place. Maro owned everything.

What is more, Katherine Mezur points out that the men of butô often cross-dressed as women in an attempt to contest the male gender categories of postwar Japan, but the women ended up enacting primarily female roles. To be sure, the women enacted a broader range of female roles than socially available to them, but in their work lives they were obliged to enact their gender in hyperstereotypical ways (Mezur 2018, 366).

Let's keep going with this inquiry. Those naked bodies were not performing just anywhere. Mainly, they performed in the cabarets in smaller cities on the periphery of Japan. We might observe that in reality, Dairakudakan ate by means of the paychecks of people from rural Japan. This fact allows us to connect the finances of butô to larger urbanizing and globalizing forces. In that original vignette about the cabaret that refused to pay Maro's dancers, the production company complained that the dancers were doing a poor job. Maro admits that the training and costumes were initially rather slapdash, but then says something telling:

> But for all that, in today's world in which traveling strippers, dancers or other artisans from the sex-work world were aging, and becoming more and more scarce, wasn't it hard for them to forego the entertainment in which lively youngsters from Tokyo . . . would dance wildly? (Maro 2011, 174)

Urbanization was bleeding rural Japan of its youngsters, so Maro thought they could not be so choosy about his product, because he was bringing youngsters back. Youth mattered a great deal in the success of butô burlesque performers and having a young vibrant (and naked) body trumped other concerns. Ironically, the very process of industrialization and urbanization that bleached out the countryside, is the same process that created the possibility for Hijikata/Motofuji/Maro to send young naked bodies back to the smaller cities in the countryside to raise cash for their endeavors in the capital.[6]

The corollary was that other than butô dancers, peripheral cities were only able to attract "traveling" workers. While waiting for the show to start in Sapporo, Maro reminisced about his own days as a cabaret dancer. Apparently, the hostesses he met were drifters. He tells his manager that "it was completely normal for them to have Osaka accents, or be from Okinawa via Kumamoto, or Hiroshima via Ibaragi" (Maro 2011, 198). Because most of the local talent was gone to the major metropolises, show clubs in smaller cities could only attract unmoored women from across Japan to serve as hostesses and sex workers. Butô's focus on marginalized populations may stem in part from the fact that the dancers themselves felt marginalized, but they also spent time with migrant people on the periphery of society. What is more, the cabaret may have served as a harbinger for the peripatetic career-arcs of the women of butô, who eventually traveled (not just Japan but) the world teaching workshops and training dancers.

To look at this same system from the side of the dancers, when we couple this system with the fact that many butô companies lived communally, basically the companies had a system to provide room and board for everyone who studied with them. This is in contrast to the usual system, often called the *iemoto* system, used in many traditional arts. In the iemoto system, the head of the school charges for individual classes, materials, and performance and critiquing fees.[7] The head teacher does not care where you find your next meal, what your living conditions are, and what your source of money is (many parents pay for lessons that are considered finishing arts for young women). They just expect the participant to pay to play. Butô artists contrived a way to enable people with no financial means to participate: They sent them out to do cabaret shows, and in the process they fed and housed everyone and funded the butô shows as well. The upside was that anyone could join, regardless of financial circumstances, and they could gain valuable performance skills on stage. The downside was that it feels exploitative, because much of the money is funneling to the top.

In conclusion, the cabaret was immensely important for the development of butô. It served to train the dancers in how to attract and hold the attention of audiences. It enabled the dancers to raise money to feed and house themselves and stage their (sometimes extravagant) avant-garde shows. It put the dancers in constant contact with the rural and migrant sectors of Japanese society. It reinforced gender stereotypes for the women, while allowing them to step outside other stifling gender roles. When the cabaret dried up in the early 1990s, most of the dancers began to rely on international performances to make up the difference, while some also turned to appearances in cinema as a major source of income.

7

Interlude

Butô's Success in France

Without the success of butô in France, there might not be a butô today, or it might be a smaller localized art form confined to the side streets of Japanese cities. Understanding the role of Paris in the evolution of butô is crucial for understanding how it came to have a worldwide reach. This chapter considers the various aspects of butô's reception that led to its phenomenal rise from obscurity to the main stage.

Some people in Europe were aware of butô, but the first recorded use of the term "butô" for a performance in Europe referred to Butô-sha, a performance group created by Miura Isso[1] that performed "The Door" (*La Porte*) at the 1977 Nancy Festival. The choreography by Miura and Koseki Sumako used various aikido or shintaido techniques and also perhaps some Suzuki method, as Koseki had been a student of Suzuki Tadashi.[2] Neither Miura nor Koseki had studied within the main group of butô performers, but the performance apparently had some of the visual images that were later to become associated with butô, such as "the evocation of birth, communication with the universe and with animals, nudity, slowness, and eroticism" (Aslan 2002, 23). The dance reviewer for *Le Monde*, Marcelle Michel, singled out Butô-sha:

> This is a Japanese group that uses Aikido training to release generally repressed unconscious forces. The dancers' bodies, superheated through breathing techniques, explode and release in leaps and movements of communicative dynamism. (Michel 1977)

Miura may have sought to capitalize on the growing awareness of butô in the European audience by appropriating the word for the name of his company. His dance may also portray what he saw as the primary components of butô. Even if the underlying technique is different from Hijikata's, birth, slowness, nudity, and eroticism have been staples of butô. Thus, the European introduction to the term "butô" contained some stereotypical content of butô, as well as a focus on the energy of the performer that dovetailed nicely with the experiments of other performers.

Half a year later, Murobushi, Ikeda, and Yoshioka opened the floodgates for butô with *The Last Eden*.[3] As I noted in the introduction, they treated a wide range of topics. They possibly reconfigured Theseus and Ariadne's trip through the labyrinth to encounter the minotaur to double it up with a long-standing interest in the Ox-head

A History of Butô. Bruce Baird, Oxford University Press. © Oxford University Press 2022.
DOI: 10.1093/oso/9780197630273.003.0007

Horse-head theme (Centonze 2018b, 230). Another scene features a wooden-faced figure and a woman in a kimono holding a Japanese sword. This figure was Murobushi's embodiment of a mummy (Figure 7.1). The mummy was based on his research into *yamabushi* (itinerant mountain priests) and *sokushinbutsu* (a practice by which Buddhist monks would close themselves in a cave or pit and starve themselves to the point of desiccation to become mummies).[4] Murobushi emphasizes the dubiousness and disreputability of the priests, but he was also likely attracted to the intense physicality of monks who starved themselves to death (Murobushi and Ishii 2011, 4).

The program lists the "Voice of Mishima" as part of the soundscape for Scenes 5 and 6. This was Mishima Yukio's speech to the self-defense forces to try to foment a revolution. The speech is strange.[5] Mishima became increasingly right wing through the 1960s and eventually tried to instigate a coup d'état to return the emperor to power. Predictably, right-wing elements pepper the speech. Mishima laments the fact that the Japanese constitution (which he argues was foisted on Japan by the United States) prohibits the Japanese Self Defense Forces from being a national army. He also

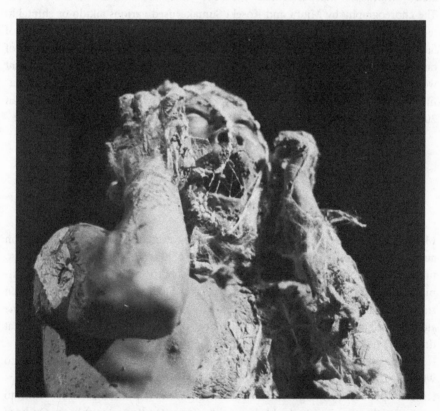

Figure 7.1 Murobushi Kô as a *sokushinbutsu* mummy in *Last Eden: Gate to the Beyond*, 1978. Courtesy of Fonds Jean-Marie Gourreau-Médiathèque du Centre national de la danse.

argues that Japanese culture is centered on the emperor. But ironically, the tipping point for Mishima appears to have been the recent subjugation of an antiwar demonstration. Since Mishima wanted to strengthen the military, it might seem surprising that he was angered by the quelling of an antiwar protest. But Mishima interpreted this action as the state employing its tools of repression (the police force) to solidify the power of the state bureaucracy and paradoxically weaken the military. He thought that the incident placed the military more firmly in bureaucratic control. He further argued that Japan would be nothing more than a pawn of the United States unless someone acted to upend the status quo.

However, we should understand Murobushi and Ikeda's use of Mishima, it is clear that they were engaging in a complex negotiation of Japanese identity. While they were possibly addressing European culture in their treatment of Theseus, Ariadne, and the Minotaur, they were locked in a wrestling match with their own culture and how that culture would develop, and they were not going to give up that wrestling match just because they were performing elsewhere. However, most of the complexity of the dance was beyond the Parisian audience. They likely knew who Mishima was, but could not understand his words, nor could they know anything about *yamabushi* and *sokushinbutsu*.

Sylviane Pagès observes that without the cultural and historical context to make sense of the performance, the audience defaulted to misunderstandings and exoticism (Pagès 2018, 257). The worst of these misunderstandings tied butô to the atomic bomb. The dancers may have inadvertently exacerbated this misunderstanding by their choice of costumes. It was easy for audiences to make a mental leap from the tattered costumes of Murobushi's mummy to the tattered costumes of mannequins in the Hiroshima Peace Memorial (Centonze 2018b, 230; Pagès 2018, 257). Pagès notes that because the atomic bomb was understood as a singular phenomenon that is incapable of being compared with other events, this misunderstanding "lock[ed] butoh into an intransigent Japanese otherness" (2018, 257). Once Japanese bodies and culture were rendered completely other by the bomb, the only available response was exoticism, because one could not claim to understand them. It is possible that butô was successful precisely because of such exoticism. The audience may have been less interested had they known that Murobushi and Ikeda were staging a treatment of Theseus and Ariadne. And undoubtedly, some performers capitalized on that exoticism, by intentionally offering up incomprehensible spectacles to the audience.

Close on the heels of that performance came the appearance of Ashikawa Yôko and Tanaka Min at the exhibition "MA: Space-Time in Japan," at the Museum of Decorative Arts, in connection with the Festival d'Automne in October 1978 (see Figure 7.2). Available photographs show Tanaka dancing naked both in the venue and outdoors in much the same manner as his *Drive* series (Fuller 2016, 75; Imura undated).[6] French intellectuals such as Henri Michaux, Michel Foucault, and Roger Caillois were drawn to Tanaka's sparse style, and Tanaka soon became acquainted with Gilles Deleuze and Felix Guattari (Pagès 2015, 35). These intellectuals gave butô a respectability that Murobushi and Ikeda had not been given. The irony was that the

Figure 7.2 Tanaka Min at the MA Exhibition, 1978. Courtesy of Fonds Jean-Marie Gourreau-Médiathèque du Centre national de la danse.

French intellectuals were promoting the version of butô that was the least invested in contesting and negotiating Japanese culture. The audience may have exoticized Murobushi and Ikeda, but it is worth noting that the artists were caught in a conundrum. To the extent that the artists treated problems in Japan, they might be seen as currying exotic favor, but not dealing with Japan resulted in its own set of problems and benefits. They would obviously lose their ability to critique Japanese culture, but they could also be taken as embodying universals or they could be seen as conforming to an international style much like the style of architecture so in vogue at the time. *The Last Eden* was a far cry from the "deodorized" style that was to form another face of Japanese culture starting with the release of the Sony Walkman the following year.[7] It was certainly this "deodorized" style that led to the European success of Tanaka and Sankai Juku.

Reasons for the Success of Butô in France

Butô did not succeed just on the basis of *Last Eden*. Pagès outlines many of the larger currents that contributed to the success of butô. One of these was simply the length of the run. *The Last Eden* ran for a month, and Ashikawa and Tanaka danced for two weeks. As I have noted, Ashikawa was compelled to perform an increasing number of times each day. This long exposure gave time for word of mouth to take effect and for the performers to reach larger audiences (Pagès 2009, 42).

Of course, the performers needed a venue. Initially the French dance world was closed to butô, because it was monopolized by ballet and Merce Cunningham–style currents of American modern dance (Pagès 2015, 46–47). In contrast, the theater world was receptive to non-Western performance. The programmers of the various theater festivals (Festival d'Automne, Nancy, and Avignon) took pride in including non-Western performances. The Autumn Festival, where Ashikawa and Tanaka had made their mark, was founded with the help of the future French minister of culture, Michel Guy. Pagès quotes him as vowing that "national borders will never on any account be cultural limits" and also saying "it is necessary to escape any form of ethnocentrism, to get out of the habit of believing that the West is the center of the world" (Pagés 2015, 43). The Festival of Nancy (that had shown Miura Isso's Butô-sha), also featured Mwondo Zaire Theater and the Shanghai Ballet. A press release for *The Last Eden* also included information about the concurrently playing Balinese topeng by I Made Djimat.[8]

Festival producers were reinforced by well-placed critics and agents, including the producer Martyne Matyas and Marcelle Michel. Amagatsu and Sankai Juku were personal favorites of Gérard Coste (the cultural attaché at the French Embassy in Tokyo in the 1970s), Thomas Erdos (the agent for Pina Bausch, Carolyn Carson, and Alwin Nikolais), and Gérard Violette (director of the Théâtre de la Ville in Paris for over 35 years).[9] These were some of the most powerful people within the world of French arts, and they all lent their support and connections to the new dance form. The organizer of the MA Festival, Isozaki Arata, was similarly well connected. He had met Foucault and Claude Lévi-Strauss in Japan, and both had apparently expressed interest in the exhibition (Pagès 2015, 35). Therefore, butô's success in Europe was premised on Hijikata and Tanaka's friendship with Isozaki, who was more widely connected internationally and domestically than they were.

Pagès also mentions that Isozaki found a willing partner in the Japanese government. Japanese artistic diplomacy has a long history, including participation in world fairs and universal expositions from the Universal Exposition of Paris in 1867. These venues provided the Japanese state the opportunity to advertise itself on the world stage. In the postwar era, such diplomacy came to be used for increasingly nationalistic aims as Japan sought to demonstrate both outside and at home an image of a unique culture with a rich history (Winther-Tamaki 2001, esp. 5–11). Isozaki worked with the Japanese government to provide funding for the Autumn Festival and the MA Exhibition. Pagès even presents the amusing image of French diplomats pressuring Japanese diplomats to increase Japanese funding, because Japanese diplomats did not want to present avant-garde dance as at the core of Japanese life (Pagès 2007, 44). The success of butô was, in part, the unintended result of the efforts of Japanese diplomats to promote Japan to the world (even if those diplomats did not like butô).

Beyond the efforts of specific producers and promoters of theater festivals, Pagès points out that the theater world itself was undergoing a transformation in which various different strands of theater were all, broadly speaking, questing in a similar direction. These were the ideas of Artaud; the physical theater of Grotowski, Barba, and Kantor; and the mime of Decroux and Marceau (Pagès 2007, 45–46). Early butô artists were drawing explicitly on the ideas of Artaud and on French mime through the mediation of Oikawa Hironobu. The similarity of butô artists with Grotowski, Barba, and Kantor may be no more than an indication that butô served as a kind of Rorschach inkblot onto which Europeans could project whatever was most on their minds. But it may also serve as a mark of the simultaneity of avant-garde practice, as butô performers were responding to conditions similar to those of their European counterparts.

Pagès indicates that although the dance world was closed to butô, it was in a flux similar to that of the theater world, in which all of the definitions and categories of dance were being contested and reconfigured. This revolution was predominantly led by American modern dancers such as Merce Cunningham, Alwin Nikolais, and Carolyn Carson, with a second-generation including Trisha Brown, David Gordon, and Steve Paxton (Pagès 2007, 46–47). Even though they could not perform in dance venues, butô artists benefited from and contributed to a widening of acceptable practice, so that any sort of body could dance (old, weak, small) and any movement or gesture could be included in the category of dance (including simple, slow, or ugly movements). In addition, the fact that Murobushi and Ikeda, Ashikawa, and Tanaka took different approaches to choreography and improvisation contributed to altering the definitions of what constitutes a dance piece and how choreography happens.

Pagès also posits a deep (but unstated) affinity between the bones of French dance and the butô's roots in German Expressionist dance (Pagès 2010, 2018, 258). Because Mary Wigman had been discredited by her association with Naziism, no one in France was willing to publicly acknowledge the German expressionist roots of French dance. Butô was also presented as a sui generis art form, or sometimes even mistaken as descendant from noh and kabuki, rather than in the genealogy of Ishii, Eguchi, and Miya (whom the French audience were not familiar with). This leads Pagès to speculate that audiences and dancers may have felt something uncannily familiar with butô, even if they could not identify it consciously.

Through all of this, Japanese arts were seen as standing out even among the various non-Western arts. There is a long history of European and American artists admiring Japanese arts. An incomplete list from the world of painting and printmaking would include Whistler, Van Gogh, Toulouse-Lautrec, Klimt, and Beardsley.[10] The theatrical world was similarly infatuated with Japan. Well known are the explorations by Brecht, Britten, and Yeats of the noh theater, and to these we can add the contemporaneous use of kabuki by Barrault, the puppet theater by Barthes, and Zen-inspired ideas by John Cage and Merce Cunningham.[11] Pagès quotes Michel Guy saying that when he visited Japan in 1976, he sensed "a perception of space and time radically different from ours" which he sought to introduce to his audiences (Pagès 2015, 43). Recall that Ashikawa and Tanaka rotated with shakuhachi players, lute players, and chanting monks, all a testament to the special place that Japanese art and culture occupied in the French imagination in the 1970s.

For all these reasons, the performers found a welcome home in Paris. But another factor was important: the difference between the structure of the theater world in Paris and Tokyo. In Paris, the theater owners pay the performers. In Japan, the performers pay the owners. Although there are exceptions, the world of the theater runs primarily on the *noruma* system (from the Russian *norma*). In Japanese, this indicates half-voluntary half-pressured work quotas (Martin, 2011). In the performing arts, it describes the system by which performers rent the theater and sell the tickets themselves.[12] Motofuji tells of passing the hat at the intermission of an early show (after the audience had already paid admission) to receive enough money for the owner to let them continue with the second half (Motofuji 1990, 99). In practice, this means that the theater owners do not assume any risk, because they are guaranteed their revenue regardless. The performer bears the risk. If no one comes, they pay for the privilege of performing to an empty house. Of course, this means that in Japan anyone with enough moola can perform, but the Parisian system has its own upsides.

The first has to do with the composition of the audience. In Japan, performers often recruit their friends and family to buy tickets. Many artists know the reality of hustling for an audience, but individual artists usually have fewer resources for cultivating an audience than a theater. In general, small Tokyo theaters do not cultivate relationships with clientele such that a person takes a chance on an unknown show. In Paris, theaters usually cultivate audiences that will come to shows they would not ordinarily attend. The poster nicely reveals this (see Figure 7.3). The top features the logo and the name of the theater (Nouveau Carré Silvia Monfort) in the largest typeface, with the promoter Martine Matyas directly beneath. The name of Ariadone's 1975 performance, (*Mesukazan* misspelled as Meskazan) from which some of the content was taken and the name of Murobushi's group (Sebi) are in the middle. The poster presents a visual indication that the theater is invested in the outcome, rather than just serving as a rental space. The theater and producer were trying to lend their prestige to the show. Such being the case, the butô artists performed in front of a wider audience than they could normally expect in Japan.

The second upside of Paris: Murobushi and Ikeda were paid no matter the size of the audience. They were initially only engaged for two weeks, so if they had not drawn a crowd, the show would have ended after the second week.[13] But they did not need to advertise for their own show or arm-twist their friends into paying for tickets. They could spend their time working on their craft. That is good for any artist—to be able to concentrate on creating art rather than drumming up support.

Owing to these specific circumstances, butô was successful in France, and the performers were able to parlay that achievement into a ticket across Europe and around the globe. This happened to varying degrees. Sankai Juku hit the biggest jackpot with a contract to produce a show from the Théâtre de la Ville. The other artists still had to

Figure 7.3 Program prominently featuring the name of the theater and the promoter. *Last Eden: Gate to the Beyond, 1978.* Courtesy of the Murobushi Kô Archive and Watanabe Kimiko.

work plenty hard to realize their visions, but conditions in France made it easier for them to do so. And European sexism notwithstanding, it was easier for the women to succeed in Europe than it was back in Japan. As noted in the last chapter, when income from the cabaret dried up, international touring took the place of the cabaret as a primary source of income for many butô dancers, making the European reception even more important to the long-term success of butô.

8

Ôno Kazuo

Ôno Kazuo was once called the "Soul of Butô," and this moniker certainly captures his status within the butô community, in scholarship, and for audiences at large. Ôno traveled to Europe as part of the butô wave in the 1980s and was received rapturously by crowds who did not care for Murobushi and Ikeda's more arcane experiments. Many people confess to having been moved to tears by his performances. Even people who professed not to understand him always came away convinced of his sincerity. Among the butô world, other artists have detractors, but everyone claims Ôno for their own. Unlike some of the other dancers, within scholarly circles, he has been the subject of nuanced and rich academic analysis. More than anyone else, Ôno served as the embodiment of what butô should and could be.

This chapter sketches out a starting point for Ôno in his pre-butô dances up to 1959. Passing over his time with Hijikata quickly, I turn to his solo career starting in 1977. Part of Ôno's success lay in conveying an idiosyncratic worldview to his audiences through movement. In brief, Ôno held that the universe is endlessly generative, but prodigal in discarding people and things along the way. In response, he expressed a combination of gratitude and guilt in his dances. I close with an analysis of his dances in terms of five intertwined themes: gender, ethnicity, age, eccentricity, and the extent to which he relied on technique or improvisation in his performances. Following other scholars, I argue that part of his success was rooted in the audience seeing him as having contested these categories and rendered them less operative in his own life, in his dance, and by extension in the world at large.

Biography

Ôno was born to a well-to-do family in 1906 in Hakodate on the northernmost island Hokkaido.[1] His father led a fishing cooperative, spoke Russian, and fished throughout the north Pacific. His mother was an organist, a fan of ghost stories, and a specialist of European cuisine. Owing to a downturn in the fishing economy, in junior high school, Ôno moved to Odate, Akita prefecture, to live with a wealthy childless relative. He was apparently a standout track and field athlete and star baseball player. Photographs show Ôno and others swimming and canoeing. In 1926, he moved to Tokyo and enrolled in the Japan Physical Education and Exercise School (present-day Nippon Sports Science University). While in college, he saw Antonia Mercé y Luque

A History of Butô. Bruce Baird, Oxford University Press. © Oxford University Press 2022.
DOI: 10.1093/oso/9780197630273.003.0008

(La Argentina) dance. His education was interrupted for 16 months owing to his conscription for military service in Sapporo, and he finally graduated in 1929. After graduation, he taught physical education at Kanto Gakuin High School, a private Christian school (associated with the moderate American Baptist Churches). A photograph shows him leading what appears to be an outdoor calisthenics class. Under the tutelage of the school principal, Sakata Tasuke (a disciple of Uchimura Kanzô), he joined the Christian faith at this time.[2]

Ôno's choice of a moderate Protestantism may have helped later European audiences appreciate his dances (Takahashi 2012, 18). Christianity may have also bolstered Ôno's mystical tendencies. Ôno claimed to see visions, and he gave credence to them, rather than dismiss them. His mother similarly claimed to see a vision of Buddhist monks at the moment his younger sister died in a train accident. Whether because of his mother or his religion, visions and other sorts of supernatural experiences were formative throughout his life.

In 1933, he got a permanent job at the Soshin Girls School (also associated with the American Baptist Churches). Photographs show him overseeing a student performance as part of a sports day (field day, *undôkai*).[3] The girls spell out the letters S-O-S-H-I-N (in the way a marching band does during a half-time show) and march around the field smartly making circles and radii and deftly crisscrossing with each other. As part of his employment, Ôno was required to teach dance, so he took lessons from the dance pioneer Ishii Baku for a year. In 1934, he saw Harald Kreutzberg dance, and then in 1936 he began to study dance with the duo Eguchi Takaya and Miya Misako. Thus, Ôno studied with three of the pioneers of Japanese modern dance.

As noted earlier, all three of these pioneers had studied with Mary Wigman, but they had learned radically different approaches to dance (Kuniyoshi 2018, 26). Kuniyoshi argues that

> Ishii felt the strength of Wigman in her attempt to express through bodily movements the internal transformations of the spirit and the dramatic transformations in the emotion of the individual, and not in the specific transformations of the movements themselves. Ishii thought the task of dance expression was not the expression of the truth of the human through the trivia of daily life, or the details of real life, but through taking the matters of daily experience, purifying them, strengthening them, and elevating them into a more universal movement. (Kuniyoshi 2018, 27)

Eguchi and Miya understood expressionism differently from Ishii. Kuniyoshi quotes Eguchi to give an idea of his abstract dances:

> One day, I sat in a chair, and while I was idly moving the fingers on my right hand (which was resting on my knee), when I tried to bend my wrists almost to the square and stand my middle and ring fingers up firmly, I became aware of a sharp and severe sensation, and thought to make that into the basis for creating a "Movement."

This "hand movement" that I had made with no particular purpose in mind became a "stimulus" and I was able to give birth to various movements all at once using this movement as a base. (Kuniyoshi 2018, 25–26)

It appears that Eguchi's dance was based purely on a range of hand movements. Later, Ôno claims he was dissatisfied with Ishii's dances and training, which he describes somewhat dismissively as "pantomime, . . . drama, and theater" (Kuniyoshi 2018, 25). He says that he was more interested in the abstract movement of Eguchi and Miya.

Ôno's budding dance career was interrupted by the war, in which he participated in campaigns in northern China and in New Guinea. Ôno did not leave behind much information about his war experience, but once wrote, "My New Guinea experience. When about 6,000 soldiers had to move from the east to the west in a terrible rush because we lost the battle, we were informed that 2,000 died. When someone in front lost their way in the jungle, the others following behind them were lost" (Ôno 1998, 22). Here, Ôno focuses on accidental loss of life, but New Guinea was not just an average war theater with the average horrors of war. Because Japanese military leaders were completely inept in their management of the war and willfully refused to learn from their mistakes, New Guinea was a special kind of purgatory. Yoshito writes that Ôno told them about being "so terrified that the hair on his head would positively stand on end," about wild dogs devouring abandoned corpses, and about Japanese soldiers plundering "money and goods belonging to the local population" (Ohno and Ohno 2004, 110). Even worse than this, the very fact of Ôno's location suggests that he would have been exposed to cannibalism, and war atrocities. He may not have participated personally in any of these, but at the very least, he had to have been aware of them, and he would have been subjected to prolonged extreme hunger.[4]

Ôno's Early Career as Head of His Own Company

After the war, he spent a year in a POW camp, before returning to Japan and resuming his training with Eguchi and Miya. He acted as a substitute teacher in place of Eguchi/Miya and appeared in their dances throughout the 1950s. At some point, Soshin gave him lumber from a demolished building, and he built a dance studio right next to his house. In 1949, he began taking students and choreographing his own dances, while continuing to appear in Eguchi and Miya's dances. There was a luxury tax on ticket sales, which started at 150% of the total sales in 1949, fell to 100% in 1950, and then fell further to 20% in 1952, so Ôno was sufficiently invested in dancing to go into debt in order to stage shows (Kuniyoshi 2012, 54).

From the dance programs, we can see that early in his career, Ôno choreographed (or cochoreographed) approximately 23 dances between 1949 and 1959. Eight were rooted in artistic and literary sources: in 1949 "First Flower of Linden Tree" based on Rilke's poem "Softly Drifts a First Blossom," "Statues of the Ernst Family" based on the sculptures of Max Ernst," and "Devil's Cry" based on Matsuzumi Yuichirô's works;[5] in 1951 "Rain on the Town" based on Verlaine's poem "Il Pleure dans Mon Coeur" and "Across the Fields" based on the Hesse poem; in 1953 "Fox and Statue" based on Rilke's poem "Song of the Statue," and "Fruit from Heaven" based in part on Takami Jun's poem "Heaven"; and in 1959 "Old Man and the Sea" based on Hemingway's novel. A second set of dances was based on religious themes, including: "Jacob's Hymn" (1949), and "Seven Songs of Thunder and Lightning" (1949). The other dances are not easily categorized, but it seems clear that some dances were short, single-themed etudes such as "Tango" (1949, 1950, 1951).

One dance, *Jellyfish*, apparently was a requiem to soldiers who survived the war only to die on the voyage home and be thrown overboard. Focusing on the sad fate of soldiers who made it through the war and then died on the journey home is typical of Japanese attitudes, which minimize Japanese wartime atrocities and focus on Japanese as victims of the war. This experience may also have been an early building block of his worldview.

Kuniyoshi points out that the reviews of Ôno's dances were mixed. Over and over between 1949 and 1953, critics complained about his lack of technique and that his dances were "eccentric," and "conceptual" (Kuniyoshi 2018, 26–28). During that time, he appeared as a guest performer in other dances, and it was there that he met (1954) and danced with Hijikata (1955). He also engaged in deep self-study to try to figure out what to do next. In a letter written sometime in late 1958 or early 1959, Ôno wrote, "Since 1953, I have been exceedingly troubled while researching the relationship between dance pieces and expressive techniques" (Kuniyoshi 2012, 69). In 1959 he choreographed the story-based dance *Old Man and the Sea*. It was based on the Earnest Hemingway novel and John Sturges's film adaptation. This was to be Ôno's magnum opus, the dance that would enable him to finally break through. Alas, it was not to be.

Again, the reviews were mixed. One reviewer wrote,

> It appears that there is a clear mismatch between Ono's strong personality and the other dancers, and particularly during the second and third acts, I felt temporal gaps. To put this another way, this is because the undulations in the radiation of Ôno's personality are too excessive. (Kuniyoshi 2012, 76)

Writing for the national newspaper, the *Mainichi Shinbun*, Mitsuyoshi Natsuya wrote,

> Ôno Kazuo, who is more of a poet than a dancer, held his first recital in a long time. This unique performer dances pregnant with internal images brought about by his poetic disposition. Sometimes they are so excessive as to be unmanageable, and so fully submerged as to be unconnectable to concrete embodiment.... Despite this, he adhered closely to his poetic images.
>
> Of course, Hemingway's *Old Man and the Sea* is a difficult work to embody concretely.... when it comes to depicting this on a flat stage without water or waves, the only thing that one can rely on is the internal images of the dancer. It was

structurally too long, . . . and here also, Ôno embraced ever further into himself his own images, and did not pay enough attention to external embodiment. However, it is fun to follow along with his writhing bountiful images which are whirling around inside him. This is what sustained this piece.

Although, there are many dancers who only dance superficial outward forms and have nothing inside themselves, Ôno is the exact opposite. He is quite awkward and as a rule not stylish, but he is without a doubt a unique dancer. (Kuniyoshi 2008, 75).

Although there were some positives, Ôno was deeply discouraged by the overall response.

There are several possibilities for why the performance was not a success. Later in life, Ôno said that he was interested in studying with Eguchi and Miya because of the abstract quality of their dances. Mitsuyoshi observed that *Old Man and the Sea* "is a difficult work to embody concretely" (Kuniyoshi 2008, 75). In a letter to a friend, Ôno also wrote that he was experimenting with a dance style of "new representational painting" (Kuniyoshi 2012, 74). Perhaps the gears would not mesh between the narrative-based source material, Ôno's training in abstraction, and his experiments with a new more representational kind of dance.

It is difficult to judge a dance from photos, but my impression of *Old Man and the Sea* is not that the problem was the choreography. Rather, as I see it, Ôno did not give his character sufficient depth to be convincing (Figure 8.1). Perhaps it was a mistake to try to dance a story that relies heavily on internal monologue, but to successfully dance *Old Man and the Sea*, the main character must be able to convey several things:

a. fear of poverty and starvation
b. respect and admiration for a worthy adversary
c. determination that the sea and the fish will not get the best of him
d. utter exhaustion
e. slight senility or madness, and the accompanying effort to keep one's mind clear
f. despair when the other sharks get the best of him, resulting in the waste of a worthy adversary (and valuable source of income)

All the physical events were present according to the scenario: the pair of marlins, the arm-wrestling match, landing the fish, and the attack of the sharks. If Ôno did not execute these properly, the dance would not work; but even if he did get these right, if he did not create a convincing character, the dance could not succeed.

Ôno apparently wrote a letter to Hemingway to alert him of the plans to adapt his novel (although it is not clear if he sent it). In it Ôno anticipated some difficulties:

If the old man's entire world doesn't show through in each of his steps, the role won't come alive. As you can see from this picture, I am a slender man. But I am frantically wagering my whole personality as a dancer on this old man. I want to

Figure 8.1 Collage of facial expressions of Ôno Kazuo in *Old Man and the Sea*, 1959. Photographer unknown. Courtesy of the NPO Dance Archive Network and the Ôno Kazuo Dance Studio.

create a stage space so that the audience will not notice the meager size of my physique, that I can't change anyway at this point, and I am determined to do this by understanding the old man, and his world. (Kuniyoshi 2012, 70–71)

Ôno worries that his body is not suitable for playing the lead role. I am not convinced. Ashikawa could do any age or any emotion, regardless of her stature. So, Ôno's size should not have mattered. But before the performance even took place Ôno was keenly aware of another problem: "If the old man's entire world doesn't show through" at each moment, not only will the role not come alive, but the performance as a whole will not succeed. His solution was to thoroughly understand the old man and his world, and Mitsuyoshi wrote that he "dances pregnant with internal images," but neither comes through in the photos. Why? Why was this role beyond Ôno? I think it was that he simply did not have the right techniques to bring depth to his performance.

The Era of Butô

After the tepid response to *Old Man and the Sea*, Ôno quit choreographing dances. Hijikata invited Ôno to appear in the revised *Forbidden Colors* in a role based on the characters O-kyô, a male prostitute from the Ueno district of Tokyo, and Divine, the aging prostitute from Genet's *Our Lady of the Flowers*. Dressed in a green negligee, a brick-red sweater, a white lace gown, and cheap vinyl shoes bedecked with fake red flowers, Ôno entered the stage from the audience where, after some time, some young men killed him with makeshift arrows, and carted him away (Goda 1988, 40–46). Observers speculate that it must have been strange for the Christian Ôno to portray a gay man (Ohno and Ohno 2004, 134–135; Kuniyoshi 2012, 80–86). That is likely true and did not end there. Ôno appeared in a homoerotic duet with Hijikata in *Rose-Colored Dance*. Hijikata likely reoriented Ôno toward many aspects of existence, such as (homo)eroticism, death, and darkness. This undoubtedly contributed to Ôno later challenging dichotomies of gender and ethnicity.

One dance from this era yields another aperture into Hijikata's possible use of blackness in *Forbidden Colors*. Ôno, Hijikata, Motofuji, and Yoshito teamed up with the long-time collaborators Ikemiya Nobuo, Kobayashi Shinji, and the Fujii Kunihiko Creative Dance Studio to stage *Negro and River* (*Niguro to kawa*, July 1, 1961). The front cover says that the dance was choreographed by Fujii Kunihiko, with a script by Ikemiya Nobuo, but inside, it also says that Ôno choreographed the dance, so we may presume some sort of co-choreography. This dance was in part based on the Langston Hughes anthology *Weary Blues* (Arimitsu 2018, 45). The cover of the program features smiling dancing black people, making it seem as if the dance echoed a narrative of the happy black person so prevalent in Hollywood movies (see Figure 8.2). However, the synopsis of the dance complicates this overly happy picture. In Scene 1, "Memory of a Parade," two young "negroes" are "visited by a tragedy that calls to mind the death of Patrice Lumumba, but they do not get flustered. Music, parade and cakewalk are signs of the memories in their hearts." Scene 2, "Black Pierrot," apparently featured "men who can never get enough sleep no matter how much they sleep," because they "work non-stop." Scene 3, "The Bus Stop," referred to "5000 negroes walking for one year in the Southern city of Montgomery" and a "nameless old woman singing, 'Don't ride this bus. Walk.'" The synopsis closes with the description: "The resistance to racial discrimination causes those who have lost humanity to quake." Along with this scene

Figure 8.2 Program cover. Fujii Kunihiko and Ikemiya Nobuo. *Negro and River*, 1961. Courtesy of the NPO Dance Archive Network and the Ôno Kazuo Dance Studio.

synopsis, the dancers appended a minimanifesto that read, in part, "Our intention in dancing negroes [sic] is simple. It is a repudiation of weak, dirty humanism.... The images which are giving rise to subterranean rumblings throughout the world cause our muscles to warp refreshingly." The dancers were clearly aware of current events such as the Montgomery Bus Boycott of 1956, and the assassination of the African nationalist revolutionary Lumumba six months before. No photographs of the dance currently remain, but from the cover of the program, the synopses, and the minimanifesto, we can see a complicated, sometimes stereotypical and naïve but sometimes informed understanding of blackness.

Turn to Solo Career and Foundation for a Cosmology

Ôno appeared in Hijikata's choreography for the next eight years, but then left the stage. Rumor is that he had a falling out with Hijikata, but it is possible that he was merely busy with other projects. He appeared in a series of three experimental movies entitled Mr. O (O-Shi) directed by Nagano Chiaki: *The Portrait of Mr. O* (1969), *Mandala of Mr. O* (1971), and *Mr. O's Book of the Dead* (1973). Yoshito writes that the shooting of these movies was formative for Ôno and points out that he did things such as sucking the teat of pig wallowing in manure (Ohno and Ohno 2004, 144). Yoshito surmises that Ôno more fully embraced the impetus to explore other aspects of life and his own identity. It might be equally accurate to see this as an ongoing process of Ôno creating a new identity for himself.

Schwellinger argues that during this era, Ôno consolidated a personal cosmology (Schwellinger 2018, 114). According to her, his cosmology was rooted in a decisive experience from 1962. On his mother's deathbed, she allegedly said "A flatfish is swimming in my body." Rather than dismiss this as incoherent rambling, Ôno understood these words as a final gift from his mother. He interpreted the flatfish as a metaphor for thriving (or at least managing) under overwhelming pressure. In his telling, "under the pressure of living deep in the ocean" a kind of fish that was originally more spherical "over time became flat" (1981, reprinted in Ôno 1998, 117). A related evolutionary process migrated one eye over to the other side of the body so the flatfish can see with both eyes while resting on the bottom of the ocean. Despite living in what Ôno terms an "undesirable place" (the sand at the bottom of the ocean), the flatfish can "kick up the earth" with its hidden pectoral fin, and "wriggle its entire body" to dart out of the sand to catch prey, and thus "receives much from the ocean" (117; compare with Ohno and Ohno 2004, 21). He also drew a connection between his mother's struggles caring for her children and the conditions of a flatfish. As Schwellinger noted, for Ôno, the flatfish was "the gestalt of life itself" (Schwellinger 2018, 114, quoting Ôno 1998, 116).

Chantal Aubry relates another foundational experience in Ôno's life.

One day, more than twenty years ago, Kazuo Oono had a dream, a waking dream, a kind of hallucination. An enormous star fell right beside him. There it was, a gigantic mass of energy, incredibly powerful. He wanted to flee, but he couldn't, he was nailed there. Then he woke up. And it was from this experience that everything became clear to him. The molten matter, the tangible vision of expanding molecules, the steam, the sudden change in temperature, the water, the sea—he sensed completely what took place at the birth of the world. And he understood that love and the birth of a child are the same [as the birth of the world], the same chemistry, the same molten matter, the same flow of energy, the same telluric force. (Aubry 1986, n.p. "Special Suite 4")

This experience must have happened sometime during or before 1965, not long after his mother's death. From it, we see that Ôno was quick to draw connections between geological and evolutionary processes and everyday occurrences such as creating new human life. I will return to this cosmology shortly, but let's first consider the performance that eventually made Ôno famous.

Admiring La Argentina, 1977

In 1977 Ôno returned to the stage with *Admiring La Argentina*. Originally, Ôno choreographed a dance featuring his students interspersed with his own solos. Hijikata edited out the group dances and suggested that Ôno add the tangos and reprise Hijikata's own choreography from *Forbidden Colors, revised version* (conversation with Yoshito, September 15, 2009). The dance was transformed into a retrospective of the "sum and substance" of Ôno's own "individual trajectory through life," paired with a somewhat improvisational homage to the flamenco dancer Antonia Mercé, whom Ôno had seen 47 years previously (Ohno and Ohno 2004, 150).

The first two scenes reprised Hijikata's choreography from eighteen years before, and show Divine dying and being reborn. Wearing a shawl over a dark seemingly soiled dress (perhaps bespeaking a life of penury), Ôno sits several rows back in the audience.[6] Bach's *Toccata and Fugue* pierces the darkness, and the lights come up on Ôno. He stands but seems indecisive. After false starts and retreats, he kneels in front of the stage as if to pray. Finally on stage, he backs into the sidewall as if he has been skewered, head lolling, arms dangling, right shoulder shrugged up. He appears to be enacting the pain of the dying male prostitute. Eventually he totters away from the wall and lays a shawl on the ground. Then he kneels (perhaps representing the tubercular Divine vomiting into a toilet), falls on his side, and dies. One member of the audience said that Ôno "deepened the darkness with every moment," and drowned in a "pitch-black lake" like the lake of shit in which Genet's Divine drowned (Schwellinger 2018, 118; quoting Nagao 1978).

The lights go down, and after a costume change Ôno sits with a bow in her hair in a short shift with shoulder straps. Reborn as a young girl, she draws her skirt to her mouth and nibbles it. She moves off the gown, lifts it, and shyly puts it on. She looks tentative, clumps around in short steps, and makes her way off stage.

Another scene (provisionally "Daily Bread") features Ôno in a pair of black trunks miming everyday activities, such as stretching his neck (perhaps mirroring the calisthenics he taught at Soshin), or engaging in janitorial duties (his job when he got too old to teach physical education). After some falls, crouches, slumps and s-curves, he clomps off stage, only to be propelled back on stage in front of a swiftly moving grand piano that threatens to bowl him over. Rumor has it that acting on a cue from Hijikata to keep the performance fresh, the stagehands pushed it onstage prematurely. In the scene (provisionally "The Marriage of Heaven and Earth"), he leans back (knock-kneed) against the crook of the piano (where a lounge singer might usually stand), looks up and breathes raggedly with his arms splayed out on the piano and his mouth open, as the pianist plays Bach's *Prelude and Fugue No. 1* in C Major (see Figure 8.3). He looks as if the weight of a hard life might grind him to the ground. One later reviewer writes of "his skin looking as if it had been removed, wrung out and then glued back on" (Temin 1986). In the second half, Ôno dances an homage to Mercé with vaguely flamenco movements to tango music such as Alfred Hauze's version of Arie Maasland's "Ole Guapa" and Juan de Dios Filiberto's "Quejas de Bandoneon."[7] In the finale, wearing a frumpy dress, he cycles through off-balance depictions of shyness, sadness, and menace (see Figure 8.4). He concludes with a military salute.

Possible Reasons for the Success of *Admiring La Argentina*

Admiring La Argentina was a fantastic, but also intriguing, dance. Yoshito says Ôno danced self-portrait, but the self Ôno depicted was a collection of personal memories (physical education teacher, janitor, and soldier) and in part, a collage of reenactments of past performances, both his roles choreographed by Hijikata and dances that he had seen. Mizohata Toshio suggests that it is possible that even the scenes that seem to stem from Ôno's personal life, such as those featuring janitorial work, were in fact quotations from the Mr. O movies (pers. conversation, October 5, 2016). *The Portrait of Mr. O* contains a scene of Ôno in a boiler room opening and closing valves, very much like a janitor might. Whatever the case, the self of the dance was a complex combination of quotations and memories.

Before considering anything else about it, let's think about what could have changed to make this dance successful in comparison with *Old Man and the Sea*:

1. Ôno does something closer to his own personal experience.
   —Genet's Divine, and La Argentina do not seem any closer to his own experience than Santiago.

Figure 8.3 Arms splayed out in "Marriage of Heaven and Earth." Ôno Kazuo, *Admiring La Argentina*, 1977. Courtesy of the photographer Ikegami Naoya, the NPO Dance Archive Network, and the Ôno Kazuo Dance Studio.

Figure 8.4 "Finale." Ôno Kazuo, *Admiring La Argentina*, 1977. Courtesy of the photographer Tsukamoto Hiroaki, the NPO Dance Archive Network, and the Ôno Kazuo Dance Studio.

2. Nothing changed in him, but the butô movement changed his audience so they accepted something previously unacceptable.
—This is possible. Butô definitely changed the expectations of audiences. But this cannot be the whole story, because even though we only have descriptions of the dances, none of the pre-1959 dances seem anything like *Argentina*.

3. He changes, so that in fact, he is dancing something closer to his own personal experience. Hijikata encouraged him to explore other aspects of existence, and then the process continued through the Mr. O series of movies. Eventually, he coalesced around his new worldview.
—This is possible. It had been 16 years since he first danced Divine, long enough for Divine to become a part of him. Much longer than the gap between the October 1958 release of the movie *The Old Man and the Sea*, and the dance version in April 1959.

4. Ôno learns to use evocative methods to deepen his performance.
—This seems most likely to me.

I argue that what happened between *Old Man and the Sea* and *Admiring La Argentina* is a combination of Numbers 2–4. Ôno changes; audience expectations change; and he acquires richer character preparation skills. We do not have Ôno's creation notes for the 1977 *La Argentina*, but if the 1981 notes that Ôno created with Hijikata for *My Mother* are any indication, Ôno drew on a rich set of imagery prompts while dancing the series of characters/selves.

Changes in *Admiring La Argentina*

For all the brilliance of the original *Admiring La Argentina*, it was not yet historically significant in the history of butô or dance. The reception of Ôno in France was a necessary part of the dance becoming important. In 1980, Ôno appeared in the Nancy Theater Festival, and made stops in London, Paris, and Stockholm. For a septuagenarian, who performed approximately twenty-five times between 1949 and 1976, the response was overwhelming: He was in demand. D'Orazi even notes that he was celebrated as the founder of modern dance in Japan (D'Orazi 2018, 262). However, in the three years since the premier, Ôno's cosmology had percolated and evolved. Moreover, Ôno's encounter with Europe changed both him and his choreography. The chronology of these changes is hard to sort out, because there are only a few recordings of the dance, and even fewer records of Ôno's thoughts until after he had become famous. Whatever the case, the way Ôno conceived of the dance gradually changed, and his internal transformations were accompanied by dramatic alterations in lighting, costumes, and changes in the choreography.

For starters, the connection to La Argentina in the title was not straightforward. In 1977, in a preview for the dance, a G (certainly Goda Nario) and another reviewer, Nagao Kazuo, both mentioned Genet's Divine in their descriptions of the dances (G 1977, 5; Nagao 1998, 269). This makes it seem like Genet's work (filtered through Hijikata) was still very important. After the fact, Ôno maintained that he was astounded by Mercé when he saw her dance 47 years previously, but Yoshito confesses that Ôno had never mentioned Mercé during the intervening years (Ohno and Ohno 2004, 145). Ôno reported that he was reminded of her one day while looking at the Nakanishi painting *Shape of Painting 13-h*. This is an abstract painting featuring a two-dimensional sheet layered under a pale metallic blue three-dimensional cylinder that looks as if someone has used tin snips to peel back circular holes in the bottom corners. Nothing in the painting would seem to suggest La Argentina, but somehow the painting suggested Mercé to Ôno. Meanwhile, the Japanese American dancers Eiko and Koma coincidentally sent Ôno some materials and a photograph of Mercé (Ohno and Ohno 2004, 147, 266). Prone to attributing meaning to such serendipitous occurrences, Ôno says he decided on the spot to choreograph a dance to/for her.

However Ôno came to Mercé, the promotional materials, ticket, and program of the original performance relegate her to a partial focus. The flyers and postcards feature a photograph of hunched Ôno dressed in ripped clothing with his clenched hands crossed over his feet. The text mentions an "exiled Carman" (perhaps a typo for "Carmen," the hero of Bizet's eponymous opera) as the "Spanish dancer" who will pour a "holy nostrum" into Ôno's "fevered aged body." The reverse side gives Ôno's bio, information about the show, and mentions that Ôno had been obsessed with Mercé for nearly five decades. The tickets feature a photograph of a young Ôno in full soldier gear standing smartly at attention, hands on his sword. The program first refers to Mercé on page 16: a photograph of Ôno by Hosoe Eikô is superimposed on an upside-down and backward program of La Argentina's Tokyo performance, such that she smiles up at him from his right knee. These materials show that Argentina was not an afterthought, but neither was she the sole focus of the original dance.

In the Japanese promotional materials for the Nancy performance three years later, there are four scene names: "Birth," "Daily Bread," "Together with Tangos," and "With Gratitude." These names were not conveyed to the audience, who were only given information about Ôno's infatuation with La Argentina. But from the promotional materials, we can see that prior to the Nancy performance, Hijikata's "Death of Divine," and the rebirth as Culafroy were lumped into one scene titled "Birth." It appears that Ôno was already reconfiguring the performance in his mind to de-emphasize the death of Divine.

On the tour in France, Ôno met Mercé's family, and received a pair of her castanets. He subsequently added scenes of dancing to recordings of Mercé playing castanets. He also visited Mercé's grave and fervently felt that she was his bride (Ohno and Ohno 2004, 185, fn 9). In later rehearsal notes, he identified the "Birth" scene as a "Rebirth" scene and thought of it as his *own rebirth as* La Argentina, rather than a rebirth as Culafroy. He also imagined himself as having been "born from Argentina" (Ôno 1989, 106). Thus, Argentina traveled a winding path in Ôno's mind from inspiration (for half of the dance), to bride, to self, to mother. Over time, the "La Argentina" of the title became a greater presence in the dance, by taking over (at least in Ôno's mind) scenes that had concerned Divine and Culafroy and with the addition of scenes devoted to her. These changes influenced the reception of the dance. All audiences need some way into a work, and for Western audiences, Mercé proved to be a handle that viewers could latch onto to help them grasp the performance.

There were actual changes in the choreography that were not just conceptual or additive. Ôno's originally out-splayed hands in the "Marriage of Heaven and Earth" were redirected upward and thus transformed into a reaching for the heavens, perhaps in yearning or in a call for help. The section was also shortened by dropping the Fugue, leaving only the Prelude, perhaps more readily suggesting to the Western audience the Bach/Gounod/Heugel "Ave Maria." When the critic Jennifer Dunning reviewed his performance at La Mama in 1981 for the *New York Times*, her religiously charged description of Ôno as "messianic" in this sequence seems apt, whereas this description would have been more a stretch in 1977.

The original costumes tended toward plain, dowdy, or even unkempt and seemingly soiled garments, but Ôno switched to camp, frilly costumes (Ohno and Ohno 2004, 78). The cyclorama (or opera-style) lighting of 1977, with Ôno in front of a red-tinged backdrop, caused his face to seem yellowish-green and thus rather sickly.[8] Over time, lighting designers dropped the cyclorama lighting and opted for washes that filled the entire space. Later lighting designers used washes of neutral white, or blue and lavender light, making him look more ruddy. The original color temperature was created with diffuse pools of white light with yellow hues, but over time, designers gradually gave Ôno star treatment in sharply focused white spotlights with cooler blue hues.[9] The exact steps in the transformation of the lighting are not clear, but Ôno was lit at Nancy by the internationally famous lighting designer Jean Kalman. His pupil, Mizohata Toshio, remembers that Kalman used a blue wash for Ôno, setting a precedent for future lighting. Perhaps Western lighting designers instinctively gravitated to a flashier lighting scheme.

As Lucia Schwellinger has noted, the upshot of the transformations was that *Admiring La Argentina* became more abstract over time and much lighter in tone (Schwellinger 1998, 153). Schwellinger remarks that for the audience in Nancy, the dance was less about the horror of the death of an indigent male prostitute, and more a kitschy-beautiful performance of an elderly woman. Dunning echoes this sentiment in 1981 when she wrote of a posing, preening "glittering old hag" conveying "glints of humor" (Dunning 1981). To be sure, Dunning was drawn to the power of Ôno's performance—and indeed the various versions are magnificent in their own ways—but there is no denying that the dance changed from addressing a sick and dying male prostitute, custodial tasks and physical education, exhaustion, dowdiness, and war to conveying humor, theatricality, and the campy glamour of an aging—but still very elegant—drag queen striving for redemption. If the original dance was a meditation between three (or four) characters—the Divine/Culafroy of Genet/Hijikata; Ôno himself as a teacher, janitor, and soldier (or as the lead role in the Mr. O films); and La Argentina (and possibly Bizet's Carmen)—over time, the suffering of Divine got left behind, the hints at custodial work became less recognizable, and La Argentina came to prominence.

Considering *Admiring La Argentina*

The dance scholar Mark Franko has commented perceptively on *Admiring La Argentina*. Franko seems unaware of the transformations in the dance, and apparently only saw the Mercé-forward version(s) from 1982 and later. He thus spends considerable time discussing Ôno's use of La Argentina, but nonetheless makes two extremely valuable observations about this dance. The first deals with intercultural interactions, and the second deals with what we might call the interpersonal interaction that Ôno stages between himself and Mercé.

Franko's first observation is that we cannot understand Ôno and this dance without considering a web of exoticizing behaviors. The Argentine Mercé exoticized Spanish Romani dance(r)s. Japanese people exoticized Argentina and tango in the 1920s. Ôno exoticized Mercé. The Western audience exoticized Ôno (Franko 2011, 114–119). Within that web, Franko explores three options for understanding Ôno's relationship to Mercé.

One possibility is spirit possession. Mercé possesses Ôno: She "becomes animate again, through Ohno" and controls him (Franko 2011, 121). Conversely, Ôno might be taken to metaphorically devour Mercé, so that "As Ohno reproduces La Argentina on stage he gains a part of her strength" (123). Franko continues, "One could say that his consumption of La Argentina made the Kazuo Ohno phenomenon possible, that he consumed her to produce himself" (123). For Franko, the possibility that Ôno devours Mercé and puts her energy to use for himself is important, because he acknowledges that "the international success of *Admiring La Argentina* . . . launched his second, by far more important, dance career" (123). Franko was not suggesting that Ôno was anything less than sincere in his admiration for La Argentina. But we must remember that no matter how else we understand Ôno, his international success rests on his appropriation of Mercé, and the way this enabled European audiences to access his dance. The performance fees for dancing in Western venues were an important part of the income of many butô dancers and the roughly 5,000 dollars Ôno received as a performer fee from each venue would have been a significant portion of his annual pension-based income (Ashikawa 2018, Section 7).

As Franko and others have observed, however, the question of possession is not so straightforward with Ôno and Mercé. Yoshito had mused long before, "I am never sure whether [Ôno] is quietly possessing her spirit, or if La Argentina herself has entered his body" (Ohno and Ohno 2004, 166). Franko concurs and identifies a curious aspect of Ôno's dance: "intermittent or delayed mimesis" (Franko 2011, 110).[10] This leads him to argue that "what we are given to see is neither La Argentina impersonated nor Ohno appropriating her image, but rather his own identification with her as a process of self-dispossession" (Franko 2011, 124). Incidentally, this likely applies to Ôno's embodiment of Genet's Divine as well. Franko presses on to argue that Ôno "willfully exiled himself" because of his "will to self-estrangement" (125).

Franko's idea of "self-dispossession" is uncannily similar to one theme of postwar Japanese thought that focused on regret, repentance, self-criticism, and self-dispossession. The philosopher Tanabe Hajime's thought had been used to justify Japanese aggression during the war (Sakai 2000).[11] In his 1946 *Philosophy as Metanoetics* (more prosaically, "Philosophy as the Way of Repentance"), the philosopher acknowledged his complicity in the war effort, and his need to engage in self-criticism and repentance (Tanabe 1990; Dower 1999, 496–501). In 1961, Tanabe was echoed by another philosopher, Nishitani Keiji, who was less interested in Japan's wartime behavior than in exploring the possibilities of Christian-Buddhist dialogue through a discussion of the *ekkenosis* (self-emptying) of Jesus in light of the Buddhist concept of emptiness (*sunyata, kû*). According to Nishitani, the understanding of God as all-powerful has it exactly backward. Nishitani argues that the very nature of God lies in self-emptying, which he associates with the idea of *anātman*, non-ego (Nishitani 1982, 58–60).

This is not the place for an extended look at the respective philosophies of Tanabe and Nishitani. Rather, I wish to provide a cultural background for what Franko terms Ôno's "self-estrangement" by highlighting parallel concepts in the work of contemporary Japanese philosophers. It may be that the regret, repentance, and self-criticism of Tanabe are echoed in Ôno's practice of remembering those lost in the war and apologizing for having lived on. In the 1981 program for *My Mother*, Ôno wrote, "I am living with the incorrigible mistakes that I have made. Pardon me. Thank you." Given Ôno's adoption of Christianity, it is possible to see his "self-estrangement" as both a cultural- *and* Christian-motivated *ekkenosis* (self-emptying).

We find corroboration for such a thesis in Ôno's remarks about Jesus and Judas. Ôno balks at the interpretation that Jesus felt betrayed by Judas, and rather emphasizes that Jesus considered Judas a friend. He implies that Judas should feel betrayed by the reception he received when he just did what Jesus wanted. Ôno then says, "Jesus, you too made me realize the true meaning of God when you were nailed to the cross" (Ohno and Ohno 2004, 212). The true meaning of God for Ôno does not lie in omnipotence, but in asking for help with the task of self-emptying.

It is probably impossible for any of us to ever truly lose our self-interest when interacting with others. This is particularly the case when we interact with people from different cultures, because we may be predisposed to exoticize (or demonize) each other. Ôno's dances hint at how to handle ourselves in such encounters. To the extent that we can do some self-emptying, self-estrangement, or even some careful "intermittent or delayed mimesis" of others, we may come closer to a nuanced interaction with them.

My Mother

Ôno toured *O-Zen* (Table) on the same tour as *Argentina*. It included the group choreography that Hijikata had cut from *Argentina*. However, it did not attract as much attention. Perhaps for this reason, thereafter Ôno appeared in the solos that audiences craved. The first of these was *My Mother* (Watashi no okâsan, 1981), which toured with the evolving *Admiring La Argentina*. The Japanese program notes display Ôno's personal cosmology, with essays about Jesus and Judas Iscariot, improvisation, and the last words of his mother. In programs for Western venues, short excerpts were repurposed into paragraphs for each scene, which were given distinct titles: "A Dream of the Fetus," "Mother's Dream," "The Will," "I Shall Not Correct It," and "Finale." Sometimes, the notes do not clarify much, as when the program for the La Mama performance (1981), identifies Ôno's costume as a "cat's hospital gown." Many viewers likely reacted similarly to the dance critic Jill Sykes, who wrote that for one scene, the title, subtitle, and brief description "conveyed nothing . . . to my mind, though the creative artist's actions were presumably shaped by these images" but that "another note, however, was extremely helpful" (Sykes 1986, 30).[12]

In the Copenhagen 1982 version, Ôno appears in a white minidress (the "Cat's hospital gown"?) holding an artificial flower, accompanied by wind sounds (see Figure 8.5). The movements are slow: He creeps, totters, and often looks like he is being dragged by the flower. The sounds of the tsugarujamisen player Takabayashi Chikuzan's "Jûsangata" (Thirteen River Lagoon) fill the air. Still in the white shift, Ôno drops the flower and seems to comb his hair. At times it seems as if he is pulling himself through some thick medium. He sports a silly grin, and seemingly mimes eating something, and scooping his hand in or dangling it in water. Sometimes he looks inquisitive, sometimes anguished, and sometimes as if he is about to pounce on something. After a costume change, he appears in a yellow kimono with burgundy undersleeves. The kimono is not folded under an obi to take up the extra slack but rather extends several inches onto the ground. His movements are more inward-directed. He shuffles, stoops, hunches over, and wanders. He removes the kimono, revealing a burgundy flowered *happi*. He hides behind the kimono, drapes it over his shoulder, and bundles it on his head. Then he stumbles forward and lies on the ground with his face pressed into the floor. The lights go down. Regular shamisen music fills the space, and when the lights come back up, Ôno lies awkwardly facing the audience atop something supporting his legs with his face close to the ground. He rolls off it, to reveal a small gold-lacquered table. He mimes an effort to lift it, stands protectively over it, kneels atop it, eats off it, looks down on it with tenderness almost as if to pray to it. After another blackout, he wanders the stage in low light seemingly dragging stuff toward himself, pushing it away, gathering it together again, and lifting it and pouring it on his head. He seems to be searching for something or wandering aimlessly.[13]

Figure 8.5 Ôno Kazuo in *My Mother*, 1986. "A Dream of the Fetus." Copyright by and courtesy of the photographer Nourit Masson-Sekine, the NPO Dance Archive Network, and the Ôno Kazuo Dance Studio.

The program notes suggest that, among other things, Ôno was thinking about the death of a sister who was hit by a train and killed in 1914, his mother's final bequest to him (the remark about the flatfish), and Ophelia. It also appears as though Ôno used Hijikata's evocative work to help him embody these characters. Here, for example, is a brief excerpt from the *My Mother* notebook (for the June 6, 1981, performance):

1. Dream of a Fetus
Just who are you?   I am the dead   Will you go to eat bugs and butterflies?
Monet's waterlilies   A fetus watching intently as if it has a veil over its face
That artificial flower of snow within the color of a twilight spirit
A monster's dwelling in which moss is growing   Nonchalant pebble
The surface of water of a flower garden   The gently lapping flower garden
    To the extent that one squats   Blake's beard (photograph of peerage)   Mother's
    halo (nimbus)

(Ôno 1998, 124)

Ôno toured the two performances for the next two years, and in the process visited the Dead Sea. From his experience there, he, Hijikata, and Yoshito created another work that premiered at the 1985 Butoh Festival.

The Dead Sea: Viennese Waltz and Ghosts

The Dead Sea was ostensibly divided into four scenes:

1. In Place of a Spoken Prologue.
2. The Dead Sea.
3. Toys.
4. Viennese Waltz and Ghosts.

Ôno again created material through various associative means: weasels, generals, mothers, dead angels. To give time for costume changes and to accommodate Ôno's stamina, he alternates (and sometimes overlaps) with Yoshito, who generally moves slowly and precisely, in contrast to Ôno's more varied styles. Ôno starts in a white dress, long white robe, with white leggings underneath, and white shoes, all topped by a katsura wig. He wanders a tight circle holding his robe out, embraces the back wall, and peers into his hands as if moaning (see Figure 8.6). One reviewer saw in him the miserable figure of Dickens's Miss Havisham (Supree 1985b, 78). Sometimes he crouches and sometimes he looks up. This is followed by deprecations, searching, caressing. He returns to the stage with a satchel or apron, blacklined cape, scarf, an artificial flower in his hair that appears to be constructed of United Nations flags, and a doll strapped to his shoulder. Ôno seems like a knight or courtier prodding a horse (see Figure 8.7). Kisselgoff described this character as "the lost musketeer" (Kisselgoff

Figure 8.6 Ôno Kazuo in *Dead Sea*, 1986. Photographer unknown. Courtesy of the NPO Dance Archive Network and the Ôno Kazuo Dance Studio.

Figure 8.7 Ôno Kazuo in *Dead Sea*, 1986. Copyright by and courtesy of the photographer Nourit Masson-Sekine, the NPO Dance Archive Network, and the Ôno Kazuo Dance Studio.

1985, 19). Suddenly diffident, he recoils, wraps a shawl around himself, and shrinks back with marionette-like movements. Then he is coy, prodding his horse again, and throwing his wrists out and letting his hands snap forward. Yoshito appears and slowly spins with one arm out, gradually raising it up to the sky. He kneels and bows his head. His movements are very much like Sankai Juku throughout.

Ôno returns in a puffy white outfit with bunched, pleated sleeves. Many of the movements repeat previous ones, but at one point he falls on his back and thrusts his hands and his feet into the air. Yoshito takes a turn again, slowly swaying and rotating. Then Ôno reappears in a skirt and blouse with an obi. With his pinky finger extended elegantly, he stomps and stamps around the stage. Next, he throws his hands out (as before) with mincing steps. For a moment, he looks positively ungainly. Then he leaves and after a turn by Yoshito, he reappears clad in a black tuxedo and black patent leather shoes. Again, he throws his hands up, and lies on the floor with his legs and arms up. Upright again he kicks a leg out with an arm over his head.

Reviewers each saw different characters in Ôno's performance, and all understood that the dance meant different things to different people. Mainly they focused on their overall impressions, centered around Ôno's emotion and his honesty. Burt Supree commented, "His piquant gestures and his emotional potency have the power to fascinate, but his absolute authenticity, his amazing truthfulness is all that gives form to the work" (Supree 1985b, 78). Jill Sykes marveled at "a performer whose compelling stage presence carries a wealth of authority, self-examination, experience, and conviction" (Sykes 1986, 30). Kisselgoff observed, "there is an enduring humanity about Mr. Ohno, which in no way runs counter to the seriousness of his meditation upon the universe" (Kisselgoff 1985, C19). By 1985, Ôno had fully become a symbol of authenticity, truthfulness, and humanity.

Ôno's Worldview

The program notes for *O-Zen*, *My Mother*, and *The Dead Sea* reveal that Ôno was imagining a rich world behind his dances. In the same way that Ôno's conception of Mercé changed through his encounter with the traces of Mercé, his imagined world gradually snowballed through a process of association. This world was peopled with a growing cast: a general peering out of "moss gully," a lake melting into angels, an enormous phantom Argentina hovering over the Manhattan skyline doubled with the image of a fighting bull, et cetera (Schwellinger 2018, 116; Ôno 1998, 104). More broadly, these visions and particularly the experience of seeing fellow soldiers die on the way home from the war, the observation about the flatfish, and the experience of the contiguity between the birth of a child and the birth of a star gelled into a four-part worldview, which was communicated to Ôno through mystical experience (Schwellinger 2018, 114, 116). It starts with two initial premises:

1. The universe brims with vitality, which manifests itself in various ways in diverse conditions.
2. However, in this vortex of vitality, some elements are sacrificed or sacrifice themselves.

For example, the vitality of the universe is manifest in a species of fish evolving into an outlandish flatfish and succeeding in its environment. Mothers and wombs embody the second premise. They act as microcosms of the generative universe, but they also serve as examples of self-sacrifice in creation. According to Ôno, his mother let him absorb her energy while he was gestating in the womb. She suffered immense pain while birthing him. And she put up with his egotistical and selfish demands as she raised him and his nine siblings. Ôno felt a combination of gratitude and guilt toward his mother and to the world at large. These feelings led to two prescriptive elements of the worldview:

3. We should all feel a mixture of gratitude and guilt toward those beings that sacrifice themselves for us or fall by the wayside in the ever-constant churn of the cosmos.
4. We should repay those beings (and the universe itself) by creating new life and new art (which according to Ôno are the same things).

Dancers and choreographers shoulder a special role in his worldview. In the words of Schwellinger, they "should recognize the continuity of life, and the related emotions" that come from these realizations "such as gratefulness, guilt, [awe, wonder, joy], etc., and turn them into movement" (Schwellinger 2018, 114).

By now, the reader should have a good sense of Ôno's dances. Each contains a series of solos (sometimes alternating with scenes featuring Yoshito to accommodate costume changes or to give Ôno a breather). In these, Ôno embodies different characters in different outfits generally scored to different pieces of Western music. The movement palette varied from scene to scene, but was relatively constant across the dances as a whole. It is almost possible to see Ôno as dancing different versions of the same dance throughout his buto career, each a manifestation of a widening set of associations surrounding the four-part worldview.

Considering Ôno's Dance

I turn now to think about Ôno's dances within dance, Japanese, and world history. There are five main categories in which to think about Ôno's dances: gender, ethnicity, age, technique, and improvisation.

Gender

Audiences were amazed by Ôno's unabashed cross-dressing. Franko analyzes Ôno's drag in his consideration of *Water Lilies* (1988). Franko observes that Ôno attempts to divorce drag from sexual desire. Usually, drag relies on desire, specifically the heterosexual male's scopophilic desire for the woman. The transvestite exploits this desire through the reveal of sexual characteristics that shocks and disorients the heterosexual male who has desired someone he thought was woman, who is now shown to be a man (Franko 1992, 594–596).

Counter to that trend, Franko argues that Ôno explores drag (and gender) without also entailing desire. In this regard, Ôno matches the broader configuration of gender/sexuality in Japan, in which there is a disconnect between gender presentation and sexual preference (McLelland 2000, 11). To be sure, reviewers frequently cite Hollywood sex symbols such as Jean Harlow, Marlene Dietrich, and Gloria Swanson when referring to Ôno (Kisselgoff 1985; Sykes 1986; Temin 1986). This indicates that his drag still creates a frisson of sexual charge, and that Franko overstates the degree to which Ôno escapes the boundaries of sexuality and desire. Yet, Franko is correct that desire is largely unimportant in Ôno's dances. For example, in the opening scene of *My Mother*, Ôno appears in a minidress. Ôno starts with the minidress pulled down to cover his underwear, but over time the dress hikes up. Ôno seems completely unconcerned about the moment of exposure of his underwear (see Figure 8.8). What is more, glimpsing Ôno's underwear has nothing in common with the "ubiquitous 'panty shot' of manga and anime" captured from a low camera angle (Lamarre 2013, 135). Ôno could have played up the reveal, but he simply does not assign his genitalia any special status or importance, or presume that his audience would or should.

Quoting several passages will capture the extent of Franko's argument. Ôno "attempts simultaneously to perform and demystify cross-dressing" (Franko 1992, 596). The result is that "Ohno's performance is not concerned with the fixing and supporting of identities that usually occurs in Western theatrical cross dressing. His cross dressing does not play into or explore the prestige of those solutions; rather by playing 'away' from them, Ohno abandons both illusion and delusion" (602). Instead, his performance "speaks of disparate sexes in one body without invoking paradox" (603). The effect is that Ôno's "performance suggests . . . the range of differences that bodies lay claim to." (603). Further on, "Ohno's 'truth' . . . is the death of gender as *the* theatrical polarity founding public space. Ohno asserts his maleness in middle voices . . . and he traverses innumerable unmarked positions free of reactive parody" (604). Finally, Ôno suggests "a voluminous or depth model in which any and all gender attributes—biological, dispositional, sexual, vestimentary, gestural—are subject to recombination at uneven intervals and to unequal degrees" (604). The upshot is that Ôno allows a "range of differences," and "innumerable unmarked positions." In the process, he opens up space for all kinds of "unconventional sexualities" and masculinities (without the usual baggage that masculinity entails). Through this,

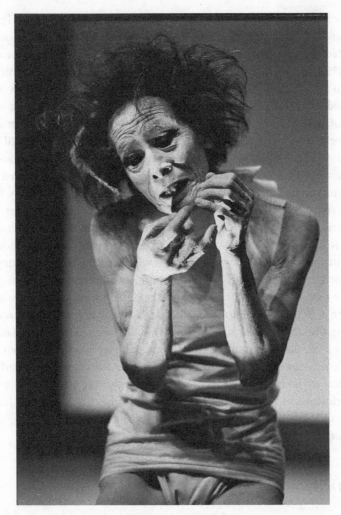

Figure 8.8 Ôno Kazuo unconcerned with (his) sexuality, *My Mother*, 1986. Courtesy of Nourit Masson-Sekine, the NPO Dance Archive Network, and the Ôno Kazuo Dance Studio.

Ôno contributed to the realization that gender norms are not as monolithic as people might have thought and appealed to audiences who were looking for ways out of constricting gender norms.

Ethnicity

Franko's argument about ethnicity is more veiled. He assumes that Ôno's ethnicity critique is fundamentally linked to his gender critique, and even that culture and gender are so thoroughly entwined that it is impossible to divorce them. He then observes that Ôno purposefully adopts "anachronistic stereotypes" when embodying Western females and employs the "hackneyed body language of feminine delicacy" (Franko 1992, 602–603). I would add that Ôno does the same thing with stereotypes of Western men, such as "the lost musketeer" (Kisselgoff 1985, 19) or the ever-present black-tuxedoed man. Franko juxtaposes these choices with Ôno's citation of Monet, who "constructed his own water-lily pond, Japanese footbridge, and garden," creating an "orientalist landscape [that] was Monet's life model from 1899 until his death in 1926" (600). Ôno thus cites a Westerner's overly romanticized and anachronistic view of Japan right alongside his own overly romanticized and hackneyed views of Western characters, suggesting that both are equally separate from reality. Ôno can, thus, be seen to suggest that ethnicity is just as much a fabrication as gender.

Ôno's critique of ethnicity lies in his refusal to assign a frisson to ethnic cross-dressing, just as he refused to assign one to gender cross-dressing. Once we understand that Ôno does not depend on the reveal ("Aha, I was a man faking I was a woman and I fooled you into desiring me") for the effectiveness of his cross-dressing, we can see that neither does he depend on the reveal for his ethnic cross-dressing. His gender performance amounts to "I happen to enjoy dressing like a woman and embodying the stereotypical attributes of a woman (such as gentleness, nurturing, or delicacy), but that says nothing about my sexual preferences, nor about whether or not I identify as a man in other moments of my life, nor even about whether those stereotypical attributes apply to all women. I just enjoy playing (female) roles." His ethnic performances seem to convey, "I happen to like dressing up like hackneyed portrayals of Western women and men of all sorts, but that says nothing about my ethnicity or their ethnicity. I just enjoy playing (Western) roles."

Eccentricity

Franko celebrates Ôno as "eccentric" (1992, 600, 603), but he does not follow this conclusion to another radical end. I have frequently noted that butô puts characters on stage who were not hitherto thought worthy of representation. I have been at such pains to emphasize the way that Ôno frequently looks dowdy or frumpy, because Ôno does not just embody various genders or ethnicities. He presents all sorts of eccentric alternative modes of being, including those of dowdiness and frumpiness. The history of performing arts is full of people playing frumpy for a laugh (which usually barely conceals disdain). But Ôno's refusal to play drag for any parodic purposes extends to his refusal to play frumpy as parody or with animus. Just as he takes alternative genders seriously, he also presents eccentric characters seriously.

My assertion that the eccentric aspect of Ôno's performance is as radical as his gender critique is not to take away anything from the gender critique. It was (and continues to be) urgent. There are still young people committing suicide in my own country, the United States, because of stifling gender norms and homo- and transphobia. But even so, in the 1980s it was as big a step to present conventionally unattractive women with sympathy on the dance stage, as it was for a drag queen to approximate conventionally attractive women.[14] In this respect, we should be reading Ôno's work in light of Anna I of Pina Bausch's *Seven Deadly Sins* (1976), although the gender politics of Bausch and Ôno differ markedly.[15]

Now, I hasten to add that most of Ôno's eccentric characters (such as frumpy or dowdy) are female-coded by their clothing. Ôno's male characters span a smaller spectrum. In part, this reflects the underlying truth of gender differences in the eccentric modes. We do not have the same categories for men as for women, because men have been less likely to be solely characterized in terms of their looks, fashion, and sexuality in the first place. So, sexism is at work in Ôno's presentation of eccentricity. However, many of the male eccentric modes involve an aggressive (or even toxic) masculinity that is fundamentally at odds with other aspects of Ôno's program. Ôno was not an equal-opportunity impersonator exploring and taking seriously all aspects of masculinity and femininity. You will not encounter the fat slob, the chauvinist pig, or the abusive drunk in his repertoire. Rather, he adopted a wide range of stereotypically female modes without submerging what Franko calls his "middle voice" masculinity.

Age

Concert dance has nearly always been the kingdom of the young. Part of Ôno's appeal is the sheer novelty of watching an old man dancing into his nineties, and making no attempt to hide his age. Watching Ôno in 1986, Marcia B. Seigel remarks, "All the artifice is not meant to disguise the fact that he is 75 years of age, but to make us more aware of it" (Seigel 1981, 34). Given the generally low expectations about the physical abilities of old people, observers cannot help but be amazed at how well he can dance. Reviewer Mindy Aloff writes, "Ohno seems to have made a pact with the devil, for he exhibits [a] lean muscled body" (Aloff 1982, 48). Part of our reaction rests on admiration for him being able to do so much more than we expect at his age.

Age is more than just a kind of costume, though. Japan has the longest life-expectancy in the world, and the problems and benefits of an aging society have been a part of Japanese discourse for some time. Considering Japan's low birth rate, two observers pointedly note that "Japan simply cannot afford having older adults not working" and as a result that "Japan has high labor participation rates among older adults" (Muramatsu and Akiyama 2011, 429–430). Ôno mirrored this larger trend by performing until the age of ninety-seven.[16] We might observe that Ôno could dance well, and certainly wanted to dance (and craved the limelight), but that he also *had* to dance. He lived more than forty years after the usual retirement age. The income he gained from performing internationally might have constituted from one-fifth to one-half of his yearly pension based income.

The scholar of aging and performance Anne Basting interprets Ôno's age in a way that parallels Franko's investigations. Basting argues that we have come to see age similarly to gender and ethnicity. Previously, we routinely associated old age with essentialist states such as decline or fulfillment, but more recently we associate age with "a more realistic view of ongoing, always dynamic re-involvement, reviewing, renewing, and reworking" of the self (Kivnick quoted in Basting 1998, 18). Basting claims that Ôno offers "the possibility for a model of age that embraces change" (134). She continues, "What is too often imagined to be the *ravages* of time on the body in Western culture, Ôno re-creates as beauty, not only in the present moment, but as an accumulation of the moments across the life course and across generations" (140). She then refers to Ôno's "overflowing of binaries of youth and age," and concludes by observing that "if there is parody in Ohno's performance it is . . . aimed at the notion that binaries alone dictate the possibilities for humankind" (143). That is, just as Ôno challenges male/female and East/West dichotomies, he refused to observe a young/old dichotomy.

However, Basting acknowledges that this dichotomy is more "sticky" than the others (1998, 142). In this she is echoed by the dance scholar Kimura Satoru. He identifies what he terms the "most Ôno-like" movements:

Those are hand (or arm), and eye (or head) movements. Both the hands (which are out in front of every part of his body), and the pupils (which direct the thoughts forward) wander about in mid-air. Accordingly, the trunk comes along later as if following these two, and the legs chase after. (Kimura 107–108)[17]

I would add that Ôno often leads with his wrists or throws his wrists out and lets his arms follow and fingers snap forward as the extension of the movement of his wrists. Based on several comments by Ôno that the "spirit [or soul] leads," Kimura says that these types of movements give the impression that Ôno's "thoughts separate from his body, and the left-behind immobile old body just endures the yearnings that it cannot fulfill" (Kimura 108; but compare with Ohno and Ohno 2004, 230 and 295). I take Kimura to indicate that despite Ôno's ability to embody many different ages in his dance, he still faced an obstacle in his own body. In this, Kimura's response parallels what the performance scholar Kathleen Woodward terms the response of "sentimental compassion" that often accrues to portrayals of age (Woodward 2006, 164). From Kimura's observations, we can conclude that part of our reaction to Ôno is sympathy because his age has conspired against him so that he can no longer do everything he wants to do.

Gender, ethnicity, and age are the three axes of Ôno's dance. We could map them like this:

Male—female (but with masculinity always showing through)
Japanese—Western
Old—varying ages (but with old age always showing through)

Statistically, Ōno played more female roles than male roles, but he maintained his masculinity throughout while adopting various aspects of femininity. He played more Western-coded roles than Japan-coded roles. While he often embodied someone younger than himself (such as the young girl in *Admiring La Argentina*), mostly he played his age straight up. This disparity between how Ōno played gender, ethnicity, and age provides an important clue for the further understanding of Ōno's dance. Something undeniable happens to bodies as they age. I am certainly not the same body I was as a wrestler in high school or as a modern dancer in college. I cannot do three hundred pushups anymore. Age is not entirely a construct. Basting even makes light of the "science fiction fantasies of worlds perpetually frozen in glory days of young adulthood" (Basting 1998, 144). We can understand Ōno as offering an anti-essentialist embodiment of gender and ethnicity, but age is more "sticky." Age is part social construct, but also (so far) inevitable, despite what we might want to make of it. Perhaps realizing this, Ōno owned his age (and his "middle voice" masculinity) more than he owned his ethnicity.

Universality and Improvisation

In his portrayal of eccentric characters, between Japan and West, female and male, Ōno articulated a remarkably individual worldview. At the same time, he was often seen (and often saw himself) as articulating universals. For example, Kisselgoff refers to him fusing "the universal symbol with a portrait in miniature," and Ōno claims "dance springs from that universal womb where death and life intertwine" (Kisselgoff 1985; Ohno and Ohno 2004, 199). We distrust most claims to universality, because we suspect that the universal is merely a code for all the unquestioned assumptions of a dominant group. However, another part of Ōno's appeal lies in this tension between the extreme individual and the universal.

Kuniyoshi argues that this tension has its roots in Ōno's training with both Ishii Baku and Eguchi and Miya. She depicts Ōno feeling torn between the "exalted dramatic dance" and "universality that surpasses everyday human emotion" of his first teacher Ishii, and the abstract dance of his second mentors Eguchi and Miya (Kuniyoshi 2018, 27).[18] But She argues that he came to see both as misguided and was searching for something more aligned with his own experience. She depicts Ōno as searching for movement that is not so universal as to be removed from the self, and not so abstract as to be removed from the self, but rather a kind of movement that is intimately connected to the self.

Kuniyoshi observes that Ōno retained from Eguchi and Miya the idea that introducing small variations in movement could produce new movements. She quotes Ōno saying that he "understands what Eguchi means when he says that all the body's parts are connected to each other, so even in the movement of one joint, there are innumerable movements." But she argues that Ōno goes beyond this to the realization that "movement is also naturally related to problems of the heart/mind, soul, and life"

(Kuniyoshi 2018, 27–28). Essentially, Ôno posited an intimate connection between body and mind. Rather than taking one movement as a well-spring for hundreds of other movements because the entire *body* is connected, he supposed that any transformation (no matter how minute) in any part of the body/mind has the potential to elicit ripples throughout the whole.

We think this is a given now. Forcing a smile can lighten your mood; stretching your neck or slowing your breathing can make you feel calm. The reverse works as well. Imagining being happy can flood physiological ease through your body and perhaps a smile will appear on your face. Ôno extended this idea past the boundaries of the individual to the universe. In a workshop, Ôno said, "Since each and every one of us is born in and of this universe, we're linked to every single thing in it. There's nothing to stop us from reaching out and touching the entire universe" (Ohno and Ohno 2004, 239). Because Ôno thought that the body-mind and the universe were intimately connected, he was searching for or enacting a universality rooted in his own everyday experience.

The issue of Ôno's relationship to individuality and universality is also related to Ôno's relationship to improvisation. Takahashi Kazuko gives some indication of the parameters of Ôno's practice:

> Although Ôno's performances are thought out beforehand in terms of spatial configuration, movement directives, and intentions, it is not the case that the movements are fixed choreographically. The performances have the characteristic of being danced improvisationally.... Whenever, Ôno is creating works, he writes several pages of creative memos on B4 sized paper with colored markers. He writes and moves and moves and writes. Writing on sheets of paper becomes/is image training for movement, and out of that larger process the work is born. (Takahashi 2011 8)

The performances "have the characteristic of being danced improvisationally." They look like they are improvisational. But to a certain extent, Ôno used a similar method to Hijikata's late-era imagery work to create and reproduce movements. Ôno's notebooks reference art, abound in fragments of poetry, and contain evocative prompts, although it is clear that Ôno sometimes changed his motivations when restaging his dances.[19] In his quest to hit the sweet spot between abstraction and universality-beyond-the-everyday, Ôno used structured improvisations in which any physical or mental change anywhere had the potential to ripple everywhere.

Conclusion

Ôno's dance changed as he encountered Europe, but he captured the hearts and minds of audiences around the world because like the flatfish on the ocean floor living under extreme pressure, he "illustrate[d] the possibility of living in seemingly adverse circumstances" (Schwellinger 2018, 120). Managing under pressure is the essence of Ôno. It is why his performances struck such a chord, why people were inexplicably moved to tears when they saw him. Who among us cannot relate to feeling overwhelming pressure? He managed that overwhelming pressure, like the flatfish, by improvising within and challenging structures. His structured improvisations helped him to go beyond gender and ethnic stereotypes and represent a way out for others. He lived both within and beyond the confines of his bodily and social age. And he modeled what to do when you have managed to live (and thrive) under pressure: show gratitude for what you manage to eke out, give thanks for the evolutionary changes that allow you to eke something out, acknowledge the efforts of others that came before you, and feel survival guilt because you made it when others did not. The next step for us: do our part to add to the life and art of the universe.

9

Ikeda Sanae/Carlotta Ikeda and Compagnie Ariadone

Carlotta Ikeda was one of the three dancers in the eventful 1978 performance *The Last Eden*. Even more than Murobushi and Yoshioka, she caught the eye of dance critics. One raved:

> Naked whitened body, spiky hair in the red rays of the sun, a dagger coming out of her crotch, muscles retracted, she escapes from a fetal coil by twitching. Her impassive face, transparent like porcelain, her eyes rolled back into an inner trance.... She comes and goes on all fours with the impatience of a feline . . . , rushes at a musician as if to bite the sounds and offers her arched back to a shower of falling white sand. . . . Mad visions cross our imagination: Amazon, panther woman, sea flower, sphinx. Carlotta Ikeda creates from scratch her own mythology, which is unlike anything ever seen before. (Michel 1982a)

The reviewer, Marcelle Michel, strains to describe her, "Amazon, panther woman, sea flower, sphinx." Finally, Michel gives up, and summarizes: "unlike anything ever seen before." A few years later, Michel identified her as one of the three faces of butô in France (Michel 1986). It might be tempting to chalk this up to butô being unlike anything ever seen before, but Ikeda kept trying to be "unlike anything ever seen before" through her entire career. Odette Aslan suggests that she remained betwixt and between for her entire career (Aslan 2002a, 149; Druet unpublished). In this chapter, I sketch Ikeda's career with a special emphasis on her attempts to dance betwixt and between butô and other dance and to train Western dancers.

Ikeda began her dance career studying ballet and modern dance with Eguchi and Miya, and also learned Graham technique (Aslan 2002a, 149). She says, however, that she felt like she had encountered a wall. When she saw Hijikata's dance, she realized that there was a way over the wall (Boisseau 2004). She was recruited for Dairakudakan in 1973, but apparently Maro was nervous because she already had a dance background, so she formed an all-women's troupe, Ariadone no Kai (Compagnie Ariadone), under the supervision of Murobushi.[1] By 1974, she began going by the name Carlotta Ikeda. Almost from her name, one can feel Ikeda as betwixt and between. Ikeda was her given Japanese surname; Carlotta, the name she chose, a reference to the romantic ballet dancer Carlotta Grisi (Aslan 2002a, 149).

A History of Butô. Bruce Baird, Oxford University Press. © Oxford University Press 2022.
DOI: 10.1093/oso/9780197630273.003.0009

Despite the fact that she felt that Hijikata's dance was the way over the wall she faced, she did not turn her back entirely on ballet or Graham technique but used her name to mark herself as still having one foot in ballet and modern dance (Druet unpublished). Her company name, Ariadone (Japanese pronunciation of Ariadne), echoed this bifurcation. In one promotional flier, Ariadone is identified as the wife of Dionysus, *and* "the god of dance who unspooled a coiled thread in the labyrinth of Daedalus." In another, Ariadone is "the princess of the crazed emperor, or rather, she is already the crazed emperor herself."[2] Ariadone was thus seen as a person who helps people out of danger and as a manifestation of ecstatic celebration (Druet unpublished). Ikeda retained the Japanese pronunciation, Ariadone, throughout her career, perhaps to signal that her conception of Ariadone was different from Ariadne.

By 1975, Ariadone was ready to present their own show. The media headlines gushed over the all-female avant-garde dance troupe:

Even the Osaka Strippers are Surprised
What! Nudes at Kyoto University!?
Art? Superior to Art? Whatever, Nude Nude Nude. . . . 8 Woman Lez Tag.[3]

The gap between the cabaret dances and the "butô" dances seems particularly small in this case. Aslan notes that work in the cabaret and in such shows gave Ikeda an approach to eroticism that does not accord with Western attitudes toward sexuality, because she learned to be not the least bit self-conscious about her body and nudity (Aslan 2002a, 149). Ikeda continued to work with Murobushi for several years, including the trip to France. Soon she went back to France and stayed for good. Having worked in concert with Murobushi for so many years makes it difficult to sort out choreographic credit for many of the dances until after 1985. In 1984, a dance critic reported that Ikeda said that "She improvises and then Murobushi picks the movements, orders them, and decides on the lights and music" (Michel 1984). As with the other women of butô, she likely deserves partial choreographic credit for the dances, whatever it might say in the program. With *Blackgraywhite* (1988), she struck out on her own (although she co-choreographed with Murobushi again in *Ai-Amour*, 1993, and *A Rite of Spring*, 1999).

Yvonne Ténenbaum carefully outlines many of the elements that likely made Michel feel that Ikeda was so unclassifiable. She observes that Ikeda concentrates or contracts her muscles while exhaling, so that she can create a fascinating interplay of opposing energies and directions in her dance (Ténenbaum 2002, 204). In the case of Ikeda, Ténenbaum also observes, "The entire body dances: the toes . . . , but also the hands, fingers, mouth, tongue, and the whole face, as well as the legs and arms" (2006). In addition, she argues that Ikeda introduces "imperceptible" movements to the "visible" movements ("macro-movements"), so as to transform the impression that the viewer receives without the viewer being aware of the precise cause of the impression (209). Ténenbaum asserts that "this imperceptible movement creates something infinitely alive and also disturbing" (209).

To complement these specific movement strategies, Ténenbaum notes, Ikeda blurs the boundary between humans, animals, minerals, and vegetation (the French press never seem to tire of pointing out that her given name, Sanae, means "Rice Seedling"). Ikeda's animal movements are not mere imitations or representations of an animal, but rather the result of working to "find the animal" in herself. Ikeda "rediscovers [the] mechanical principle" of the animal so that she "moves the knee forward with a deep flexion of the hip that does not engage the pelvis," thereby leaving her torso nearly independent of the motion of the legs (Ténenbaum 2002, 210).[4]

As with animals, so with language. Odette Aslan notes that Ikeda has a different relationship to the act of reading than most choreographers (Aslan 2002a, 153). An interviewer asks Ikeda if she uses texts as inspiration. She answers, saying that she does not use texts directly, but rather that during reading a "relationship between text and movement happens" when she "allow[s] the feeling [she] experience[s] to express itself through movement and dance." She continues, referring to a dance of hers, *Waiting*, which was inspired by the works of Marguerite Duras: "Marguerite Duras wrote with her whole body and ... I read her with my whole body. Marguerite Duras' words have bone and muscle" (Ikeda and Bastien 2001, 64). Here Ikeda can be seen as articulating and practicing a different relationship between language, body, and movement from Hijikata/Noguchi's imagery work, which was often more unidirectional with the mind suggesting to the body what to do.

In the same way that Michel had found her work unclassifiable, so was her life. She straddled boundary lines between France and Japan, male and female, and muddied sexual categories. Some dances feature moments of strong heterosexual sexual tension, as well as moments when, like Ôno, the dancers draw near stereotype, but Ikeda ultimately refuses these binaries. This refusal is most explicit in two dances, *A White Day* (Une journée blanche, 1991, co-choreographed with Hervé Diasnas) and *Ai-Amour* (1993, co-choreographed with Murobushi). In *A White Day*, Ikeda and Diasnas enact a strange relationship with each other (Dalmau 1991). In one scene, Diasnas squats inside a huge box-like carapace, as if he is a dwarfish tin-woodman. He seems to timidly pine for the impossible object of his desire, and even at one point gathers up objects Ikeda discards as if all her trash is sacred treasure. She opens her robe and flashes him, ignores him, flirts with him. The entire scene is like beauty and the beast in which the beast has an Asian woman fetish. But the performance refuses to condemn him for his fetish. After all, she might have a dwarfish tin-woodman fetish. But the performance rejects a happy ending as well. Through different scenes, the two come close, connect, and then break apart. At one moment (no longer the squatty, boxy tin woodman), he dives for her but she rolls out of the way so that he crashes on the floor. But lightning fast, she rolls back over and dives on him. He stands up carrying her, but then she pushes herself off and runs away. In the end, they approach each other with arms out, their chests touch, but they do not embrace each other. They slowly turn, their torsos brushing against each other, with their arms reaching beyond each other.

Ai-Amour (1993) depicts a similar unease about relationships (Ikeda and Musale 1994, 26:44).[5] The "ai" of the title is a bilingual wordplay on the present tense conjugation "ai" of the French verb "avoir" (to have, to possess) and the Japanese "ai" (love). So, the first word of the title suggests a mashup of love and possession. Ikeda and Murobushi crawl and circle around each other as if they might devour each other (in both the sexual and literal sense as food), but for that very reason, they are also wary of each other (see Figures 9.1 and 9.2). She hoists him in the air, smashes heads with him, and kisses him. They curl up, spooning each other. He crawls away and she clings to him. In the end, the two spoon in white clothes that Willems takes to be funerary clothes and in some place that Musale cinematically reconceives, in the version staged for the documentary, as outside of time, space, and gravity (Willems 1993; Ikeda and Musale 1994, 36:00).

These two dances momentarily borrow gender stereotypes, but then subvert them in the next moments. Lamolière argues that while Ikeda sometimes seems to accept gender roles, she has trouble defining exactly what those roles might be when pressed and never talks about gender in her notebooks (Lamolière 2020, sections 13, 14, and 16). She quotes Ikeda,

> It would be too simplistic, even vulgar, to equate women with eros. While one can easily associate the passivity or flexibility of a woman's body with eros, eroticism that is confined to one sex does not interest me. What attracts me is an eroticism that emerges in a close relationship, a relationship that does not suppose the man and the woman [. . .] On the stage, the dancer is too often a woman instead of being the one who dances.
>
> **(Lamolière 2020, section 16)**

In this light, we can see that Ikeda's dances refuse any sort of tidy heterosexual romance, but rather presume a kind of ongoing tension within relationships and erotic attraction. In the documentary Ai-Amour, the narrator echoes this, observing "Carlotta Ikeda has created a new way of thinking, where eroticism is no longer linked to a sexual gender. In this state one forgets sexual limitations" (Ikeda and Musale 1994, 4:15).

Ikeda's group choreographies for Ariadone extend her understanding of gender and sexuality but at the same time seem to express more fully the brute reality of being a woman. One reviewer felt that Ikeda's first solo choreography, Blackgraywhite, was an embodiment of the "discomfort of the modern world and more particularly that of women" (François 1990, 22). Another felt that in Blackgraywhite Ikeda attempted to present women's flesh "outside of commerce with men" (Ténenbaum 1989, 27). The Language of the Sphinx (1992) features women bound in what might be bondage

Figure 9.1 Ikeda and Murobushi in *Ai-Amour*, 1993. Courtesy of Fonds Jean-Marie Gourreau—Médiathèque du Centre national de la danse.

bands (with Elizabethan collars that might suggest dog collars around their necks) gasping for air and flopping like fish (see Figure 9.3 and Ikeda and Musale 1994, 1:20–4:10). Because it's Ikeda, and these moments usually wind their way around to recognizing some sort of complexity of desire and pain, we might expect to see the dancers enjoy their bondage, but at least in the clips available, they never do. David Jays wrote that Ikeda "suggests a fairly dispiriting, if strikingly staged, progress.... Girlhood is as good as it gets.... Adult life [is] downhill all the way" (Jays 1995, 273). Later, the women scurry about like hens. They bite, hit, chase, head-butt, and scold each other, but when faced with danger they crowd together to protect each other (see Figure 9.4 and Ikeda and Musale 1994, 18:00–20:00). Emi Slater was slightly more upbeat,

> At times it felt like a Greek drama, at others, like a farce or a parody on womanhood. It remained throughout however an extraordinarily strong expression of the locked-in frustrations of being a woman.... The piece overall for me, was about the power of the energy of one woman among many. One woman trying to understand herself and finding strength in herself and other women. (Slater 1997, 24)

Ann Nugent echoed, "The triumph of the piece is that at the same time the women are conscripted, they are also liberated. They have found strength in the group, strength in their energy" (Nugent 1995, 17). A moment in *Togué* (with live music of the hardcore band Spina, 2002) suggests a similar outlook.[6] In one scene, the women line up

Figure 9.2 Ikeda and Murobushi in *Ai-Amour*, 1993. Courtesy of Fonds Jean-Marie Gourreau-Médiathèque du Centre national de la danse.

across the front of the stage and give what looks like a row of chin flicks, thumb biting, or giving the bírd all directed to the audience.

In an interview accompanying *Togué*, Ikeda says that she never really cared about the label "butoh," and that she does not want to get caught in the past (Ikeda 2002a). Because of the forceful nature of Ikeda's attempts to straddle the boundaries between categories, Lamolière argues that her dances force viewers to recalibrate viewing positions and assumptions, and "invent new modalities of reading and reception in order to be able to talk about the dance presented to them" (Lamolière 2020, section 42).

Unlike Amagatsu with his biennial contract with the Théâtre de la Ville, life was much harder for Ikeda. In 1998, an unnamed critic pointedly noted that Ikeda was triply damned because the men who manage the theaters do not schedule much dance, she did not have an artist's subsidy, and her work was unclassifiable. The critic concluded, she "fights, with her handful of people, so that her work is seen" (*Le Monde* 1998). Even that may not have been enough. Lamolière notes that there was a gap between the way that critics talk about her and the actual visibility of her company, which was not that great (Lamolière 2020, section 7). Sadly, she passed away in 2014.

However, Ikeda lives on. As with the other women in this book, part of Ikeda's legacy lies in the myriad people she taught. She spent fifteen years teaching at the ImPulsTanz—Vienna International Dance Festival at the invitation of Ismael Ivo (Regensberger and Ivo, 2014). In her hometown of Bordeaux and across the world, she conducted a range of different kinds of dance- and writing-training aimed at

Figure 9.3 Women in bondage in the *Language of the Sphinx*, 1992. Screen capture from Ikeda and Musale, *Ai-Amour, Carlotta Ikeda and Her Butoh*, 1994.

Figure 9.4 Women banding together in the *Language of the Sphinx*, 1992. Screen capture from Ikeda and Musale, *Ai-Amour, Carlotta Ikeda and Her Butoh*, 1994.

different audiences, such as potential collaborators, dance professionals, and new-comers.[7] In bio after bio, dancers mention making a pilgrimage to train with her. One such dancer, Tanya Calamoneri, writes,

> in a weeklong workshop with Carlotta Ikeda at ImPulsTanz in Vienna, I had [an] insect experience in which we were to imagine being eaten alive by bugs, collapse into a riddled mess until we were completely dead, and then rise up as ghosts. By the time we got to the sweet, melodic music at the end, I had thoroughly ex-hausted myself, and so what did rise up for my spirit dance was just a fraction of my strength. I felt like I was dancing almost weightlessly, truly like a floating ghost. (Calamoneri 2012, 15)

Ténenbaum writes that in her training, Ikeda subjects dancers to fatigue, exhaustion, and pain, but that her training forces the dancer to "find an economy different from" normal, in which the will "makes the decision to continue" (Ténenbaum 2002, 207). Here also, a dancer somehow pushed through exhaustion, using her imagination of being a ghost to pull herself upward and to enable herself to float in the air. It was not just her muscles that got her upright. It was Ikeda's combination of training, muscles, imagination, and music that had her floating in the air.

10

Yoshioka Yumiko

Yoshioka Yumiko encountered butô during an indecisive moment as a college student.[1] She answered a flier with various pictures (Bellmer, Marilyn Monroe, etc.) on it advertising for dancers and met Amagatsu and Maro. Within three days, she moved into the Dairakudakan theater/dormitory and started training with Amagatsu for a burlesque show. This training included movements taken from Noguchi taisô and specific movements named "beast" and "Marilyn Monroe." Amagatsu told her that if she ever forgot her movements, she should just freeze, and he would dance around her. Sure enough, on the first day, she forgot her movements for about five minutes and just stood motionless staring at a green exit sign. After some time, she recalled her choreography and finished the set. That green exit sign has played an important role over her entire (still-ongoing) career. This chapter traces the career arc of Yoshioka, an important proponent of mixed-media butô, and one of the dancers who has most embodied what it means to practice butô as an itinerant woman.

Eventually Yoshioka was chosen as the dancer to accompany Murobushi and Ikeda on their foray to Paris, where she appeared under the stage name Hanaoka Mizelle. After that show, she continued dancing with Ikeda in Ariadone until 1981, when Ikeda temporarily disbanded her company. Yoshioka worked as a hostess and in striptease acts for several years, before finally teaming up with Seki Minako and Delta RA'i (Raimund Dischner) to form tatoeba Théâtre Danse Grotesque. Seki and RA'i had both danced with Tamura Tetsuro and Furukawa Anzu of Dance Love Machine, who both choreographed early performances. RA'i had also studied with Maro and taken classes from Ôno. Van Hensbergen notes that their dances found a happy coincidence with the dance theater of Pina Bausch (van Hensbergen 2018a, 282). The Japanese word *tatoeba* means "for example" and they used this term as an indication that they would take example movements from daily life and deform them. The three tried to define butô, but at the same time, expand on butô by focusing more on humor, nonsense, and exploring improvisation (which Yoshioka was never allowed to do in Ikeda's strict choreography).

A 1989 dance, *All Moonshine*, co-choreographed with Seki Minako, features the two kneeling back on their heels on the stage with their backs facing the audience and their hands across their chests and poking out the opposite sides.[2] The program notes spool out Yoshioka's daydream of the pit toilet of her grandmother's house transforming into an ocean, suggesting that Yoshioka conceived of the figures as nearly immobile sea creatures such as snails or anemone. The creatures rise to their knees and almost keel over precariously and then rise to their feet and pursue each other trying

A History of Butô. Bruce Baird, Oxford University Press. © Oxford University Press 2022.
DOI: 10.1093/oso/9780197630273.003.0010

to kiss each other. Dances such as these caught the attention of the German press and the three appeared on television extensively.[3]

In 1995, she founded TEN PEN CHIi Art Labor with the visual artist JoaXhim Manger. One half of the title, "Art Labor," serves as a micromanifesto recognizing the labor that goes into creating art. Butô does not magically gush forth from the artist as Hijikata's chauvinistic rural-Japan worshipers or Ôno's Italian audience thought. It takes labor. Katherine Mezur further observed that the "art labor" of Yoshioka (and other female butô artists such as Kaseki Yuko and Seki Minako) is disconnected from traditional communities and nations (Mezur 2014, 217–220). Many contemporary artists lead a deracinated existence, but Yoshioka (like her fellow female butô artists) seems particularly homeless as she keeps up a grueling schedule of international travel (Mezur calls it "migrant art labour") in order to teach and practice her art (217). You might think it would be better when she goes back to Japan, but in fact, she finds herself "erased from the current arts scene or cast as [an] outsider[], in a separate category from 'Japanese artists'" (219).

TEN PEN CHIi literally means, "sky transforms, earth [becomes] different" and is a four-character Chinese phrase (天変地異) that means "natural disaster." Yoshioka intended to use the concept to explore a multidirectional understanding of the world, in which natural changes influence mental states, just as mental states shape natural states. According to her, humans are invited at every moment to understand and evaluate the changes that happen as humans affect nature and nature affects humans. Yoshioka understands this concept in a distinctly ecological way. When I listen to Yoshioka talk about the connection between humans, the environment and "natural" disasters, I cannot help but think about the thousands of earthquakes caused by fracking or the increasing number of hurricanes and wildfires as the oceans warm, but the deserts and forests dry out.

In keeping with the implicit multidirectionality of Yoshioka's conception of TEN PEN CHIi ("sky transforms, earth different"), she and Manger have explored the relationship between dance, installation art, and the interactions between bodies and technology in pieces featuring complex machinery. Her choreography now is a mix of structured improvisation and minutely crafted dance using imagery work.

I-Ki: An Interactive Body-Dance Machine (1999) features Yoshioka caught in a huge clear plastic tent.[4] The tent is connected by tubes to a huge pneumatic pumping apparatus. The apparatus begins to pump air out of the tent and sends bursts of electricity that shock her at intervals. She seems like she will be simultaneously asphyxiated and electrocuted (see Figure 10.1). Indeed, the title *I-Ki* is homophonous for "breathing," "liveliness," and "life." She fights through the plastic tubing as if she is struggling to get out. Finally, she finds a hole and escapes. She seems unsure of what to do with herself on the outside. She is excited, but then increasingly nervous. She scratches herself and makes fish breathing motions with her hands, as if in fact now on the outside she is asphyxiating. She re-enters the plastic tubing and a bearded man appears on stage. She and she snuggles with him safely within her plastic tubing.

Figure 10.1 Yoshioka Yumiko asphyxiating in TEN PEN CHIi: Art Labor, *I-Ki: An Interactive Body-Dance Machine*, 1999. Direction JoaXhim Manger, and choreogr. Yoshioka Yumiko. Courtesy of the photographer Klaus Rabian.

I-Ki suggests several narrative arcs. One is the "boy in the bubble" narratives of patients with aplastic anemia or severe combined immunodeficiency (SCID) who have such severely weakened immune systems that they cannot survive outside bubbles. Another is the lack of oxygen narrative, in which a character is trapped in a small chamber (outer space, submarine) and running out of oxygen and we watch anxiously to see if they will escape. Finally, there is the narrative of someone who is trapped in some place and escapes only to realize that they liked it all along and want to go back.

Test Labor (2001) appears to depict the laboratory of a mad scientist. Naked bodies lie on shelves, and more bodies are half-submerged in tanks of water (see Figure 10.2).[5] The corpse-like bodies on the shelves climb out of their individual shelves and move around on top of and inside the shelves. The bodies in the pool move around, sometimes crawling over each other and sometimes sitting together spooning in a row. The mad scientist comes on with rabbits. The bodies become increasingly frenetic in their spaces, seeming like they are exploring their spaces and might find a way to escape. Is this some kind of human experimentation? Is he training these bodies to be his soldiers in an egomaniacal plot to control the world?

Figure 10.2 Bodies in the laboratory of a mad scientist? TEN PEN CHIi: Art Labor, *Test Labor*, 2001. Direction JoaXhim Manger, and choreogr. Yoshioka Yumiko. Courtesy of the photographer Klaus Rabian.

In *WA-KU: Déjà vu* (2007), Yoshioka enacts the role of a trainer/promoter/referee for three women boxers who battle it out in a boxing ring with a pool of water as the surface of the ring. She trains them, urges them on during the match, and counts them with her fingers when they are knocked down (see Figure 10.3). It is not clear whether she is counting in order to determine whether or not they have been knocked out, or holding up fingers to determine if they have had a concussion and can understand how many fingers she is holding up. At some point, the boxers turn on her and attack her. Once she has been hit, the boxers seem to accept her into their company and the four participate in a cheerful and erotic melee in the ring, but eventually they seem dazed and unsure where they are.[6] The performance toys with the conventions of female professional wrestling, but also highlights the exploitation and objectification of female bodies in such venues (with particular attention to traumatic brain injuries). Despite the fact that the women seem to genuinely enjoy their romp in the ring (once the boxers make friends with the trainer/promotor/referee), the subtitle, *Déjà vu*, is particularly chilling as it reveals that this has all happened before and will happen again. The main title *WA-KU* means "framework," which of course indicates the boxing ring, but also suggests the structural or institutional frameworks that objectify womens' bodies.

BiKa: Beautification (2009) features two men and two women at a gym with a weight machine at the back of the stage.[7] The four do aerobics, make cheerleader

Figure 10.3 Yoshioka Yumiko urging on the boxers in TEN PEN CHIi: Art Labor, *WA-KU: Déjà vu*, 2007. Direction JoaXhim Manger, and choreogr. Yoshioka Yumiko. Courtesy of the photographer Klaus Rabian.

motions, and run in place. Gradually their efforts to make themselves beautiful distort them and they combine into a series of strange creatures. One creature is formed by the four dancers bending over in a tight circle with their hands to the floor and their buttocks touching each other. Each lifts one leg up and their legs entwine in the space above their buttocks, creating this creature which has four heads facing down to the ground and one entwined leg with four feet in the air. They pulse almost like a jellyfish. In another scene, the women stretch their faces in facial exercises to strengthen their skin and keep it from aging. Meanwhile the men flex so strenuously that they bend their faces out of shape. In these scenes, Yoshioka draws on the vigorous body choreographies of Dairakudakan, and more directly on the stereotypical facial expressions of butô but gives them a context they never had before. The piece closes with the dancers getting trapped in the pulleys and cables of the weight machine, suggesting the danger of spending too much effort trying to beautify oneself.

Overlaid on her company work, Yoshioka also works as an independent dancer and choreographer. One solo dance, *100 Light Years of Solitude* (2016), features Yoshioka imagining a solitary creature 100 light years away from anything else.[8] Given the emphasis of some butô dancers on examining the socialization that forms us, it is intriguing for Yoshioka to attempt to portray a character that is exposed to no socialization whatsoever but still subject to environmental pressure. The result is a half-bug-half-reptile-half-human character in a world in which the categories of human, animal, and insect (that we use to divide our world) are nonexistent (see Figure 10.4.) Perhaps this suggests that the boundaries (or frameworks) between humans, animals, and insects (that we create on our world) are not as clear cut as we might think (or want to admit).

Along with her individual dances and company choreography, Yoshioka and RA'i act as producers of the quadrennial eX . . . it Festival at Schloss Bröllin in northeastern Germany. Much is contained in the name of the festival: the "ex" of ex-change, experience, ex-plore, and ex-it out of yourself. In this there is an impulse to communicate and collaborate between and beyond different languages and cultures and to appreciate and share with each other.

The 1995 festival was a fantastic combination of puppeteers, performing artists, and butô dancers all striving to define butô, use butô to take themselves somewhere new, but also twist and bend butô into something else.[9] There were all different kinds of workshops and all different kinds of performances in all different kinds of spaces and at different times. Dawn, day, dusk, night. Inside, upstairs, downstairs, doors, windows, cracks, outside (close to buildings where the buildings provide the backdrop and away from the buildings in nature), ponds. Choreographed work, improvisation. Large group, small group, pair, or individual work. Slow, fast, still. Wet, dry, dirty, clean, hot, cold, jumbled, prim, grotesque. It was a veritable feast for the senses. In 2007, teams of choreographers with a butô artist working with a contemporary dancer led workshops for the participants and then the teams choreographed a work on the participants as part of their residency.[10]

Figure 10.4 Yoshioka Yumiko in *100 Light Years of Solitude*, 2016. Courtesy of Francisco Amaral.

But there is also the "ex" of that initial green exit sign from Yoshioka's first time on stage when she was frozen without remembering her steps. It might sound paradoxical to advocate for an exit given the emphasis on exchange across cultural and linguistic barriers, but in her practice and teaching, Yoshioka advocates for having an exit sign or strategy as well. This is something to focus on while things are unsettled to give dancers time to collect their thoughts and mentally regroup. Of course, in the end, whether by using their own exit strategy or just because the festival is over, everyone goes to their own exits. The participants return to their own art (and life) labor, but Yoshioka hopes that each participant will take something away, so they are changed as well. Whether by artists traveling to her, or as is much more often the case, Yoshioka traveling to artists, she has provided numberless dancers and artists with chances to "ex-change, ex-perience, ex-plore, and ex-it" out of themselves and be changed in the process.

11
Kasai Akira and Tenshikan

Kasai Akira is such a wonderful enigma that it is hard to know where to begin. He can seem like the smartest person in the room by far, and then he can seem positively surreal—the next in a line of butô artists who stretch life and language beyond their breaking points. His dances are the same. You can be scratching your head thinking you have just seen the absolutely wackiest thing ever, and I always have the feeling that Kasai is never willing to settle for anything less than a performance that has been shaped by the entire universe and has the power to reshape the entire universe.

It is not just life and language that he warps out of recognition, it is also butô. Not initially willing to rubberstamp all of Hijikata's experiments, over his career, he has stood at arm's-length from the art form. At one point, he left butô (and Japan) altogether, not to return for 15 years. And his audiences and fellow dancers have never been sure that he belonged. The kerfuffle at the 1994 San Francisco Butoh Festival is now legendary. A spectator heckled, "That's not butô. You should stop." Instantaneous fury. The spat-out reply: "This is my blood. This is my life."[1] But, it was not so easy to convince people who *knew* what butô was and *knew* somehow that Kasai did not belong.

In Kasai Akira's 2007 *Butoh America*, five Caucasian female dancers wear what Megan Nicely describes as "commercially made generic wear such as that found at capitalistically-driven chain stores that outsource cheap labor" (Nicely 2012, 241). They fawn over and then unceremoniously devour the aging Kasai and dump him into a bathtub, seemingly dead. Gia Kourlas of the *New York Times* saw a "rusty" "random assemblage of scenes," which was "hardly as exhilarating as life and death" (Kourlas 2007). Aynsley Vandenbroucke felt that Kasai's dancing "resonates with my archetypal image of butoh, [but] most of the evening does not" (Vandenbroucke 2007). Nicely sees in the responses a collective search for (or assumption of) a "true butoh," but butô was already a lot of things, not all equally visible in the early years of butô. In the end, Kourlas finds something symbolic about Kasai being devoured by Caucasian women, but takes this to be an accident—a failure of Kasai's choreography—rather than something Kasai set out to do from the beginning. Nicely counters that this is intentional: "What better way to comment on America's fascination with the exotic butoh body than to eat it up?" (Nicely 2012, 241). We could even imagine that Kasai was predicting that the United States would devour him and other butô artists and remake them into what they are looking for, and that Kourlas effectively proved him right by repeating in her review what the dancers had done onstage.

A History of Butô. Bruce Baird, Oxford University Press. © Oxford University Press 2022.
DOI: 10.1093/oso/9780197630273.003.0011

Whatever the case, by dint of cussed doggedness, Kasai managed to shoehorn his way back to the center of the butô world. Butô festivals and producers are flighty creatures by nature—often dependent on schedules and timing as much as any grand vision of butô.[2] But though he failed to capture the attention of the French audience in the eighties, and watched Ôno, Sankai Juku, and Tanaka reap all the glory, more recently, Kasai has seen performers and producers come to him for a form of butô that can be tailored to any individual or circumstances and is methodologically rigorous. He has been invited back repeatedly while other performers have settled for one-year gigs. One example: a standing workshop in Rome every year for seventeen years. Something about his dance has made audiences and performers want to elbow their way back for more.

Kasai's Core Principles

Undoubtedly, much of Kasai's appeal rests on a set of interlocking convictions:

— Art is not a private individual matter, but must be (and necessarily is) connected to the entire universe.
— Everyone (not just artists) must more fully study the relationships between matter, consciousness, language, music, and movement.
— Such study will provide the methodological rigor for each individual to create personally meaningful and universally valid dances *and* allow them to tap into an alternate power, an atheistic materialist mysticism, at work in the universe.[3]
— Politics and history have been dominated by a toxic masculinity manifest in war and armament, and the world desperately requires a completely new way of thinking.
— Part of the rejection of toxic masculinity entails a recognition of alternate sexualities and gender conformations.
— Art must demonstrate a connection to underserved people.

In the coming pages, I track Kasai's dances and examine these convictions more fully.

Early Years and Dance Training

Kasai Akira was born in 1943 in Mie prefecture to an upper middle-class Protestant family. Through his formative years, he felt powerful feelings and emotions from hymns and church rites, but quit going to church in his teens. He was interested in synthetic theater and eventually studied mime and yoga with Ōta Junzō and ballet with Chiba Akinori. He also studied modern dance with Eguchi and Miya, and from 1963 studied with Ôno. He caught the attention of Hijikata because of a performance in October 1962 titled *Sacrificial Ceremony* (Gigi) (Kasai 2004a, 2004b; Kasai et al. 2005). Roughly half of the evening was a duet with and choreographed by Ôno, set to Bach's "O man, bewail thy sins so great," from *St. Matthew Passion*, and the sound of bodies burning in a crematory. In one segment conceived by Kasai, he danced inside a large glass box on stage. Five thousand chicks were suspended above the box and fluttered down into the box gradually filling it. In the course of his improvisational dance, Kasai trod on them and crushed and killed some of them. In retrospect, Kasai characterizes the dance as having been related to Dadaism, and as stemming from a desire to create something "impossible" (Kasai et al. 2005, 54–55). He also wrote that he was preoccupied with treating "human life, volition, emotions, and thoughts" as abstract material for dances "thoroughly and unnaturally separate" from his life, and that he sought to unite "in the world of imagination those things that are opposed to each other" such as life and death (Kasai 2004b, 18). Of this dance he continues, "the process of life was experienced in the thunderous roar of the crematory for dead bodies, [and] flowers bloomed only on the border between life and death" (18). Kasai certainly shared with other early butô performers a desire to remake performance.

He soon became an integral part of the butô world, joining the performances in the mid-sixties such as *Rose-Colored Dance* and *Tomato*. However, he chafed at Hijikata's controlling personality. Apparently, Kasai wanted to hold a recital and Hijikata told him that he would choreograph the entire recital (Kasai 2004a, 58). Gradually Kasai drifted away from Hijikata and Ôno and focused on creating his own dances.

Kasai Setting Out on His Own and Establishing Tenshikan

Among Kasai's early dances were *A Booklet of Acolytes* (Chigo no sôshi, Aug. 30, 1968) and *Tannhauser* (June 11, 1969). The title *A Booklet of Acolytes* is taken from a 14th-century illustrated scroll depicting Buddhist acolytes who were required to cater to the desires (including sexual desires) of high-ranking clerics (Atkins 2008, 950). In these dances, Kasai enacts several cross-dressed characters, already demonstrating his long-term interest in gender (see Figures 11.1 and 11.2). Kuniyoshi refers to this era as Kasai "getting close to spiritual existence by sublimating the physical body and exhausting it with dance" (Kunoyoshi 2004, 3).

In 1971, Kasai established Tenshikan (Angel House) named after Castel Sant'Angelo (Castle of the Holy Angel), the tomb of the Roman Emperor Hadrian, and subsequently military fortress, papal mansion, prison, and museum. He said he was drawn to Castel Sant'Angelo, because it had housed many different kinds of bodies. Kasai characterizes Tenshikan as "without any sort of social power structure or centralized governing force . . . a place for arts and cultural activity in a state of anarchy completely free of any central authority" (Kasai and Ishii 2013). That being said, Kasai clearly occupied the top spot in this antihierarchical world.

Figure 11.1 Kasai Akira in *A Booklet of Acolytes*, 1968. Photograph by Nakatani Tadao. Courtesy of Nakatani Tadashi, NPO Butoh Laboratory Japan, and the Hijikata Tatsumi Archive at the Keio University Arts Center.

As with the other butô dancers, during the 1970s Kasai was working his way through a strange mix of cultural material. In 1973, he presented *The Seven Seals*, but with Shinto zigzag paper *shide* hanging on the backdrop (Kamiyama 2014, 72–73). In 1975, he appeared in *Yomotsu Hirasaka*, the name of the slope that leads to Yomi, the underworld in Japanese myths, but with stage art prominently featuring a banner reading, "R Wagner A Beardsley A Altdorfer" (Kamiyama 2014, 79). Christian title and Japanese religious backdrop, and then Japanese mythical title and European artists. Weird concoctions to be sure.

The 1976 *Tristan and Isolde* features Kasai in a long, flowy floor-length skirt, headscarf, and shawl that look like the pop cultural stereotype of a Middle Eastern woman. His torso is bare and he sucks his stomach in constantly through the performance. He is joined by two women, one of whom is naked from the waist up but covered with white body paint, and the other who wears a dark dress. The two women move slowly and ritualistically through the entire piece, and usually arrive at a pose and then hold it for some time. Kasai also holds poses, but he sometimes moves quite quickly between poses and sometimes moves quite slowly. Many poses contain bent elbows and

Figure 11.2 Kasai Akira in *Tannhauser*, 1969. Photograph by Nakatani Tadao. Courtesy of Nakatani Tadashi, NPO Butoh Laboratory Japan, and the Hijikata Tatsumi Archive at the Keio University Arts Center.

wrists, and all the dancers invariably present striking profiles. One particular pose is taken from Nijinsky's bent-wrist pose in *The Afternoon of a Faun*. This bent-wrist pose becomes the basis for other bent-wrist poses and movements in which the wrists bend in different directions and up and down ninety degrees.

In Kasai's improvisations around and between the women, he does lots of ballet and modern dance movements including jetés, and a barrel roll. He also executes diving somersaults as in judo, backward somersaults, and forward over-the-shoulder somersaults. Unlike the performances based on Sade's works, discussed presently, it is not clear what this has to do with the Tristan and Isolde story, except for the fact that

Kasai uses music from Wagner's opera. Possibly, Kasai was attracted to the emphasis on darkness versus lightness in Wagner's opera, but also possibly just drawn to the passionate music.

As if to literalize both the mid-Eastern hint in his costume and the frequent use of profile poses, he appears for an extended curtain call dressed in an Egyptian outfit with a gold skirt, gold necklace, and stage knives. He raises the knives above his body, crosses them in front of his face, and stabs them into the floor. He repeats the Nijinsky wrist poses, and also walks across the stage sideways with his hands out mimicking the way Egyptians appear to walk on friezes. The movements here, and in the entirety of the dance, are similar to voguing in their use of angular lines and rigid poses. I do not claim that Kasai was watching voguing in 1976. It is highly unlikely that any Japanese person would have had access to images of voguing in that year, although it is possible that Kasai might have seen Crystal LaBeija in Frank Simon's 1968 documentary *The Queen*. Rather, it is likely that both Kasai's movements and the movements of the Harlem ballroom performers represent two different groups coming to terms with various Egyptian images that had flooded the world owing to the Treasures of Tutankhamun exhibit at the British Museum in 1972.

Tragic Tales

Two late 1970s dances were named after the works of Sade. *Tragic Tales* (January 1979) was either named after the short story by Sade, "Eugénie de Franval: A Tragic Tale" (Jpn. trans. 1958 Shibusawa), or possibly the subtitle of Sade's *The Crimes of Love: Heroic and Tragic Tales* (of which "Eugénie de Franval" was a part). In the story, a man has a daughter by a woman and then raises her up to be his lover. Kasai's *Tragic Tales* is divided into two parts. The first part is danced to Lou Reed's 1973 concept album *Berlin*, about a couple who take too many drugs, abuse each other, lose their kids, and then the wife commits suicide. Therefore, Sade's tragedy becomes doubled up with the tragedy of drug use, spousal abuse, and suicide.

Kasai enters a stage with white padded walls on the side and across part of the back, perhaps suggesting either the Charenton Asylum, where Sade was imprisoned twice, or that the husband of the *Berlin* album has gone insane now that he has lost his family. He is dressed in a black suit, white shirt, white scarf, and white face paint, with an orange ribbon in his hair (see Figure 11.3 and Kamiyama 2014, 84–87). His movements are by turns despondent, energetic, and despondent again. Sometimes the energetic moments suggest that he is insane. He walks slowly with jerky movements, arches his back so much that it seems he will fall backward, spins across the floor on his knees, and does judo rolls. Sometimes it seems that he responds directly to either the meaning of the words or the quality of the music. While Lou Reed sings about taking the kids away in "The Kids," Kasai perhaps cradles a child. When Reed croons about the wife slitting her wrists, Kasai seems to be holding something in bed beside him. When Reed's voice climbs "oh oh oh oh oh oh oh what a feeling," Kasai

Figure 11.3 Kasai Akira in *Tragic Tales*, 1979. Photograph by Kamiyama Teijirô. Courtesy of Ikeda Hayato and Minami Shôkichi.

floats through the air, and then drops to the ground and tremors his hands as if he is an addict going through withdrawal. During "Sad Song," Kasai grows wild and frenetic and throws himself around. Then he jumps to grab the top of the side wall with one hand and twists his body to the side in such a way that it looks as if his body is suspended by the neck and he has committed suicide by hanging himself. Back on the floor, he does weird jumping-jack stretches and wanders the stage aimlessly with his hands outstretched.

The second and third sections pick up the general theme of the tragedy but turn the tragedy into a lack of contact between humans even in the moments when they come near each other. Three women in brightly colored blouses, tutus, and tights share the stage with Kasai, who wears a long red gown and then later a dark blue gown with silver spots. The movement characteristic of the three is stiff-torso doll poses with hands out to the sides or in front, and they often arrive at a pose and then hold it. In one moment, one of the women pulls a large black cloth with white splotches from behind the wall. The three wrap themselves in the cloth and walk together, but they do not look at each other, so their interaction is cold even though they are in the same cloth and holding each other. In another moment, they leave the stage and return dressed in huge white robes and walk slowly back and forth across the stage while Kasai glides around and between them. Back in their colorful outfits, at one point, one of them drags the other across the stage by her heels.

Kasai sometimes interacts with the three and sometimes moves among them without any seeming connection to them. In one scene, he kneels behind one of the dancers and she leans backward over him with one leg up in parallel attitude. He briefly lifts her, and then sets her on her knees while she holds her backward arch. He straddles her face, so it is directly in his crotch and then lightly pushes her to the ground. Kasai's movements are hard to characterize. He is alternatingly slow, fast, smooth, and jerky. Flowing movements come from modern dance and ballet. Like the women, sometimes he stops and holds a pose. Kasai also has a tendency in this dance to lean in some direction and then fall out of the lean onto his haunches or to a prone position. He also makes frequent use of knee slides throughout the dance.

In *Tragic Tales*, Kasai straddles the lines between abstraction and narrative dance, and between improvisation and choreography. Frequently, the dance seems like pure abstraction, but then Kasai seemingly hangs himself just as the music refers to a man's regrets because his wife committed suicide. Most of Kasai's own movements seem improvisational, but many of the three women are choreographed. We see a continued emphasis on sexuality and violence. Citing Lou Reed's character (in the song "Oh Jim") who beats his wife when she is unfaithful to show her who is boss, raises the issue of masculinity.

The 120 Days of Sodom

The 120 Days of Sodom (March 1979) was like the early experimental works of butô.[4] The lights come up on a table surrounded by three cushioned wooden chairs, with three black plastic chairs on the other side of the stage. Kasai, dressed in an all black suit, sits behind the table while four other dancers all in long dresses (white, black, brown, and blue) are already improvising. Their moves throughout the dance are generally low to the ground, slow, and blocky. Sometimes they interact almost like slugs mashing into each other. Kasai's movements by contrast are often quite athletic, such as when he leaps into the air from a kneeling position (see Figure 11.4). Kasai also acts as the stage manager through the performance, speaking into a microphone on the table, or wandering the stage dragging the microphone and cord with him (see Figure 11.5). He tells the other performers what to do, indicates to the technicians

Figure 11.4 Kasai Akira leaping into the air from a kneeling position in *100 Days of Sodom*, 1979. Screen Capture.

when to start and stop music, and from time to time speaks to the audience. Most of the time he conducts his stage manager business with a heightened theatrical presence, but sometimes he seems to drop out of character to deliver instructions to his fellow dancers or a technician. Early on, he pushes all the dancers into a pile and then jumps atop them. Later, the dancers with the red and black dresses are tangled up together and Kasai leaps up and lands on them on his knees twice in a row. A moment later, he opens the legs of the dancer in white and mimes penetrating him. Then the dancer in black comes over and simulates anal sex with Kasai. The dancer in brown then comes and jealously pulls the dancer in black off Kasai, and the dancer in white fights off Kasai from below. Perhaps these men are the four of Sade's *The 120 Days of Sodom*, and these moments are abstractions of the sex and violence of Sade's book. From early on, we see Kasai exploring alternate sexualities and particularly the nexus between sex and violence.

In 1980, Kasai performed at the Nancy Festival alongside Ôno, Sankai Juku, and Tanaka Min. However, while Ôno and Sankai Juku were well received, Kasai was largely ignored. Maria Pia D'Orazi argues that the French audiences understood Ôno (with his Western attire and music) in relation to the dance-theater of Pina Bausch

Figure 11.5 Kasai Akira as stage manager in *100 Days of Sodom*, 1979. Screen Capture.

(who also caused quite a stir), but were not ready for the more intense experiments in the relationship between consciousness and matter that characterized the butô of Kasai (D'Orazi 2015).

Studying Eurythmy in Germany

In 1979, Kasai abandoned Tenshikan and traveled to Germany to study eurythmy with Rudolf Steiner. Eurythmy posits a one-to-one connection between movement, music, voice, and speech. Speaking to an audience who had already watched a eurythmy performance and were set to watch another, Steiner said, "The movements all those people were making with their arms, the movements they were making together in a circle, and everything else that they were doing—that was all speech; it was all speaking though not so that you could hear it. It was speaking so that you could see it! What spoke was not the people's mouths, it was their whole being" (Steiner 1984, iii). Talking to his dancers, Kasai echoes, "When you're just about to speak and your hands are going wiggle wiggle wiggle wiggle and you haven't yet said any words, this action is the root of language. If you take that wiggle wiggle wiggle and don't put it into words but keep moving then you dance" (Ito 2014, approximately 33:00).

Kasai returned to Japan in 1986 and conducted eurythmy courses, choreographed eurythmy performances for his students, and lectured on anthroposophy, the philosophy related to eurythmy, and also created by Steiner. It postulates a spiritual world connected to the physical world and supposes that the spiritual world can be studied with precisely the same rigor as the world of the natural sciences. Kasai's eurythmy performances were the polar opposite of butô performances with choruses of dancers dressed in long brightly colored robes sweeping and gliding through the space in time with Western classical music.[5]

He restarted choreographing butô performances in 1994 with *Séraphîta: My Girl with the Mirror Genitalia* with the title taken from Balzac's novel about an androgyne beloved by both a man and a woman. Kuniyoshi notes that in 1999, Kasai started to collaborate with contemporary dancers in Japan in such works as *Yes No No Yes* and *Spinning, Spiral, Shaking, Strobe*. Collaborators were Kisanuki Kuniko and Kondo Ryohei (of the Condors). In this way, Kasai has refused any strictures that one might feel from butô and continued to develop his dances in various ways.

Kasai Techniques (as Experienced in a Workshop)

After his study of eurythmy, Kasai developed his own unique approach to butô based on improvisation, eurythmy, and the continual quest to understand the connection between consciousness and matter (D'Orazi 2019). The best way to understand the attraction and power of Kasai? Spend time training with him.[6] Training with Kasai is a riveting goulash of physical exercises and stream-of-consciousness minilectures about philosophical issues pertaining to dance, history, the body, and living in the modern world.

In a weeklong session in Italy in December 2016, Kasai starts with a discussion of what he calls "original verbs": being, thinking, feeling, and moving. To this, he couples a classification of "original grammar": noun, verb, adjective. These are not, according to Kasai, just categories imposed on the world by language but correspond to ways of being in the world, and to different ways of bodily perception. There is a noun way of being in the world. A verb way. And an adjective way. Humans started our existence as verbs (or so Kasai asserts) and then 500 years ago advanced to an adjective way of being, and currently we are a noun culture. What is more, the "original verbs" correspond to the "original grammar," such that verbs correspond to moving, adjectives to feeling, and nouns to thinking. Kasai then uses these categories as prompts to alter the quality of movements. In the process, he gives two injunctions: "Don't let the original verbs mix but make them independent"; and "Dance is not moving or making form, but creating energy."

He proposes a Latin sentence: "Miseram servitutem falso pacem vocatis" and supplies his own English translation, "Humans mistake enslaved misery for peace."[7] We chant the sentence while moving backward, forward, up, down, right or left, and then say the same words while pushing forward, pushing upward, and backing up and pushing downward. Speaking from personal experience, the phrase seemed to alter the quality of the movements. And conversely, it seemed that the bodily movements accrued some significance or sensation, so that when you moved backward, for example, while chanting about being enslaved, that would alter the way the words come out. It is hard to feel enslaved while driving forward and pushing upward with all of one's might, and conversely it is easier to feel that humans might trade slavery for peace while moving backward.

Next day. Kasai muses about how the world appears to a rock, and then he encourages us to "allow rocks to dance." Segueing to Homer, Kasai wonders, "did he dance, or did he speak?" Homer, he clarifies, "danced a dance and from that words were born." He continues, "To speak is for the throat to dance. First the throat dances, then there is voice, and then there are words." He then proclaims that the "voice comes from the other side of the universe." As if to explain, he contends, "If the Trojan war hadn't happened, we wouldn't be here. If the Persian war hadn't happened, we wouldn't be here. So, my voice speaks from the other side of the Trojan war. And my voice comes from the other side of the universe."

In an exercise, Kasai explores grammatical person. This is the distinction between the speaker, addressee, and other people and things, commonly manifest in English in first person (I), second person (you), and third person (he, she, they, it). Kasai identifies the phrase "I am" as indicative of a first-person viewpoint, while the phrase "The body is X" or "There are some trees" are examples of third-person perspective.[8] We then imagine walking in a forest as if in first person ("I am walking in the forest"). We try to sense the trees around us but always as third-person objects. Then we walk in the imaginary forest again, but as if the forest were the first-person I. As with the previous exercise, trying to move while imagining oneself as a third-person object moving inside a first-person forest produces a strange alteration in the quality of the movement when compared with the sensation of imagining moving through a forest as a first-person I. Peppered into these exercises is Kasai's observation, "There is a grammar of the body. I want you to read the book of the grammar of the body."

Another moment finds Kasai identifying the plié and the arabesque as two fundamental movements with a variety of characteristics. Kasai associates the plié with Mars, the power of ancestors; the power of wrestling, stamping, and war; and with the body or putting on the body. The arabesque, in Kasai's interpretation, is associated with Mercury, culture, waking up, taking off the body, and dying and leaving the body. Kasai is quick to assert that these associations are not ballet-specific, but applicable to all dance.[9] We practice doing pliés and arabesques and feeling respectively Mars/ancestors/wrestling/war/body or Mercury/culture/wakening/leaving the body.

Then we preserve the sensation while doing something else. That is, we try to keep the plié (war/wrestling) sensation while doing something that is not a plié.

We break into small circles and hold hands and each of us tries to imagine that rather than being five separate bodies, we are one entire body. Then we drop our hands but are instructed to retain the sense of being one entire body. Next, we improvise going out from and back into that one entire body, becoming detached (in our imagination) into five separate bodies, and then becoming fused into that one entire body again. Then we mix these sensations with the pliés. We first do pliés with outstretched arms as a group while imagining being five separate people, and then one entire body. Finally, we improvise, experimenting with mixing the sensation of the pliés (ancestors/wrestling/war/etc.) with merging with and going out from the group (one entire body as opposed to five individual bodies).

At this point, Kasai gives a minilecture on the difference between himself and the two founders of butô, Hijikata and Ôno. In his retrospective analysis, Kasai presents Hijikata as having been interested in experience, Ôno as interested in his own bodily perceptions, and he himself as the culmination, because he is interested in the creation of an "infinite number" of bodily sensations. He acknowledges that when you try to pay attention to bodily sensation, you get "separated from experience." Ôno, he says, told him once that he thought too much. But, he proclaims, his goal is to "read body sensations."

Yet another day finds Kasai exploring what he calls "directionality" and "orientation." First Kasai introduces "orientation," which is basically the intentionality of a movement or one's attitude toward the movement. The examples Kasai gives are you doing what you choose (pushing your way up a river), you wishing that something would happen (a mother thinking or saying, "Child, come out of me already"), you being resigned and saying "God's will be done" about something, or even a plant growing. Later, Kasai links these orientations with what he conceives as the twelve fundamental directions: forward, backward, rightward, leftward, diagonally (in four directions, right forward, left forward, right backward, and left backward), inward, outward, upward, and downward. We then mix directionalities and orientations by combining movements: throwing one's hands up or pushing upward while moving forward or pushing down while moving backward. Next, he has us try to feel and isolate the specific energy of each of these directions. He bids us be conscious of how it feels to move forward or be oriented to the front. Kasai then asks us to move backward while holding in our minds the sensation of moving forward to see if this changes the quality of backward movement.

Another day finds Kasai using the famous passage, "In the beginning was the Word," to propose that breath and voice predate humans or deities. He recasts the Bible to say, "In the beginning there was voice." Then he has us voice a sound, and then stop vocalizing but continue exhaling. We try to maintain the sensation that the sound continues even when we have stopped physically vocalizing. One technique for doing this is to cup one's hands at the sides of the head to redirect sound to reverberate back to the ears more than normal. Then he proposes that the AEIOU vowel sounds (pronounced as in Italian or Japanese) are related to breath and voice, and thus are the first elements of language, and are precognitive sounds. As evidence, he postulates that the "Ah" in "Ah, I get it" happens before thought, and necessarily before "I get it," which is an articulation of something that has already happened. Then he has us move in different directions while voicing different vowel sounds.[10] Next he adds specific bodily postures that are taken to correspond to the vowels.

A—arms up and balancing on one leg with the other leg in a triangle with the toe pointing down.
E—arms crossed in front.
I—arms outstretched but right one up diagonally and left one down diagonally.
O—arms out front in a circle.
U—arms pointing down and slightly out to sides.[11]

After we learn the body positions corresponding to the vowels, we execute the vowel positions to the words of the previous phrase "Miseram servitutem falso pacem vocatis." The A-position corresponds to the "a" of "miseram" and the U-position with arms in an inverted U accompanies the "u" of "tutem," et cetera. Finally, we drop out some of the sounds, but try to imagine that all of the sounds (even the unvoiced ones) reverberate all the way to Palermo (266 miles over the ocean).

Considering Kasai's Ideas and Techniques

I hope I have not taxed the reader's patience too much in reproducing Kasai's workshop in such detail, but I trust that you can feel the wonderfully inventive methods of Kasai. Now I turn to what it all means for dance, performance, and all the other issues that Kasai values so deeply.

Interconnected Universe

For starters, influenced by a combination of eurythmy and anthroposophy (with perhaps chaos mathematics and Buddhist philosophy thrown in), Kasai holds that the universe is interconnected in far-reaching but infinitesimally minute ways. As already noted, Kasai asserted that all of us owed some of the peculiarities of our existence to the Trojan and Persian Wars, and then made the much greater claim that voices speak to us from the other side of the universe. The world would certainly be different in the counterfactual in which the Trojan or Persian wars ended differently. It's harder to see how voices can reach across the universe or reach us from the beginning of the universe. But given the way that quantum mechanics holds open the possibility of quantum effect happening at great distances, perhaps it is not surprising that Kasai believes this and it affects how he sees dance and our relationship to it.

Masculine History

For Kasai, there is a darker side to these interconnections. In a conversation with the poet Kawamura Satoru, Kasai identifies a tension at play in history between "universalism" and "individuality, or perhaps diversity" (Kasai and Kawamura 1992, II. 4). Kasai asserts that so-called universalism is actually a European masculinist combination of capitalism and Protestantism that seeks to destroy other peoples and cultures through colonialist policy (II. 5). Later in the conversation, Kasai observes that the Japanese military used Korean women as sex slaves ("comfort women" *ianfu*) and that Africans were brought to the Americas as slaves. Both of these manifest what Kasai calls "male dominated history" (II. 9). Kasai says that in order to "heal the remaining scars" of male-dominated history, the Americas should compensate Africans for being ripped from their homes and sold as slaves in the Americas, and that Japan should compensate the Korean women for forcing them into prostitution (II. 10). Kasai looks forward to a completely new way of thinking of politics and the relationship between politics and art. Part of the work of art for Kasai is to address underserved peoples and contest toxic forms of militarist and colonialist masculinity. What is more, as one can see in Kasai's critique of Japan's sex slavery, Kasai, like most other aware people, is conscious of the way that his own country and culture have participated in male-dominated history by silencing and effacing indigenous populations, outcasts, minorities, and Koreans, but he is also aware of the fact that Japan has suffered at the hands of Western imperialism.

Gender

Many people have noted a preoccupation with gender-bending performances in Kasai's work. However, we should remember that for Kasai, a focus on alternate forms of sexuality is not just a matter of seeing people with alternate sexualities and gender conformations as one more underserved population that art should address, as important as that is. It is as much about the political act of rejecting a certain kind of dominant toxic masculinity (which is taken to infect the recording of history as well).

Understanding Matter and Material

Kasai seeks not just a transformation in the relationship between art and politics but also a transformation in how artists understand matter and material in themselves. Kasai refers to the "riddle of matter" and stresses that there are an "infinite number of existences which cannot be seen by the eye and are of a lower order than matter" (II. 36). Studying matter and material should, according to Kasai, heal the rift between science and religion (which Kasai regards as an unfortunate detour occasioned by the inability of people to properly understand the world around them). Moreover, such study should enable a new relationship between art and political activity so that they become linked and more powerful. Artists who properly understand matter and material will be able to tap into a kind of mystical power at work in the universe. We should carefully distinguish between this mystical power and religious power. Kasai can be understood to ascribe to a secular mysticism or atheistic materialist mysticism. Of course, Kasai often refers to God in his workshops and writings, but he always seems more interested in the dead-God of Nietzsche. In short Kasai seems more interested in the idea of "God" as a shorthand for talking about powers that we do not yet fully understand. One task of the artist is to access such powers, not through the study of religion, and certainly not by getting fooled by an easy-going mysticism, but through the ever-deeper study of matter and material.

Voice Power

One such material is the voice. Nicely observes that for Kasai, there is a "quality inherent in language before it solidifies into forms (such as words or meanings) that dancers can use for movement." She continues, Kasai "understands words to live in the air, and the moving body's encounter with them creates both dance and the body itself" (Nicely 2012, 192–193). In an interview, Kasai talks about how this works in a practical way:

> [Question]: In the 1980's when you were talking about eurhythmy, you would voice a vowel sound and then try to match the reverberations of the sound to your bodily movement. Sometimes shout, sometimes groan, but make sound and body become one.
>
> Kasai: I voice when I am stuck in an improv movement. Sometimes, no matter how hard I try, when I am doing improv, I get stuck. At those moments, what I can manage to produce is words/language (*kotoba*). By voicing, the throat dances. Then it's not a tsunami, but reverberations go out over the whole body. And then another movement is born. I am often helped in this way. (Kasai and Ishii 2013)

Elsewhere, Nicely sums up Kasai's view of voice power as a "vibration-based encounter that resonates long after an initial sound is heard. These ripples or after-effects are the forces that can then be used to act—or dance" (Nicely 2018, 197).

Kasai's Categories

If we step back from the specific exercises, we can think of Kasai as having explored the following categories:[12]

Basic orientations (active, desiring passive, resigned passive, neutral)

Basic directionalities (forward, backward, rightward, leftward, diagonally [right forward, left forward, right backward, and left backward], inward, outward, upward, and downward)

Levels of reality (reality, virtual reality, imagination, dream)

Kinds of bodily perception corresponding to categories of grammar (noun, verb, adjective)

Sexuality (bisexual, heterosexual, homosexual)

Gender (female, hermaphrodite, male)

Grammatical gender (masculine, feminine, neuter—as in *der*, *die*, *das* in German)

Grammatical person (first person, second person, third person)

Types of breathing (inhaling, exhaling, holding breath)

Primal or original verbs (being, thinking, feeling, moving)

Archetypes (Apollo, Mars, Mercury)

Original vowel sounds (AEIOU)

Relationships to places (Dancing in a place, dancing the place,[13] and having a place dance inside oneself [Nicely 2012, 190])

Kinds of matter (mineral, vegetal, animal) (Nicely 2012, 195, 225)

Kinds of power (voice power, thinking power, song power, muscle power, mechanical power)

Musical keys (major, minor[14])

Types of body's age ("The body before conception, the fetal body before birth, the infant body during the period when the child is absorbing its mother language, and then the adult body . . . [and] the body after death" [Kasai and Ishii 2013])

I will not unpack each of these, but take "Kinds of bodily perception that correspond to categories of grammar." Kasai presumes there is a noun, adjective, and verb way of being in the world. These purportedly correspond to specific eras (Kasai claims for example that currently humanity perceives in a noun way, but that 500 years ago humanity perceived in an adjective way, and that before that humanity perceived in a verb way). He thinks these ways of perceiving correspond to being, feeling, and moving.[15] Then he asks the dancer to feel, perceive or move in a noun, verb, or adjective way.

Earlier, I noted that Hijikata had a nearly infinite number of modifications he could make to a movement. Kasai also seeks to create an "infinite number" of operations he can perform on a movement in order to modify it.[16] He can move while imagining being male, female, bisexual, straight, or gay, and see what happens to the movement. He can move while imagining that he is dreaming or in virtual reality. He can move while inhaling or exhaling. He can move while imagining himself as an unknowable third-person he/she/it, or he can imagine himself as an omniscient third-person narrator surveying his own movement from above. He can move while imaging himself to be a fetus, corpse, child, or adult. In each case, the energy of what is being imagined changes the movement in subtle or sometimes quite obvious (but always very real) ways. To continue the comparison, we saw that Hijikata explored the minute segmenting and particalization of the body (can dancers spread attention out to 3,000 spots on the body and feel an insect biting them in 3,000 distinct places?). Kasai parallels this with attention to minute sensations of the voice and its reverberations.

Even before Kasai, via the study of Ishii Baku, Eguchi, and Miya with Wigman, butô already had one root in Rudolf Laban's (1879–1958) idea of cataloging a universal transcultural psychophysical vocabulary. Perhaps this basic orientation was strengthened by Kasai's study in Germany with Steiner. Kasai claims a core part of his dance is exploring ways to create new types of energy, and that one way in which he has built on the dance of Hijikata and Ôno is to create a classification system for every interaction between the body, language, and mind as a tool for creating new energy and new movements. Then, as part of this exploration, Kasai tries to see what kind of energy he can create or what new movement he can find by applying each element of each classificatory scheme to all the elements of all the other schemes.

Pollen Revolution

Two of Kasai's recent performances offer more iterations of his concerns. In 2002 Kasai Akira premiered the solo *Pollen Revolution* (Kafun Kakumei).[17] Kasai started the dance dressed as and dancing as the female impersonator from the noh and kabuki play *Kyokanoko Musume Dojoji*, a play about a jilted woman. In rage, she turns into a serpent and incinerates the priest who spurned her. In the kabuki version, the female impersonator dances several aspects of the young girl's love. One reviewer describes Kasai as initially the epitome of grace and control (Mikhaila 2004). Small electronic pulses interrupt the classical Japanese music and these manifest as minute tremors disturbing the grace of Kasai's dance. Eventually things fall apart into violent twitching and spasms. Passing through a costume change, Kasai devolves into "a modern man in a gray-scale techno world" and then after another costume change, ends dancing hip-hop to the music of Run-DMC (see Figure 11.6).

It is hard to connect Kasai's movement-generation methods with any particular movement on stage. In any one moment, is he is retaining the sound of an unvoiced "e" while holding the Mars orientation while dancing like a bisexual in a dream state? Or is he rather retaining the sound of an unvoiced "e" while holding the Mars orientation while dancing like a bisexual in a virtual reality state? In truth, he has so many options that it would probably be a fool's errand to try to tease out which particular set of mental exercises belong to which movement. However, Tanya Calamoneri argues that we can see the results of Kasai's attempt to isolate and catalog kinds of energy and create new varieties of energy in the way that Kasai is able to charge the performance space with energy (Calamoneri, pers. conversation, April 28, 2021). And sure

Figure 11.6 Kasai Akira in *Pollen Revolution*, 2004. Photograph by Kamiyama Teijirô. Courtesy of Ikeda Hayato and Minami Shôkichi.

enough, one can almost feel the air crackling with energy as Kasai dances the close of the piece.

Many reviewers saw Kasai as acting out a struggle against time or some other centripetal terror. As Nicely puts it, "Kasai's revolutionary work presents a number of threats to stability, even as dance attempts to equalize them. From organic and inorganic forces to the seeming conflict between tradition and the new, and from gender difference and differences between cultures to the poles of "tradition" and the new in butoh, Kasai's work challenges human perspectives in disaster" (Nicely 2012, 234). Others saw him as incorporating into his dance various dance styles from various cultures and then disassembling these styles.

For Kasai, pollen is indicative of life force, so a "pollen revolution" is a moment when the life force of the universe causes new life. Kasai also cites with admiration the "first creature that came onto land from water." He continues, "Similar to the challenges it had leaving the safety of its familiar saltwater for land, human beings today seem to be trying to create a completely new environment" (UMS Concert Program 2004). So, we might read both the kabuki and hip-hop in this dance as moments when life force spouted anew. Kasai encourages such a reading by observing that hip-hop and butô both came from the bottom of society (as did kabuki before it) (Kasai 2004c).

For Kasai the "pollen revolution" is not just a generic manifestation of life force, but rather a transformation in life force that enables people and things to adjust to a new environment, whether that be fish surviving on land, kabuki in the 1600s, butô in 1960s Japan, or hip-hop in the 1970s Bronx. We can, however, go one step beyond understanding pollen as life force. Nicely notes that Kasai recontextualizes his dance in terms of potential harm to the human race (Nicely 2012, 234–235). She continues, "Kasai's approach is to take this threat inside and act to neutralize it, and in this way disarm what is perceived but intangible" (236). Nicely, has, in essence, turned the conception of pollen on its head: Pollen as allergen.

We can extend this conception of pollen as allergen. Deleuze considers allergens in his discussion of an exchange between Spinoza and Blyenbergh. Blyenbergh wants to find a foolproof definition of both evil acts and evil people. Spinoza resists this, and replies that evil lies not in people or actions, but in disrupting relationships (Deleuze 1988, 31–32). This is how poison works. Deleuze notes that for Spinoza poison is not evil for some transcendental reason. It is bad because it disrupts relationships (between me and other people, or between parts of my body) (32–33). Allergens are a special case because they only disrupt relationships for some people, and not for everyone, meaning that they are only poisons for some people and not for everyone.

In this light, Kasai's *Pollen Revolution* can be seen to ask pointed questions about the (originally) marginal arts of a society: Are kabuki, butô, and hip-hop allergens to society? And if so, why? And if not, why not? What is it about healthy societies that allow them to incorporate hip-hop or kabuki into themselves, as opposed to rejecting them? Do societies think of the pollens of butô and hip-hop as allergens and try to avoid them, or as a manifestation of revolutionary life force and embrace them?

I Dance the Japanese Constitution (First performance, October 27, 2013)

I Dance the Japanese Constitution provides another fascinating aperture into Kasai's understanding of the relationship of language to the body, but also his concerns about war and masculinity. The basic structure features a chorus chanting in eurythmic style excerpts from Japanese myth, different Japanese constitutions (the Meiji Constitution, and the postwar Peace Constitution), and from other notable recordings and sources such as the emperor's Jeweled Voice broadcast to Japanese citizens to announce the end of the war, and Mishima's "Voices of the Heroic Dead." Meanwhile, Kasai dances and flails about the stage constantly talking. Sometimes he voices the same words as the chorus, sometimes he exhorts them to voice more strongly, sometimes he talks about how he felt about proposed changes to the Japanese constitution (see Figure 11.7).

In a conversation in 1992, Kasai addressed what he saw as some of the problems of the postwar Japanese constitution. Principal among those was that the constitution did not stem from what Kasai termed "custom law" (Kasai and Kawamura 1992, 24–27). By 2013, Kasai had come to see the postwar constitution in a different light. Earlier that same year, Kasai organized a eurythmy retreat in which the topic was "Creating the Japanese Constitution from the Body through Eurythmy" (Kasai 2013), so he must have been thinking about how people could make the constitution their own. In the promotional materials, he wrote:

> The constitution is not a gift from God. It is the result of the laws of the body being created as the skeletal structure of the body of the country through the flow of history. It is not just a fabrication created by the Occupation Authorities in the past.

Figure 11.7 Kasai Akira in *I Dance the Japanese Constitution*, 2013. Photograph by Kamiyama Teijirô. Courtesy of Ikeda Hayato and Minami Shôkichi.

It is something that is born out of the human body which passes through three stages of development. By moving our bodies to several passages of the constitution in a eurythmic manner, I want participants to have a bodily sensation of the connection between the constitution and their bodies, and to create connections between the individual body and the social body. (Mikka 2013)

In a blog post at roughly the same time, Kasai wrote:

Reading the LDP Constitutional Revision Proposal, I feel keenly that we are moving from the sovereignty of the people to the sovereignty of the state. Originally the constitution let the human live to its utmost as an individual, not only through the ability of citizens to restrict the power of the state through the constitution, but through the ability of a single individual to do so. The constitution which was promulgated on Nov. 3, 1946, enlivens thoroughly and to the utmost extent possible an ideal and an idealism, which is not the human as abstract entity, but the human as an individual. The constitution is the power of "true language" not born from within our country but brought to us from outside our country by those who have lost their homeland. The proposed changes to the constitution by the LDP do not break free from the realm of custom law, and it is a constitution that does not have any ideals or idealism. As Chikushi Tetsuya says, a country that doesn't have ideals or idealism will collapse. (Kasai 2013)

In the program for the performance, Kasai wrote:

I have never seriously encountered the Japanese government nor the 1946 Japanese constitution in my 50 years of dance life. But recently when I read that the Liberal Democratic Party was proposing to revise the constitution, I felt my blood rustle noisily in my body. When I inclined my ear to that wordless voice, I intuited that the 1946 constitution was my skeletal structure. And I had the conviction that the fundamental ideas of Liberty, Equality, and Fraternity are applicable not just to those living today but were applicable for all those who have passed on, and that they are the law of the universe. The constitution should always be imbued with the most supreme ideals. I aim to give one bodily form to my ideas. (BankArt 2013)

From this information, we can see that Kasai had come to think of the constitution as grounded in universe-al ideals.[18] Rather than worrying about the constitution as an imposition from without, he had come to think of the constitution as intimately connected to his body and properly expressed through it. For Kasai, because each minute bit of language/voice matters and language connects to bodily configurations, the words of a constitution will form the "skeletal structure" of the people within the sphere of that constitution. Kasai might be dancing the idea that you cannot change the (words of the) constitution without changing everyone in (Japanese) society as well. This fits with Kasai's critique of masculinity, because the constitutional revisionists seek to enable Japan to adopt an aggressive military policy, rather than the defensive posture they now have.[19] If that is the case, Kasai is basically arguing (in dance form) that if you change the very words a society is organized by and create a constitution that is much more "masculine" and enables Japan to engage in offen-sive warfare, then you change the "skeletal structure" of the people. One viewer inter-preted the show as depicting the "Constitution emerg[ing] to sweep away the dark atmosphere covered in images of death since the Imperial Constitution" (Ito 2014).

In subsequent years, Kasai expanded the dance to include more performers and the recitation came to include excerpts from Rudolf Steiner's "Prayers for Mother and Child," Yosano Akiko's antiwar poem "Thou Shalt not Die," and the Preamble and 1st, 2nd, 9th, 12th, 13th, 14th, 19th, 20th, 24th, 66th, 96th, 97th, 98th, and 99th articles of the Constitution.[20] Again observers interpreted the reading of the postwar constitution as the pinnacle of the performance. I only saw the first version, but from the tone of sub-sequent reviews, it was deeply moving to see the ferocity of Kasai's dancing while the chorus recited the Articles dictating that the emperor is a symbol of the state (rather than the sovereign), the renunciation of war, the exhortation that the people must endeavor to preserve their rights, the guarantee that people will be respected as individuals, the equality of the people, freedom of thought, freedom of religion, equality of the sexes, necessity of all the ministers of state to be civilians, and the declaration that the human rights guaranteed by the constitution are age-old and time-tested.

Kasai repeated the dance, usually each May 3rd on Constitution Memorial Day. And thus, in Kasai's hands, butô became the vehicle by which both dancers and audiences re-considered their relationship to the constitution and to the ideals they want their country to embody. Moreover, in Kasai, butô continues as a means by which dancers and audi-ences explore what kind of body-mind (skeletal structure) they want to inhabit.

Conclusion

Kasai trained an important crop of dancers. They include Yamada Setsuko, Yamazaki Kota, and Omori Masahide. They have continued Kasai's quest to remake dance and butô at each and every turn. For example, Yamazaki Kota relocated to France and studied nouvelle danse, and then moved to the United States, where he has col-laborated with African American and African choreographers such as Charles O. Anderson (Dance Theatre X) and Germaine Acogny. At the same time, Kasai him-self has been active in promoting his understanding of dance, language, music, and the body. Maria Pia D'Orazi describes a shift in the understanding of butô in Italy, which in my experience is paralleled by a general shift in the understanding of butô by many dancers throughout the world. First, she says that dancers were captivated by Ôno and took from him an understanding that butô took no skill, but rather stemmed from improvisational expression of one's deepest urges and emotions (D'Orazi 2018, 263). Then, people became interested in the bodily technique of Iwana Masaki. Iwana was a butô outsider, but his approach to dance was close to Hijikata's with a classification of bodily states and the use of images to evoke energy to realize such states (266). However, she argues the dancers could not make his techniques their own. Rather, she argues that they ended up embodying Iwana's "internal landscape rather than their own" (269). There was a similar risk in studying with other butô dancers. Eventually, many Italian dancers (as well as other dancers around the world) gravitated to Kasai. He presented his techniques "as a way to connect motion to the energy of bodily sensations and to the energy of words" (269). And he communicated an urgency about the proper scope and purview of dance with his emphasis on dismantling masculinist history and recognizing and creating alternate modes of being that appealed to dancers who wanted their own performances to speak to the ends of the universe in much the way that Kasai's performances had the potential to do. In this way, Kasai's techniques could be used by anyone to create their own dances. As D'Orazi observes, "the possible results of Kasai's scattered seeds are still wide open" (274).

12
Amagatsu Ushio and Sankai Juku

One evening at a cocktail party, I was chatting with a fellow who had successfully lobbied UNESCO to alter the criteria for the "Mixed" designation so that Pimachiowin Aki indigenous ancestral lands could qualify as a World Heritage site. He was obviously cosmopolitan and had a concern for the environment and diversity that anyone would welcome. Eventually, the conversation wound its way around to me and I introduced myself as a scholar of butô. He looked at me with astonishment and blurted out that the most amazing performance he had ever seen was butô. He had clearly seen many performances, so this was not trivial praise. I asked who he had seen, but I already knew the answer: Sankai Juku.[1]

I start here because Sankai Juku was the public face of butô for decades. They have performed in 47 countries and in more than 700 cities. It is no small thing to reach that many people and to make a performance that is the most amazing performance of a person's life. In this chapter, I start with their first major dance, *Kumquat Boy*, in order to sketch a starting point for head-choreographer Amagatsu Ushio after he split from Dairakudakan. Then I switch to dances created in Paris and seek to describe what made their performances appealing to so many people. Part of their success lay in tapping into an Orientalist fascination with Japanese religion and thought. They benefited from an association with New Age thought and music. They were also exploring the same issues as the other butô choreographers, such as nature, universality, and the place of the body in the world. Specifically, I explore the ideas of Amagatsu with a special emphasis on his idea of synchronization with gravity and the lowest possible effort.

Biography and Early Dance Training

Amagatsu Ushio (real name, Ueshima Masakazu, 1949–) was born and raised in a seaside fishing village near Yokosuka, Japan.[2] The shadow of the war lingered over the town, but his father sustained the family comfortably as an electrical engineer. Amagatsu reflects on his upbringing in idyllic terms, mostly focusing on his encounters with the vastness, constancy, and rhythms of the ocean. In his teens, he worked in a boat rental shop and yearned to buy his own boat. It was not all sun and beach games though. At some point, he reports that he realized that his bucolic existence could not last. For the first time he felt death staring him in the face. He also felt the pressure of the educational track and longed to step off that path.

A History of Butô. Bruce Baird, Oxford University Press. © Oxford University Press 2022.
DOI: 10.1093/oso/9780197630273.003.0012

At some point, his family moved to the more upscale Kamakura, where he frequently listened to jazz. Soon it was time for college, but Amagatsu could not stomach the thought. He convinced his parents to send him to a year of college prep school but dropped out after a day. He spent a year treading water. Finally, he begged his father to send him to the Aoyama Sugisaku Memorial Actor Training School.

Amagatsu's father had been drafted at the age of 20 and then, like Ôno, was trapped in New Guinea until long after the end of the war. Having had his life ripped from him, he was determined not to do the same thing to his son. So, he paid for three years of actor training. Amagatsu studied the Stanislavski system, modern dance (Graham method), ballet, traditional Japanese dance, and above all, Noguchi taisô. He worked part time at the Nichiei Theater company, where he was exposed to Peter Brook, the Royal Shakespeare Company, the Moscow Art Theater, the German Opera Berlin, and Alvin Nikolai, among others. Eventually, even the institutional nature of the actor's school became too much, and he quit over a perceived slight.

He was free floating. Then he met Maro, who had recently quit Kara Jûrô's Situation Theater and was casting about for something new. Amagatsu was apparently dissatisfied with prior dance and theater forms, but he talks as though he was swept along by Maro, not as if he chose butô intentionally because of anything intrinsic to it (Amagatsu 2015, 14). Whatever the case, he helped cofound Dairakudakan, but he confesses that he felt intimidated and unprepared for the artistic and intellectual debates swirling around him.

Amagatsu choreographed some scenes, such as the lute scene in *The Story of a Phallic God*, but he passes over his time in Dairakudakan in relative silence (Harada 2004, 192). He casts himself as having intentionally avoided being sucked into the orbits of the giants of the community. We know that he participated in the cabaret performances, because he was the one who coached Yoshioka Yumiko on her first day on the job.

Founding Sankai Juku

The Dairakudakan motto was "One person, one troupe," so three years later, he started his own company, Sankai Juku (Mountain Sea School). Maro suggested the name, taken from the *Guideways through Mountains and Seas*, a Chinese bestiary (Strassberg 2018). Maro also gave him the stage name Amagatsu, a kind of sympathetic magic doll placed by an infant to ward off evil. Amagatsu says that for him, the name represented the dancer "portraying the shape of many people on stage" (Amagatsu 2015, 22).

Roughly 30 people showed up to his first workshop, excited to join in creating something new. Imagine their surprise to find that Amagatsu had no intention of creating a performance, but rather wanted to work on the fundamentals: ballet, modern, and Noguchi taisô. They trained like this for a year. Eventually, only three male students remained. The company has consisted entirely of males ever since.[3]

Their first performance was *Amagatsu-shô* (Homage to Amagatsu/Homage to Ancient Dolls, April 27–29, 1977). We do not have much information about this dance. The title contains a wordplay, making it sound like a narcissistic homage to Amagatsu himself, but also to the dolls referenced in his name. Amagatsu was apparently dissatisfied with it, and immediately got to work creating *Kumquat Boy* (*Kinkan shônen*), which premiered June 24–25, 1978, at the Nihon Shôbô Kaikan Hall.

Kumquat Boy

Kumquat Boy consists of seven "tableaux" and a choreographed bow (tableaux names taken from a CD of the music by Yoshizawa).[4]

1. "Kumquat Boy: the stirring of memory ... toward the beginning." A young bald boy in a school uniform appears. Behind a suspended ring, he opens his mouth in a silent scream and then falls flat on the ground. He rises slowly, twists his body, reclines. A warning gong sounds. He falls to the ground, devours grains of sand (or possibly uncooked rice grains) ravenously, and then spews them out. He makes strange accordion/jellyfish pulsations with his open fingers in front of chest (almost as if he has some kind of extreme pain in his stomach).

2. "Hands of darkness (Yami no te): through the microscope—solemnity of ritual." Four dancers stand on a platform in paint-splattered skirts with papier-mâché masks covering their faces. Hundreds of tuna tails cover the side and back walls. They gradually raise and lower themselves, swaying. They reach for each other with spidered hands. With their backs toward us, they do a provocative half-striptease, swaying so that their skirts begin to fall from the waists revealing their buttocks, but spreading their legs to keep the skirts from falling completely to the ground.

3. "Peacock: the vanity of nature." Under a huge red ring, Amagatsu appears carrying a peacock. He performs sideways lunges and King Tut hand movements.[5] He throws the peacock into the air and it perches on his shoulder. He dances with elbows out but wrists in. The bird seems to struggle to stay on him and then flies away while he gesticulates reaching into the air. He pecks like a bird, spiders his hands on his own chest, and then squats with one leg extended.

4. "Secret Pleasure (Higyô): conveying an impossible legend—some point within the town." Pairs of nearly naked men appear on a dark stage accompanied by music of Miles Davis. They strut in front of each other like peacocks. They embrace themselves like strippers, then one lies down on his side in a seductive swimsuit-model pose with his head resting on his hand. The stage right couple engage in vigorous wrestling moves mixed with homoerotic moves almost like anal sex. The movement suggests a struggle for control, but also quick reversals of control. One appears to be on top and in control, but then the other rolls into a superior position. There are moments that look like a fireman's carry

take-down followed by a pin. Moves from amateur and professional wrestling such as a headlock and leglock are recognizable. Then the two seem exhausted, with one in the lap of the other, and their heads moving toward each other as if kissing.

5. "Bean Boy (Mametarô): a creaking laugh." A smiling wide short kimono-clad character who looks as if he is a dwarf has trouble ascending a dais, because of his height (see Figure 12.1). When he finally climbs on it, he immediately falls off. He struggles to stand and does a sideways suriashi, or ticktock. Then he sheds his kimono to reveal a ratty canvas corset-dress. Rising to full height, he runs the four corners of the stage with his kimono flaring out behind. Accompanied by the sounds of "Highland Laddie" on the bagpipe, he does a sort of jig, splashing sand with his feet and kicking sand out of the way. As he does it, he cries, silently screams, or reaches for something else, almost as if his body has been taken over by something else and it is actually painful to be forced to dance.

6. "Processing/Disposal Plant (Shoriba, Romanized as "sholiba" in programs): the place of capture—endless." Three men appear in wrap skirts and bandannas with some sort of glass rod affixed to their heads. They sway back and forth with their hands out front, crossed at the waist. Mouths open, they silently scream, and then gasp like fish out of water. Then they face the back squatting on one knee and one foot with arms outstretched. They take out their wands and toss

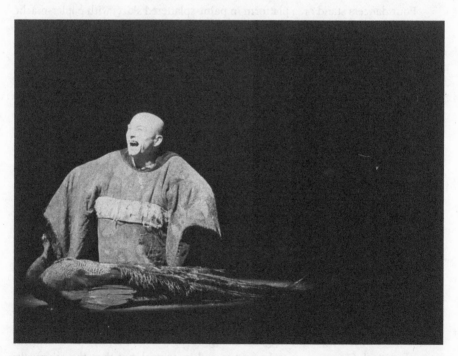

Figure 12.1 Kumquat Boy, 1980. Mametarô. Courtesy of Fonds Jean-Marie Gourreau-Médiathèque of the Centre national de la danse.

them on the ground where they stand upright. They fall to their back and sides over and over.

7. "The Iron Bird (Kinzokusei no hichô/Asuka): the stirring of memory—toward the beginning." To piercing rifling sounds over the top of a low machinic hum and samples from the Largo of Dvorak's "New World" Symphony No. 9, a single character is suspended upside down within a blue rectangle of light. His hand motions suggest a flower opening and closing. He pushes his shoulder severely out of joint, and then the rope he is attached to begins to rotate slowly. Dancers appear behind the suspended figure walking slowly downstage in half squat with arms crossed on their chests and then spreading their arms out in front and crossing them again. The hanging dancer begins to rotate more quickly with his hands crossed on his chest. The four run the fingers of one hand up the other outstretched arm. They end with a beauty queen wave, and the dance merges seamlessly into slow statue curtseys and more beauty queen waves.

Considering *Kumquat Boy*

Reviews of this dance tended to fall into three buckets. The first is attempts to find a unified narrative that would explain the entire dance. Marcelle Michel of *Le Monde* understood the dance as portraying a "regression beyond childhood memories, beyond the birth" of the boy of the first scene (Michel 1982b). In the *New York Times*, Anna Kisselgoff wrote that the dance is a "reverie on the origins of life" that "deals with evolution" (Kisselgoff 1984). The second is people who assumed that the dance is purely abstraction. The Nobel Literature Prize laureate Czesław Miłosz wrote that *Kumquat Boy* "was almost a model of Pure Form—that is, of pure dance movement for its own sake" (Miłosz 1995, 137). The third is people who just threw up their hands. Clement Crisp of the *Financial Times* and Mark Monihan of the *Telegraph* complained that the dance was incomprehensible (Monahan 2008; Crisp 2008). In keeping with my main theme of enriching our appreciation of the dances by better understanding their cultural background, I suggest that none of these three is the optimal way of approaching this dance.

The program contained notes and an "Introductory Poem." These along with the tableaux names presented quite specific images (a child standing on a beach, a species of fish evolving to walk on land) that seem to preclude a purely abstract reading. At the same time, the notes, poem, and tableaux titles present such a jumble of information that it not possible to create a coherent narrative the encompasses them all. Rather, *Kumquat Boy* offers a series of unconnected moments that each offer their own opportunities for exploration and reflection.

Going out of order, "Iron Bird" is opaque, but striking because of the dancer suspended upside down. The bird is *hichô*, which literally means "flying bird," but the Chinese characters can also be pronounced 'Asuka', which is the name of a premodern era in Japanese history (CE 538–710). Perhaps the Iron Bird is simply the suspended figure. But the next dance, *Jômon-sho* (*Homage to the Cord Pattern Era*), also has a reference to a historical period of Japan, so that reference makes it seem likely that this reference to the Asuka period was intentional, even if it is not obvious what Amagatsu might have intended by the reference.

Higyô or "Secret Pleasure(s)" is where things get really interesting. The title of the tableau is taken from the second half of Mishima's *Forbidden Colors* (Mishima 1953, incorporated into the final book as chapters 19–32), the same book that Hijikata cited in his versions of *Forbidden Colors*. In it Mishima describes a variety of male–male sexual encounters, but most notably a scene in which the protagonist Minami attends a party at the estate of a rich man. He looks out a window and is surprised by the scene: "Here and there in the grassy garden were clumps of bushes and shrubbery. In each of the shadows thrown by them there was a shadow locked in embrace" (Mishima 1968, 310; see also 329–336 and 62–63). Whereas Hijikata only borrowed the barest of hints from Mishima for his homoerotic encounter, Amagatsu explores gay encounters in much more detail. Given the reports that the pre-2005 version of "Peacock" included Amagatsu intimating humping the peacock, it is possible that "Peacock" and "Secret Pleasure(s)" are a pair. Perhaps Amagatsu substituted a peacock for Hijikata's chicken, and took his scene title from the second part of Mishima's work rather than the first. If so, it seems as though Amagatsu has initiated a conversation with Hijikata by restaging *Forbidden Colors* (which of course he had not seen) in the middle of his dance. If that is the case, the two tableaux would stand in a meta-relationship to the first quasi-butô performance. We might see Amagatsu as basically announcing a new beginning for butô.

The frankness of the portrayal in "Secret Pleasure(s)" is striking, even accounting for the fact that Hijikata and Maro had already treated the theme of male–male sexuality. These might be courtship rituals between two gay couples in the garden in Mishima's novel. Or a window into the intimate life of different gay couples, with a suggestion of the diversity of experience within the broader group. At times, the encounters look like a zero-sum game, with only one person in control and the other powerless (see Figure 12.2). At other moments, pinning combinations are easily reversible into positions of power and control for the other person. In still other moments, the men show genuine tenderness for each other. Anyone (of any sexual orientation) who has loved another person will recognize the fights, the compromises, the reversals, the raw hunger and desire, the tender moments, the movement in unison, and the movement at odds with the other, that accompany any complex relationship between equals. Anna Kisselgoff calls the wrestling couple "an extraordinary duet" (Kisselgoff 1984). On the strength of this tableau alone, Amagatsu can lay claim to being a major choreographer.

For whatever reason (perhaps he or his producers feared a negative reaction from the non-Japanese audiences to homoerotic elements), Amagatsu chose to transliterate (rather than translate) the title of the tableau as "Higyo," effectively quashing any possibility for a non-Japanese audience to catch the allusion to Mishima's work about gay men. We should be talking about this tableau as a significant moment in queer

Figure 12.2 "Secret Pleasure" (Higyô). *Kumquat Boy*, 2009. Screen Capture.

dance history. However, Amagatsu makes it almost impossible to do so. The reviewers seldom write about the dance in terms of its homoerotic content, but rather in terms of what it might say about an evolutionary progression of the species.[6] Kisselgoff refers to the peacock as "a natural creature of beauty contrasting with the succeeding images of human evolution." Then she continues, referring to the "Secret Pleasures" tableau (that she only knows as "Higyo"), "Aggression takes root" (Kisselgoff 1984). Sure, but it only makes sense to understand this tableau as a moment in evolution when two males of the same species fight each other if you do not know about the reference to Mishima's novel. She could have also written, "Secret pleasures take root," or "Love and tenderness take root." Rosemary Candelario specifically critiques Kisselgoff's Orientalism and her tendency to turn butô into an ancient ritual (Candelario 2016, 91–94). Yet, even if Kisselgoff had been prone to thinking about butô as dealing with contemporary matters, some readings were cut off from her. When Kisselgoff tried to make sense of the dance, she fell back on the other pieces of information and defaulted to an interpretation concerning ancient evolution rather than reading the individual scene as a window onto male–male sexual encounters in postwar Japan.

The title of the tableau "Mametarô" refers to a Tom Thumb–type story of a 3-centimeter-tall boy who makes good in the larger world.[7] Both Kisselgoff and Walther call the tableau a "tour de force" (Kisselgoff 1984; Walther 1984). They are right. The tableau is riveting, and it shows off Amagatsu's abilities to great effect. Critics were drawn to the complexity of the character's emotions. Godard refers to this character as "hollowed out by a smile without joy" (Godard 1980b). Later, Walther countered that it was "the best inaudible howling laughter one could ever see" (Walther 1984). Then the character sheds its thick kimono and rises to full height in a tattered canvas corset-dress. Despite the fact that the character kept smiling, critics felt an edge to the portrayal see Figure 12.3). Michel called it a "frenzied jig to a lively bagpipe tune" (Michel 1982b). Monahan termed it, "can-canning dementedly across the stage" (Monahan 2008). Clement Crisp saw it as "skipping about in a seriously unhinged reel" (Crisp 2008). The different reactions show that Amagatsu was seen as expressing

Figure 12.3 Compelled to dance. *Kumquat Boy*, 1980. Courtesy of Fonds Jean-Marie Gourreau-Médiathèque du Centre national de la danse.

different emotions. In fact, Amagatsu cycles through an impressive range of emotions. The character is inquisitive and curious, surprised, happy, sad, anguished, determined, resigned, compelled. Whoever these two characters are, they live fully complex mental lives that produce mixed emotions on their faces.

The complex personality of the Bean Boy character makes him compelling. What is more, the character has a different body type from most people, and expresses gender differently from most people. This is what butô is usually all about: trying to understand (however unsuccessfully) the inner world of someone else, and particularly someone who does not fit in with normal society. When faced with such a character, I want to know more. What is the story behind this Bean Boy that makes him determined in the face of obstacles, but also compelled to dance a jig long past when it has ceased to be fun? Are these just two moments in the life of a short folk tale character? Or are they indicative of some other pain and pleasure? For me, Amagatsu's "Bean Boy" evokes little people. The fact that the character seems obliged to put on a happy face while it falls over perhaps alludes to expectations society places on little people and the struggles they face. When the character later seems compelled to dance a gender-blurring jig, I cannot help but think about people who do not fit gender norms, and I wonder how it feels to be required to continue performing a gender you do not feel.

Kumquat Boy was still very much in the vein of Dairakudakan performances with vigorous choreography, thinly veiled political content, and spectacular stage art. I have spent so much time on the dance, because I want the reader to be aware of Amagatsu's starting point, but also the consequences of the choices he subsequently made. The most powerful parts of this dance are the ones that have the most specificity: a Japanese boy hearing a warning gong and eating and spewing out sand; postwar Japanese men hooking up in the dark and then negotiating complex relationships; a little person trying to live his life when the steps that everyone else can climb are too tall for his legs. It would have been interesting if Amagatsu had followed this dance with other dances that examined such characters who do not fit into society or have some kind of problem. However, Amagatsu did not make such dances.

Amagatsu often says that he drops away some preoccupations but expands on others. "There are issues from the previous work that still bother me or remain unsolved in my mind. These become the starting point for a new work. When I create a new work, I am always addressing the same types of issues from a different angle. Or carrying on unsolved problems from a previous work" (Amagatsu 2006c). As if to prove right the people who saw his dances as unified narrative arcs, he focused more on universals, evolutionary arcs, and a personal notion of time.

Relationship with Théâtre de la Ville, Paris

Amagatsu might come off as calm and unassuming in interviews, but he was (and is) tremendously driven to have his work seen. After the premier of *Kumquat*

Boy, Amagatsu barnstormed through small venues in Japan, such as college festivals, ever on the lookout to perform. Then he caught the eye of Gerard Coste, the Cultural Attaché for the French Embassy in Tokyo. Following on the success of Murobushi, Ikeda, and Yoshioka in February 1978, and then the later success of Ashikawa and Tanaka Min at the MA: Space-Time in Japan exhibit, Coste arranged for several butô dancers and companies to perform in France. In 1980, Sankai Juku performed for two weeks in Paris and then at the Nancy International Theater Festival.

The troupe used France as a springboard to further exposure in Europe. They earned a tremendous amount of publicity by staging hanging events in which they lowered dancers upside-down from the side of prominent public buildings much like the suspension of the dancer in the "Iron Bird" scene of *Kumquat Boy*.[8] Building on the previous barnstorming, Amagatsu decided that they were not going back to Japan, but rather staying in Europe. With a gargantuan amount of effort and a bit of luck, they turned their exposure into a grueling multicity tour through the outlying cities in France, Italy, Switzerland, Belgium, Mexico, Spain, Venezuela, and Poland. They eventually performed the show in 113 different cities over fifteen years, before retiring it (it was restaged in 2005). After a short stay in Japan, they returned to Europe. They were performing *Kumquat Boy* in Lyon and were approached by two people about performing in Paris. Playing it cool, Amagatsu told them he wanted time to think about it. Had he known who he was talking to, he might have been less coy. The two were Gerard Violette, administrator (and later director) of the Théâtre de la Ville, Paris, and Thomas Erdos, the agent of Pina Bausch and one of the most powerful agents in French performing arts. What is more, Violette wanted the Théâtre de la Ville to produce a new work by Sankai Juku (Amagatsu 2009, 2).

This meeting led to a long-term relationship with the Théâtre de la Ville. Over time, the theater produced shows for Sankai Juku roughly every other year through 2019. Amagatsu credits the Théâtre de la Ville for making his success possible. Unlike in Japan, and unlike his previous two years spent continually drumming up business, Amagatsu did not have to spend time in publicity and fundraising (which had included cabaret dancing in Japan). He routinely points out that he might have stopped dancing had he not been welcomed in France by the Théâtre de la Ville and Violette (Amagatsu 2009, 2). Considering the fates of dancers such as Ôsuka Isamu of Byakkosha, this is entirely possible.

Beyond financial and logistical support, the relationship with Théâtre de la Ville influenced Amagatsu in another important way. Amagatsu refers to the theater as an "ancient Greek type of theater, where the audience can look down on the entire stage" (Amagatsu 2006c). This enabled Amagatsu to treat the surface of the stage as a canvas on which the dancers could draw visible and lasting patterns. Over time, Amagatsu used sand and water as canvases that the dancers could interact with and draw on with their bodies.

Homage to the Cord Pattern Era II

The first dance of the Théâtre de la Ville era, usually known as *Homage to Prehistory* (Jômon-sho, April 20–24, 1982), was actually a combination of two prior works (Amagatsu 2015, 32–33). These were likely *Vague Chronicle: Ceremony for Two Huge Rings* (Bakki, 1981) and the original *Jômon sho*, which is more accurately translated as *Homage to the Cord Pattern Era*. The resulting dance was *Homage to the Cord Pattern Era II: Ceremony for Two Huge Rings* (Jômon Sho II), but the indication that this was the second version was quickly dropped. Rosemary Candelario notes that the translation of *Jômon sho* as "Homage to Pre-History" erased the fact that Jômon indicates a particular point in Japanese time, the era often dated from 14,000 BCE to 300 BCE. Candelario writes,

> Japanese avant-garde artists were interested in the Jōmon period as a mythological source of a Japanese culture untainted by outside influences (e.g., Buddhism and the Chinese writing system) and also as something pre-dating and therefore outside of Japan's recent imperialist and violent history. The past of the Jômon became for artists a source for actively imagining another present and future. (Candelario 2016, 94)

Candelario makes another important point about the title and the reception of butô: "butô was seen as prehistoric, not because it had always been that way, but rather because something had caused the prehistoric state" (94). This something was cataclysm, and specifically the atomic bomb, which effectively erased from the reviews everything in between tradition and a postapocalyptic future (94).

In the first scene, four dancers are lowered upside down into the space, featuring two huge rings by Nakanishi Natsuyuki.[9] They clasp hands and pull toward each other and then at other moments turn away from each other. Finally, they alight on stage and disengage from the ropes. It is a striking means of entering the stage space, and the company used a similar mechanism of outdoor upside-down suspension from the side of buildings as a means of publicity for years. Amagatsu follows in a solo, dancing within and around two huge rings, all the while gasping like a fish. The four men reappear with tuna tails affixed to their outfits creating fishbone rib cages (see Figure 12.4). Over and over, they sit up and gasp for air and then recline back down. Then they begin to writhe and inch across the floor like worms or slugs. Are they fish crawling up on land? Amagatsu appears again with some kind of seaweed or coral on both sides of his head, the bushy ends of which make him look like he has huge sideburns. He crouches, stands, and reclines, all the while gesticulating his arms and fumbling his fingers. The foursome returns in blue, skin-tight costumes. They use poles to push the rings around, but these poles also seem to be weapons as well as objects of worship. There are moments when they use Hijikata's exact sequences of

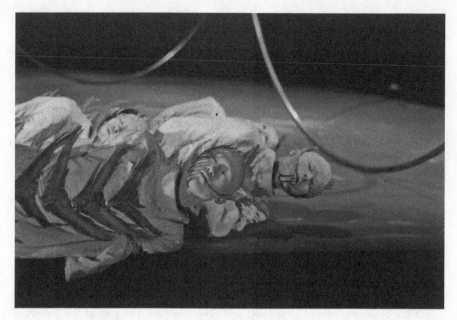

Figure 12.4 Fishtail ribcage. *Homage to the Cord Pattern Era II*, 1984. Courtesy of Fonds Jean-Marie Gourreau-Médiathèque du Centre national de la danse.

movements from *Twenty-Seven Nights for Four Seasons*. Amagatsu dances with the rings, and then is joined on stage by the other four, who use poles to spin glass panels. The five then stand in a group in the center of the two rings (with Amagatsu in the center), all pulsing inward and outward. They initiate movements that start with the wrist and allow their wrists to pull their entire bodies out and then they lean back to center again. Or they all rise up and then shrink back down again. Sometimes their movements are piston-like, with Amagatsu at the center rising up while the other four shrink down, and then the four outsiders rising up as Amagatsu shrinks down in the center. They close with a choreographed ending with their hands crossed in front of their chests, flapping slowly like birds while curtseying up and down.

There are undeniably gripping or fetching moments in this dance, such as when the dancers seem to be performing as a group the approximation of the undulations of a jellyfish, or the writhing of the skeletal fish, or even pushing the huge rings around the stage.

Ritual in the Performances of Sankai Juku

Most reviewers comment on the ritualistic or ceremonial nature of the performance. Michelle Dent nicely unpacks the ritual nature of Sankai Juku performances by noting that for the anthropologist Victor Turner, ritual was supposed to transform society from one moment of (relative) stasis to another by transporting the participants and the observers into a momentary state of "liminality." Liminality, she explains, "is the ambiguous space that opens up during the ritual; it is . . . neither here . . . nor there. It is a space loaded with import, intrigue, and danger" (Dent 2004, 179). Turner observes that the ritual momentarily "transgresses or dissolves the norms that govern structured and institutionalized relationships" (Dent 2004, 179, quoting Turner 1969, 128). For a moment during ritual, things are in flux, before settling into a new set of structures and a new hierarchy. Dent observes that Turner was worried that people would apply his theory about specific tribal societies in Africa to other places and times, so Turner suggested the term "liminoid" as a better term for most rituals in modern society (180). Dent worries that she will be seen as "hair-splitting" to maintain that a Sankai Juku performance allows an audience to occupy a *liminoid* space, but not a genuinely *liminal* one (180–181). However, this is a useful distinction for thinking about the status of ritual or ceremony in Sankai Juku.

It is certainly the case that some viewers feel as though they have passed through a liminal state while watching a Sankai Juku performance, and it is certainly true that Amagatsu was experimenting with the power of ritual. But it is not clear that he and his dancers go through the same kind of individual change as might occur in a coming-of-age ceremony or initiation. Nor is it clear that his audience goes through a similar societal change as witnesses to a ceremony. It may even be the case that Amagatsu's notion of time, in which no one moment is more important than any other, cancels out his focus on ritual, because ritual depends on one moment being perceived as definitively more important than other moments. In short, Sankai Juku's dances open up a liminoid space, in which the power of the quasi-ritual causes the audience to feel something intently, to have what Turner might call "experiences of unprecedented potency" (Dent 179; quoting Turner 128), but it is not clear that anything changes in these liminoid moments. It is perhaps for this reason that Godard concluded that *Homage to the Cord Pattern Era II* was "Less violent than *Kumquat Boy*, more homogenous, [and took] the shape of a comic strip of extreme refinement, but at the limits of aestheticism" (Godard 1982).[10]

Owing to the fact that *Homage to the Cord Pattern Era II* was a mash-up of two different dances (with choreography borrowed directly from Hijikata), different impulses push in different directions. Over time, this was to change. By the time of *Egg-Heat* (Tamago o tateru koto kara: Unetsu Premier Théâtre de la Ville, April 1–5, 1986), Amagatsu had excised the competing voices within himself and begun to present relatively unified works. Later, he proudly contrasts his own single-minded works with Dairakudakan's "proliferating energies" (Amagatsu 2006a).

Egg-Heat: From Standing an Egg on End

On nearly dark stage in which large eggs are suspended above a pool of water, a single figure (Amagatsu) kneels, facing away from us. Occasional gongs from a Buddhist begging bowl punctuate the darkness.[11] Amagatsu is lit from below so that he casts a huge shadow on the back wall. He rises slowly and reveals that he is holding a shofar. He steps into the water, and the ripples are visible climbing up the back wall. He blows the horn. Four dancers dressed in shiny white diaphanous gowns come slowly feeling their way along the sidewalls, and then out to the front of the stage. They reach up, crouch down, and then reach into the water and splash it. The lighting has changed so they no longer cast shadows on the back wall. Rather the water is side-lit such that when they splash, it shows up white in the darkness. They cup water in their hands and rub it on their arms and then mime cupping water and drinking it, and it seems to refresh them. They make their way slowly along the front and up the sides of the stage, where Buddhist begging bowls are hung just above head height. They use rods to strike the inside of the begging bowls rapidly creating a din. Stepping into the water they again reach, turn, and crouch. The lights go down.

They come upon Amagatsu in a pleated floor-length robe kneeling on a polished stone platform, in front of an egg balanced on end and surrounded with concentric circles of sand. He opens and closes his fingers (which seem to have been dipped in blood) and then uses his hands to rake through the sand. He turns on his side, and one hand repeatedly floats up into the air and slowly settles back down. At some moments he seems to be mouthing a silent scream. His movements become more animated. Sometimes he forms a cup with his hands that seems to examine the space almost like a gaping eel searching for food. On the other end of the platform an egg is suspended above a conical pile of sand. He steps into the water, where the other dancers are hunched over. Then he pushes the suspended egg and turns it into a pendulum. The dancers fall on their sides and relax down into the water. They gesticulate sinuously with both their arms and legs. The ripples are projected onto the back wall. Their garments cling to their skin and become slightly transparent, and the wrinkles of the garments echo the ripples of the water. They stand slowly dragging their limbs out of the water and collapse, and then repeat the same motion again and again. Finally, they come to standing and the lights drop.

The lights come up on Amagatsu standing beside the platform. He sways gently, seeming to synchronize himself with the pendulum, and I have the feeling that he is synchronizing his movements with the clock of the universe. He lifts the standing egg from the rings of sand and carries it in cupped hands in front of his face as if it is a sacred talisman. He seems to mime the egg passing through his body and out his crotch as if he is giving birth, and then pushes it arms-length away as if he does not want it anymore. After walking across the front of the stage, he holds a sculptural pose in which he stands in profile with the left leg bent, the right leg up in attitude, the egg cradled in his left hand, and his right hand following the S-curve of his back and body. He steps into the pool and carries the egg diagonally, crisscrossing the stage. Then he carries the egg to where water dripps from above and holds the egg above his head while the waterfall increases in intensity. The egg breaks. The other four dancers (in loose ribbed outfits) come on stage, moving quickly back and forth across the space while Amagatsu wanders about seemingly bereft over the loss of the egg.

The men come together in a group, seemingly carrying eggs, which they deposit in the water. Then they perform vase-hand movements somewhat like Amagatsu's from earlier in the dance. They continue their group movements, predominantly facing each other in a circle raising their elbows or dangling their hands. They depart, and Amagatsu comes to a platform in the middle of the pool on which sand is falling. He stands in the sand. He seems to wish the sand would stop falling but then comes to peace with it. The other dancers enter the sides of the space and ring the begging bowls. For a moment, Amagatsu seems to gain energy and gesticulates wildly upward, but then stops and lets the sand fall on him. The men walk to the back of the pool and then make their way forward through the water slowly. All of the dancers flap their arms-wings slowly in unison. The dancers begin a cycle of moving forward through the space and then running back swiftly while the lights are down and moving slowly through the space again. These moments feel like jump cuts, because each time the light comes up, they are in a slightly different place and Amagatsu is lower to the ground, until he is lying curled up on the platform with the sand falling on him as if it will eventually bury him. The men make their way back over to the sides and crawl and climb along the walls, leaving Amagatsu with sand falling on him.

There are clearly various impulses behind this dance, just as in the previous dances. One of the scenes is named after the book of Finnish folklore, the *Kalevala*. However, the impulses have been sublimated and it does not feel like any of the tableaux clashes with any other tableau. Each person will perceive the dance differently, but it would be predictable if someone were to understand the dance as the birth and hatching of an egg, and then eventually the death of the one who gave birth. This consistency was to become the pattern for the remainder of the dances in Amagatsu's career.

Amagatsu's Philosophy—"Dialogue with Gravity"

Amagatsu often refers to his work as a "Dialogue with Gravity." This is a multifaceted concept. Most obviously in his dances, gravity pulls the suspended dancers slowly to the ground in *Kumquat Boy* and *Homage to the Cord Pattern Era II* (Jômon sho). There is a sense of danger because the dancers might fall and be hurt. That danger was accidentally literalized when one of the dancers, Takada Yoshiyuki, fell to his death in Seattle in 1986.[12] There was no dialogue with gravity in the sense that dialogue usually signifies give and take. Gravity spoke and had the last word. However, in *Homage* the dancers curl in fetal balls as they drop, which creates a sense that they are floating, and suggests a state in which gravity has less pull.

Beyond the dropping scenes, Amagatsu's "Dialogue with Gravity" is any bodily position in which you react against gravity in any way. Amagatsu says, "A body that is completely relaxed is a body that is lying down, right? I begin first of all with this easiest of states and then slowly guide [dancers] to the bodily states which are in dialogue with gravity such as sitting and standing" (translation modified from Amagatsu 2009,

5). You might wonder what is so special about a dialogue with gravity. We are all in a nearly constant dialogue with gravity. To leap, spring, bounce, bob, skip, hop—all are moments in a continuous dialogue with gravity. As are cavorting, frolicking, and climbing. Even lifting a pinkie finger a millimeter is part of a dialogue with gravity. But understanding the extra nuances that Amagatsu gives to this concept is important for understanding his dance.

Horizontal Positions and Movements

For starters, Amagatsu says, "My approach looks at the body before it learns to stand as well as the process it goes through to get there" (Amagatsu 2006c). That is, Amagatsu spends more effort exploring the horizontal positions of reclining and lying down than other choreographers. The second part of his "dialogue" involves relaxation, or what Amagatsu calls "removing power" (datsuryoku). Simply put, relaxing the tension in your muscles is necessary to lower a raised limb or let it fall. A related idea is that releasing tension is necessary for the next movement. Amagatsu says,

> we think of the relaxed state as the base of our dance. It is the act of relaxing for an instant that enables a shift of the body's weight from the right leg to the left leg, and if you can't perform that shift of the body's center of gravity, you can't take a single step. (Amagatsu 2009, 5)

Releasing tension can allow gravity to resume control and pull a weight (such as a leg or arm) down, causing a movement, or free up the body for a subsequent movement.

In *Egg-Heat*, when the dancers collapse into the pool, there is a brief moment just after the apex when they appear to be controlling their movements. Then it appears that they let gravity take over and bring them down to the water. So, the movement is created by removing tension from their muscles and then letting gravity have its say. They initiate their turn back to standing with their shoulders, leaving their arms limply draped across their bodies and under the complete influence of gravity.

The ability of gravity to cause a movement is related to the idea of generating a movement that is not intentional. In an interview, Amagatsu says, "Being moved by unwilled forces or being pulled by gravity are other types of movement" (Amagatsu 2006c). In this, Amagatsu is similar to other butô dancers, such as Kobayashi, who seek to find ways for the body to be moved rather than moving of its own volition.

Gravity Effecting Evolution

Amagatsu's "dialogue with gravity" also stems from his understanding that individual embryonic development mirrors species evolution. He often quotes Haeckel's version of recapitulation theory, "ontogeny recapitulates phylogeny" (embryonic development recapitulates the evolutionary development of the species). He encountered this idea while sitting in on the college classes of Miki Shigeo (Pers. conversation, May 18, 2014). Amagatsu writes,

One month after conception, in a few days' time, the body transforms from fish to amphibian, then from reptile to mammal. In these few days, it replays the majestic drama, which lasted tens of millions of years during the second half of the Paleozoic era, the landing of vertebrates on the banks of the continent, beaten by the waves of the ocean. Ontogeny [embryonic development] recapitulates phylogeny [species evolution]; it is also said that ontogeny is the memory of the beginnings of life in its relationship to the history of the earth. (Amagatsu 2015, 80 [2000, 15–16])

Elsewhere, he says, "when an individual is born, no matter their nationality or race, all tread the same stages of the human race's evolution" (Amagatsu 2009, 4–5). Recapitulation theory has now been repudiated by the scientific community (and was fiercely attacked and not fully accepted at the time when it was proposed). However, Amagatsu (like Kobayashi) takes it seriously.

For Amagatsu, recapitulation theory suggests two things. Humans evolved from a horizontal orientation (swimming and crawling) to a vertical orientation (sitting, standing, walking). Thus, the recumbent postures in Amagatsu's choreography hearken back to the horizontal positions in our species evolution. The species dialogue with gravity becomes the process of thinking about the properties our species had when it was still horizontal. We can see concrete embodiments of these ideas in Amagatsu's hand-eel or jellyfish movements in *Kumquat Boy*, the group jellyfish movements of *Homage*, and the reclining pose in *Egg-Heat* in which one hand seems to float in the air like a piece of seaweed in the waves.

Synchronization with Gravity and the Absolute Minimum Effort Necessary

Amagatsu also characterizes his dialogue with gravity as more like a "synchronization with the [sic] gravity" (Amagatsu 2006a). Elsewhere he says, "Western dance would generally relate to the concept of liberation or rebellion from gravity while the basis of my work would be a synchronization with gravity" (Amagatsu 2006c). Synchronization with gravity is the idea that any moment when all your weight is not completely supported by something else (such as fully floating or lying on the ground) is a moment when you are expending effort. Amagatsu aims to see how little effort he can expend when doing any activity, whether that be reclining on one arm, or standing or even jumping. He calls this the "absolute minimum effort necessary" (Amagatsu 2009, 5).[13] This is precisely the movement most synchronized with the inevitable and unceasing demands of gravity. Amagatsu speaks of aligning oneself with a radius extending directly from the center of the earth: "The image of a body in which the dialogue with gravity is going well is one that, when standing up, has the center axis of the body pointing straight toward the center of the earth. In other words, the force of gravity is distributed evenly on the bottoms of the two feet and the body is standing very easily" (Amagatsu 2009, 5). If muscle tension or poor posture are shifting you out of optimal alignment with that radius pointed to the center of the earth, you will necessarily use more energy. In order to find this perfect alignment with the gravitational vector, Amagatsu has to be a veritable detective searching out any and all physical tensions and relieving them, and figuring out the most efficient way to do every movement of an entire choreography.

The quest to release tension or find the absolute minimum effort necessary made Amagatsu and his dancers increasingly nuanced observers of their own bodies and led them to develop extraordinarily minute perception. As an example, Amagatsu mentions the importance of rehearsing in the Théâtre de la Ville:

"Being able to work in a space with the same dimensions as the actual performance stage is extremely important for the dancers. Because, with the internal tension that is so important in my choreography, differences of, for example, even one step in a sequence can have a slight but perceptible effect on the emotional tension or the thread of concentration involved" (Amagatsu 2009, 8).

Of course, the dancers are professionals and perform in different sized spaces under differing conditions, but the proof of the sensitivity of the dancers is that they could sense if the theater was one step smaller or larger than their home rehearsal space.

All this attention to minimal effort paradoxically translated into extreme mental tension. Amagatsu refers to a "thread of consciousness" that the dancers must maintain in order to execute their performances (Amagatsu 2009, 5). Part of maintaining the "thread of consciousness" lies in being attentive to gravity and preserving a perfectly relaxed state, and Amagatsu observes that it has the side effect of requiring that the choreography be slow. But the "thread of consciousness" also encompasses other mental streams. Amagatsu explains,

All of the Sankai Juku choreography depends on whether or not you can keep that "thread of consciousness" unbroken.... For example, once the dancers are out on the stage, outside of them is no longer an ordinary daily-life space. Rather it becomes some type of "assumed external environment" such as the universe, the underwater world or perhaps a seashore.... Furthermore, the dancers have their own intensive internal involvement that must not be broken. What the dancer is feeling internally at the moment may be fear or hope. And if the dancer is able to pursue that feeling intently, without losing the thread, the movement will follow suit naturally. (Translation modified from Amagatsu 2009, 5–6)

The Sankai Juku dancer must be conscious of three things at every moment: the mental effort necessary to maintain the relaxed body in alignment with gravity and only using precisely the muscles needed for the current action; what we might call the "given circumstances" of the performance (supplied by Amagatsu, such as an underwater world, or the seashore), and finally each of the dancers supply their own internal motivations for each scene or movement. Their bodies might be free from some kinds of tension, but that freedom enables supreme control.

Accounting for the Success of Amagatsu: Associations with New Age Thought and Music

Of course, a great deal of the success of Amagatsu rests on the aforementioned choreography. The movements are interesting on their own. It's not surprising that reviewers throw out words like "tour de force" when raving about his dances. The other component of his success stemmed from his catering to certain desires of the audience, and also situating himself within pre-existing discourses.

One constant feature in reviews of Sankai Juku is a reference to New Age music and spirituality (see, among others, Jowitt, Ulrich, Moreno, Woodard, Parry, Sorgenfrie, Grandgeorge). New Age is a fuzzy category, and in the coming paragraphs my point is not to make an argument about the coherence or cohesiveness of New Age religion, thought, or the quasi-genre of New Age music (which includes ambient music, world music, environmental music, and meditation music). It is to point out that Amagatsu benefited from intersecting with currents in Euro-American society broadly characterized as New Age. This is not just a function of the Orientalism of his reviewers (although there is plenty of that). His dances are consciously presented with an eye to the New Age market and its music.

Titles, Subtitles, and Tableau Titles

Part of the New Age tone lies in the titles, subtitles, and tableau titles. In English each title includes an undefined Japanese word in Romanization, followed by an English subtitle: "YURAGI—In a Space of Perpetual Motion" (1993), "HIBIKI—Resonance from Far Away," and "Sakihai—Through a Rose of the Sand" (Shijima Scene 2) are typical. Very few international spectators understand the words "hibiki," "yuragi," or "sakihai," so there is a hint of exoticism in leaving one word untranslated. Sometimes the mystical nature of the titles is enhanced or altered in the English translation. The subtitle of *Egg-Heat* (UNETSU), "The Egg stands out of Curiosity" was a creative embellishment of "From Standing on End" (Tamago o tateru koto kara). It is tricky to balance an egg on end, but in the English, the egg has agency and the modicum of sentience implied by curiosity. The subtitle of "TOBARI—As if in an Inexhaustible Flux" (2008) is miles from but equally mysterious as the Japanese "within the descending." The Japanese titles reverse the order with the subtitle coming first as a title prefix, and in fact, Amagatsu says that subtitle (or title-prefix/pretitle) is more indicative of his thinking than the main title (Pers. conversation, May 18, 2014).

Sometimes in Japanese, the pretitle runs right into the main title (despite the dash or colon separating them) making the entire title one unified idea. For example, UTSUSHI's title could be more accurately run together as "Duplication (—) in the space between two mirrors facing each other." The same goes for Egg-Heat, in which the pretitle modifies the main title, revealing the cause/source of the egg-heat (whatever that is) as stemming from standing an egg on end. In general, Japanese titles are simpler, because they forego the exoticism generated by the Japanese word. "TOKI—A Moment in the Weave of Time" (2005) is more prosaically rendered as "Time inside Time—Time." Conversely, the Japanese titles sometimes contain double meanings not easily transposed into English. The title "KAGEMI—Beyond the Metaphors of Mirrors" (2000) contains a triple wordplay. Kagemi is a near homophone of *kagami*, the mirror of the subtitle, but it also means "shadow (*kage*) body (*mi*)," which refers to a person who never leaves one's side. In addition, it is also a surname meaning "viewing the scenery" or "viewing the shadow," and a given name for a woman, meaning "beautiful scenery" or "fruitful scenery." A relatively accurate translation might something like "Shadower-Beyond the Metaphor of Mirrors." Whatever the differences between the Japanese and English titles, they correspond almost perfectly with what the music critic Leslie Berman identifies as the "quasi-mystical song and album titles" of New Age music (Berman 1988, 267).

New Age Music

Next is the music. Aside from adaptations of songs (such as Miles Davis's "All Blues," or "Highland Laddie"), the music and soundscapes fit squarely within the realm of New Age music. One composer, Yoshikawa, was even featured on a Grammy-nominated album of New Age, ambient, and environmental music. The other two, Yas-Kaz (Sato Yasukazu) and Kako Takashi, are also routinely associated with New Age music. This musical context conditions the response of the audience. For all the variety within New Age music, one can discern some continuities. Berman gives the following constellation of attributes: delicate musical interplay . . . Few obtrusive junctures, no abrasions . . . Pastel wash, moody and flowing . . . Overall effect is hypnotic . . . introspective spirituality and holistic perspective (Berman 1988, 257). Zrzavy mentions the following characteristics: subtly shifting cycles of sound, a fusion of ethnic stylings, and incorporation of environmental sounds (Zrzavy 1990, 37). Hall gives a parallel description: "One never quite knows for sure where one is. . . . This music is all middle; it starts and stops, it is turned on and off, but one does not get a distinct sense of beginnings and endings" (Hall 1994, 14). These descriptions (and particularly "subtly shifting cycles of sound,") nicely fit much of the music in Amagatsu's dances, in which there are sound clusters that gradually transform almost without one being aware of a change. Listening to such music certainly changes one's relationship to time.

Interestingly, even though Kyoko Iwaki defends Amagatsu from charges of spiritual mumbo jumbo by pointing out that he never talks about such things in interviews

(Iwaki 2018, 237–238, responding to Crisp 2008), she ends up describing Amagatsu's dances in almost the same way as the musicologists describe New Age music:

> in all works of Sankai Juku, there is no linear structure of narratives; thus, a certain moment does not become obsolete with the passing of time.... Every moment seems to be ephemeral as well as eternally recurrent . . . one could argue that, in works of Sankai Juku, the concept of time is not represented in an accumulative linear or cyclic format, but rather is experienced as a pendulum pattern. (Iwaki 2018, 240)

Perhaps this suggests a structural connection between the choreography and New Age music.

Zen and Rock Gardens

New Age thought (as well as music) depended on relatively superficial contact with the "East" for its success. Theosophy, the predecessor of New Age thought, came about at a time when Hinduism and Buddhism were first introduced to Euro-American audiences (Melton 1988, 38–44). Sankai Juku's music and the costumes mirror this trend of superficial references to other cultures. One French reviewer understood the dancers in the "Treatment Plant" scene of *Kumquat Boy* to be a reference to the Berber ethnic Tuaregs (Michel 1982b). The shaved heads of the dancers also seemed to be vaguely suggestive of Buddhist monks (see Figure 12.5). Rosemary Candelario even

Figure 12.5 Suggestive of a Zen monk in a Zen garden? *Egg-Heat* (Unetsu), 1986. Courtesy of Fonds Jean-Marie Gourreau-Médiathèque du Centre national de la danse.

observes, "Butoh outside of Japan, for example, came to stand for tradition, "Zen," [and] ideas of nature (rock gardens, etc.)" (Candelario 2021, 217).

Not Too Japanese

Thus, Sankai Juku's work depends on being sufficiently Japanese/Asian to activate a certain level of exoticization in the non-Japanese audience. However, the Japanese/Asian influence could not go too far. Iwaki observes that Western audiences were "reassured . . . that nothing too unexpected would happen on the stage" (Iwaki 2018, 239). For example, Ikeda dancing in a kimono with a knife protruding from her crotch. Such an image would be too jarring for the Sankai Juku audience or require too much work to decode or endure. Iwaki notes that the other side of Sankai Juku not alienating their audiences was that Amagatsu's style "captivated non-Western audiences with its French undertone" (Iwaki 2018, 239). In this regard, the works of Sankai Juku are similar to other Japanese products that have been deodorized to remove overly specific Japaneseness (Iwabuchi 2002, Allison 2006). Sleek, cool, and well designed, but not particularly or dangerously Japanese, Sankai Juku might be fruitfully compared with the Sony Walkman or international style architecture. Even the set designs of Nakanishi are not from his early messier period of bellows, cords, and clothespins, but his later style of soft abstraction using rings, arcs, and balances.

Capitalizing on the Healing Power of Nature

Perhaps Amagatsu's choreography intersected most beneficially with New Age in the ideas of healing, wellness, and meditation. Zrzavy argues that New Age music primarily attracted people looking for an "anti-frantic alternative" to the music around them, and to people who harbor "disdain for the musical outgrowths of post-industrial society" (Zrzavy 1990, 33, 35). Such people want to get "back to the land, nature, and idealism" and to regain a "past utopia where a state of peace and centeredness can be attained" (35, 39). Similarly, Melton states that the "central vision of New Age" was "radical transformation. Individual, personal and mystical. Awakening to a new reality of the self, experience of physical or psychological healing, intimate experience within community, acceptance of a new picture of the universe" (Melton 1988, 46). Melton might just as well be describing how many in the audience experience Amagatsu's productions.

Here is an example cobbled together from quotations in a review of *Kagemi: Beyond the Metaphor of Mirrors* (2007) by the choreographer Joanna Brotman:

> In *Kagemi*, this genesis begins as dancers squat and bound in unison with one another in a primitive quality that evokes the mimicry of monkeys and evolutionary origins.... There is a sense of innocence and communion, but no core self and no individual identity. Is this an evolutionary stage in the psychology of man, an

ontogenetic recapitulation of human spiritual development? . . . As the dance pro-
gresses, the dancers' bodies and movements are increasingly obscured by their
costumes, as if marking a progressive loss of innocence. . . . The men indulge one
another gratuitously with exaggerated smiles and insincere gestures of companion-
ship. . . . Decadent laughter becomes soulless crying, joy and pain are indistinguish-
able. Emptiness leads to anger and ultimately violence. . . . The danger of finding
oneself in another is losing oneself to a soulless mass mind. . . . [The main dancer]
must assert his identity, despite the lures of a mass culture that tempt him to seek
answers in others and to lose himself in the collective. . . . Everything in *Kagemi* thus
far has been moving towards this [final] moment of wholeness, realized in the unity
of the self with something much greater than the self. (Brotman 2007, 47–49)

In this interpretation, *Kagemi* portrays the evolutionary process by which humans
began in innocence and communion, came to a vertical orientation, became civilized,
and thus became nasty to each other, leaving the human to search for an authentic self
within a newly organized authentic collective.

Amagatsu's stage design likely aids this healing process in its use of natural elements. In *Egg-Heat* (Unetsu), the rippling of water and its reflection on the back wall
seem as important for the overall effect as any part of the choreography (see Figure
12.6). A tremendous amount of research suggests that humans react favorably to such
natural elements.[14] This has led to transformations in architecture and city planning
as architects and planners have sought ways to reconnect urban dwellers to images of

Figure 12.6 Splashing in the water in *Egg-Heat* (Unetsu), 1986. Courtesy of Fonds Jean-
Marie Gourreau-Médiathèque du Centre national de la danse.

nature, whether trees with their leaves moving in the breeze, or the rippling of water. It may be that images of falling sand also activate such relaxation mechanisms.

In this regard, Amagatsu negotiated similar terrain as other butô performers. Candelario traces a history in butô which started with Hijikata's concern with how the environment, culture, and history affected bodies. Ôno took this in his own direction with a concern for "universal 'Nature' with strong connections to his ideas about the human soul and cycles of birth, life, and death" (Candelario 2021, 220). Other dancers such as Bishop Yamada, Yuki Yuko, Tanaka Min, and Oguri went out into nature and were less concerned with the long-term effects of the environment and society on bodies, and more concerned with the ability of the body to respond (immediately or over time) to the particularities of the environment. Rather than going to nature, we could think of Amagatsu as having brought nature (and faux Zen rock gardens) to his audiences.

Amagatsu's choreography anticipates a past (and maybe future) alternative to the industrial and postindustrial present, and Iwaki argues, refuses to recognize any one moment as more important than another. Amagatsu couches this choice in language that dismisses the importance of contemporary events. Iwaki observes, "For Amagatsu, immediate social components responding to the zeitgeist are cheap auxiliaries, which do not form the quintessence of an artwork" (Iwaki 2018, 237). This creates a strange tension between his choreography and his stated philosophy. The psychological healing that people seek in his dance must be a response to a contemporary problem. Thus, paradoxically, the dances address the present by seeming not to address the present.

This has two side effects. The first is that it allows him to reach thousands of people who do not want to work too hard while they watch his dances, but just want to feel uplifted in the end. The second side-effect is a little more unsettling, because it makes it seem like his dances are not really equal to the problems of the world.

Contradictions in Amagatsu's Philosophy

This happens because of contradictions in Amagatsu's philosophy itself, which are similar to the contradiction in Amagatsu forswearing all contemporaneity but depending on the audience's dissatisfaction with the present to motivate them to come to his dance. In an interview about *Egg-Heat* (Unetsu), Amagatsu says that shattering the egg under the torrent of water represents "Creation and destruction happening at the same time." This is because cracking an egg can mean two things: An egg can get cracked as a chick comes out, or an egg can get crushed. Amagatsu explicitly acknowledges this, "you can think of [the cracking] as creation or birth accompanying destruction" (Amagatsu 2006c). Later in his career, in an interview about the dance *Birth-Sand* (*Umusuna*), Amagatsu says, "*Umusuna* is a Japanese word that means a place of one's birth. When I apply this word to the whole of human being, the earth itself becomes Umusuna. I believe that the relationship between the place of birth and people is always deeply affected by a certain natural element, and I don't think this relationship changes at present, and in the future as well, as it didn't change in the past" (Pappas 2015). This is curious. His thinking during *Egg-Heat* seemed to imply continual destruction and creation. With *Birth-Sand*, he seems to imply a static relationship between us and our planet. To be sure, no one would imagine that Amagatsu remained the same for twenty years, but it is immediately obvious that both of these ideas cannot be true at the same time, unless Amagatsu is implying that the unchanging relationship between us and our umusuna is precisely continual destruction and creation. I think it is obvious that nonstop destruction and rebirth is closer to the reality of our world.

If you take the long view, you might not be worried about immediate destruction, because it should be accompanied by simultaneous creation, although most people who are the victims of the destruction find it hard to take the long view right in the middle of that destruction. But it is not clear whether or not current environmental degradation is the same as the Amagatsu's posited static relationship between us and our umusuna earth, even accounting for simultaneous destruction and creation. Geologic changes enabled our planet to sustain life. Cosmic changes will snuff out life and art again when our sun runs out of fuel and our solar system cools and darkens. Our relationship to our umusuna changes over the long term, and not just in the abstract sense of destruction accompanying creation, but in the concrete sense of us emerging from and then eventually being erased from the universe. More recently, it also changes in the short term, in part because of the massive industrialization and urbanization that necessitated the healing process that people find in Amagatsu's dances and in New Age music. We now cause atmospheric and geologic changes to our planet by extracting fossil fuels and burning them. We release byproducts into the atmosphere, causing global warming. In turn, warming causes more atmospheric events such as hurricanes and droughts. The extraction of fossil fuels also causes more earthquakes when we take so much mass from the ground that it alters plate tectonic movements. We currently think that we risk species survival, but not in one to three billion years as our sun heats up, but rather because of the atmospheric and geologic changes we are causing. There is not such a large gap between daily concerns and geologic or evolutionary concerns, because both have now become daily concerns. Perhaps some of Amagatsu's dances will help us adjust emotionally to the inevitable end, because we will imagine a new birth that will rise out of the ashes of our destruction. A different long view (influenced by eco-criticism) might reject the human-centered worry about the destruction of our species, and just see Amagatsu's dances as an affirmation that the planet will continue on long after we are gone. Maybe some of the dances will help us to appreciate the nature we have and try harder to save it from the destruction we seem hell bent on creating. But in order for that to happen, people will have to act on his dances as if they concern the present, even if he maintains that they do not. And people who want their art to openly address the present may find his dances to be unsatisfying.

Conclusion

Perhaps it is unfair to expect more from Amagatsu than this. It is possible that without his tireless self-promotion, all the other butô artists would still be toiling in obscurity. He took the spectacular (but multivoiced) aesthetics of Dairakudakan and shaped them into single-perspective dances. His methods and training result in dancers with exquisite control over their bodies. His ideas of "synchronization with gravity" and the "absolute minimum effort necessary" are important ideas in postwar Japanese discourse and as elements in the world history of the body. The sets are striking and belong with the best abstract art in the world. The dances can take your breath away with their beauty. They offer calm within the continual storm/flux of life. Hundreds of thousands of people have taken advantage of that calm and had their breaths taken away by that beauty. My cocktail party conversation partner was right to appreciate Sankai Juku's performance. And the occasional silent scream reminds us that death comes for us all.

When I sum up Amagatsu like this, it seems like a prodigious contribution to the world of dance. But in the background of butô artists who are so audacious as to imagine that they can speak to the other side of the universe, or that they can inhabit the inner states of hundreds of different people and things, or in the background of his own dance which addressed individual characters in the present, Amagatsu now seems tame by comparison. It is hard to conceive of a version of butô that thinks that no moment matters more or less than any other moment, or that no individual experience matters, but it is clear that Amagatsu fully deserves his spot in the history of dance *and* butô.

13

Tanaka Min

Tanaka Min started as an outsider to the world of butô but over time became associated with it. In part, this was due to a misunderstanding by European audiences,
but he was also in contact with dancers from Dairakudakan at one point and studied
with Hijikata for a couple of years, bringing himself into a direct relationship with
butô. He has, however, recently claimed that he does not practice butô, or rather that
there is no such thing as a butô apart from Hijikata. Tanaka believes that artists who
use the label butô are betraying the spirit of Hijikata's work. He claims he is the true
heir of Hijikata and is trying to keep alive the spirit of experimentation that has been
lost from butô.

This chapter presents a history of Tanaka. This includes his solo works of the 1970s,
his collaborations with improvisational musicians, his experiments with farming
as dance training, his involvement with Hijikata, the changes he made to Hijikata's
methods as he adjusted to choreographing for his two groups, Maijuku (active
1981–1996) and Tokason (active 2000–2006), and finally his later solo dances in the
Hijikata mode.

Early Dances

Tanaka was an athlete and then studied ballet and modern dance at the Hiraoka
Shiga Dance Academy from 1963 to 1973. Eventually, he began to experiment with
his own dances. Early on, he collaborated with Goi Teru, who later also claimed
the butô label. One of Tanaka's first dances, *Kagura* (performed three times, 1966,
1971, and 1972), consisted of him suspending himself by ropes under the arms for
five minutes while curling himself into a ball (Tanaka and Stein 1986, 144; Fuller
2016, 71–72). By the end, his body was shaking uncontrollably. About his first dance,
Tanaka said, "I tried to express nothing" (Tanaka and Stein 1986, 144–145). That
may be the case, but the dance suggests a preoccupation with the limits of bodily
strength, and even possibly with people hung against their will. Moreover, entitling a
dance by the name of a premodern performance genre also might create certain expectations on the part of the audience.

For the first couple of years, he called his dances *Subject* or *Dance Doings* (in
English, sometimes with a subtitle), and *Dance State* (*Butai*—again sometimes with
a subtitle). Fuller notes that there was no consistency between dance names and content. Sometimes content carried over while the title changed, or Tanaka recycled the

A History of Butô. Bruce Baird, Oxford University Press. © Oxford University Press 2022.
DOI: 10.1093/oso/9780197630273.003.0013

title with different content (Fuller 2016, 65). In the beginning, Tanaka often danced nude (both inside and outside), and usually slowly. Frequently, Noguchi Minoru provided the soundscapes.

For example, on June 22, 1974, Tanaka danced naked outdoors for the first time in a version of *Subject*. With his naked wife and baby seated on a chair watching, Tanaka danced on the lawn of the OAG Hall in Tokyo. One photo shows him lying on his back at some distance from his wife and child, and another shows him leaping into the air, knees clasped to his chest (Kimu 1976, unpaginated, but approximately 13–16). A third shows him having wrenched his head sideways at the apex of his jump, in order to shift his center of gravity and cause himself to fall on his side (Tanaka and Okada 2011, 21, 23).

About *Subject* (June 22, 1974), Tanaka writes,

I first danced naked in front of my wife and daughter's naked bodies. I jumped up over and over, and then landed awkwardly. There was no end to my repetitions. My wife and daughter's naked bodies were over in the distance. I thought that maybe by doing this, I might be able to finally live freely.

And then continues, "I intended to have the image of a flung-around-baby reflect in the eyes of the audience for just one second." Finally:

The shock of the weight of my body landing thump, and the shock to my mood. A clumsy body and a clumsy self. And from a distance my wife and child watching a male falling over and over. (Tanaka and Okada 2011, 21–23)

Tanaka's words reveal the ambitious aims of the dance. The audience could watch Tanaka crashing to the ground, but also they were invited to imagine what the mediated dance looked like to the two special spectators, his naked wife and daughter. Tanaka further imagined that the audience would draw a connection between himself and the baby and imagine the baby being thrown around.

Tanaka danced many site-specific improvisational versions of *Subject* and *Dance State*. *Subject: Dead* (OAG Hall, Tokyo, October 4–5, 1974) consisted of Tanaka standing, crawling, walking, and lying on wires suspended in the middle of the performance space as if it were an avant-garde high wire act (Kimu 1976, 21–30). Here as well, it seems as though Tanaka must have been preoccupied with danger and pain. *Subject: Ishikari Plain* (near Ishikari beach, Hokkaido, March 22, 1975) entailed Tanaka dancing in a recently graded construction site between small snow-covered hills. Tanaka danced on the soil imprinted with tractor tire tracks. The repeated pattern of the tire tracks gives the space a feeling of a piece of abstract art, and almost makes it seem as though the dirt is frozen in wave patterns. At one moment, Tanaka jumped into the air with his arms held stiffly at his side while bending forward at the waist. Another two photographs show him bent over in a three-point stance with one hand on the ground, and the other arm raised high in the air. One leg is underneath him and the other extended outward as if he was a speed skater ready to glide across the ribbed soil (Kimu 1976, 7–12). Apparently, it was windy and bitter cold, but Tanaka does not seem to betray any sign of the cold in his dance (Kimu 1976, 60). Fuller writes of Tanaka's "physical research of the condition of the body through the action of exposing it to the widest variety of physical stimulation possible" (Fuller 2016, 77). In the context of the previous dances, the extreme cold seems to suggest that he was again exploring limit conditions.

Some of the early dances seem planned out, but Tanaka quickly became focused on improvisation. One of Tanaka's guiding mottos was "I don't dance in the place, I dance the place."[1] Part of "dancing the place" was trying to respond to the place, rather than impose a preset choreography on it, although sometimes Tanaka danced similar movements in different places. A photo of *Dance State: Tokyo Arts University Performance* (September 28, 1975) shows Tanaka lying on his side with mud and dirt caked to his back and buttocks (Kimu 1976, 39–40). In that case, dancing the place meant coming in direct contact with the place, getting muddy. Part of the enjoyment of watching such dances must have been similar to that of enjoying outdoor sculpture. The audience must have savored watching sunlight and shadows play on Tanaka's body. They likely also felt a visceral sensation at the audaciousness of Tanaka daring to dance naked or when seeing him get all muddy.

During this time, Fuller says that Tanaka usually favored slow movements punctuated by brief periods of quick movements (Fuller 2016, 76). Sometimes he used one movement or position as a base for sensing the world around him. I would add that often Tanaka is inclined to twist his torso, and sometimes Tanaka slowly cycles from one position to the next and back (see Figure 13.1). In one dance, Tanaka starts on his hands and knees and then pushes himself backward into a sitting position. Then he relaxes down on his back, and slowly curls his legs up and over his head until he reaches the yoga plow pose. Finally, he twists his head to the side so that he can slowly somersault backward and arrive on his hands and knees again (Imura n.d., roughly, 39:00–44:00). Sometimes he goes all the way through a cycle and then reverses back through the cycle. Another prominent pose consisted of Tanaka using a backbend or bridge pose to inch slowly along the ground or up or down a staircase (Kimu 1976, 29–30, 32–34).

The 1,824-hour *Hyperdance* consisted of hundreds of site-specific improvisational dances throughout Japan spanning seventy-six days (1,824 hours) from October 8 to December 22, 1977. Fuller affirms that Tanaka danced as many as five times per day in more than 150 locations. Fuller writes:

> spaces included college campuses, temples, gymnasiums, art galleries, tent theatres, and riverbanks [. . .] stairways and city streets, a factory, an old train station, a hotel dance hall, a lumber yard, many public parks, a bulldozer, a truck, the runway of a local airport, and . . . a garbage dump. (Fuller 2016, 77)

Fuller observes that the positions and movements

Figure 13.1 Tanaka Min in unnamed and undated dance, probably about 1977. Photograph by Nakatani Tadao. Courtesy of Nakatani Tadashi, NPO Butoh Laboratory Japan, and the Hijikata Tatsumi Archive at the Keio University Arts Center.

are never static, though the movement is very slow, and the positions are often asymmetrical. Pedestrian movements of crawling, lying down, sitting, walking, and squatting occur repeatedly.... Improvisation occurs both in the ordering of these elements, and in the subtle movements of the fingers, arms, and the muscles under the skin. It also occurs in the transitions between the repeated elements, which involve subtle shifts of weight. Tanaka's muscles are fully engaged throughout, he never relaxes, and he often deliberately makes both the positions and the transitions between them difficult for himself. Subtle weight shifts and alterations occur throughout. (Fuller 2016, 77)

Tanaka was not just researching the physical aspects of a place but also engaged in social research. Twice, Tanaka danced in a garbage dump ironically named Dream Island (Yume no shima) (Tanaka and Okada 2011, photos 7, 11, 16–17, 33). Tanaka recalls the pervasive reek of ammonia and "the sea water bubbl[ing] as it ferments" (33). Beyond the stench, Tanaka observed that after having lain in the garbage for some time, he became "confused as to whether 'garbage' really is the appropriate term" for the material there (Fuller 2016, 78). That is, his physical research caused him to reconsider society's definition of garbage.

Tanaka was researching the audience as well. Because he was dancing nearly naked, he often had run-ins with the police. In an interview, Tanaka says,

Sometimes people would say, "That is bad," or telephone the police. I would observe their reactions while I was dancing. Sometimes they (the police) would come and some people would say, "Why is this wrong? Why is this illegal?" and they would argue about it. It was very interesting.... I kept dancing of course. Sometimes [the police] would roll me up in a sheet and put me in the van. This itself was a *very* interesting dance. (Fuller 2016, 232)

Obviously, this was a multipronged performance. Fuller observes that Tanaka placed "the people watching in the position of having to choose whether the action they were witnessing should be repressed or not" (Fuller 2016, 79). The performance included the movements of Tanaka and the bystanders engaging with the police force. Fuller continues, "Even those not actively engaged in calling the police, arguing with them, or vocally supporting Tanaka's arrest, would observe others doing so, and at least consider the morality or legality of whatever it was they felt he was doing" (Fuller 2016, 79). Tanaka was pushing the spectators to conduct research as well—to reconsider their own ideas about public indecency and the police's use of force. Through it all, Tanaka was doing research on the people themselves. Would they intervene, or would they stand idly by? If they did intervene, would they successfully alter the behavior of the police, or would the police remain obdurate? It is clear that 'dancing the place' was not just a simple interaction with the environment, but a complex consideration of the physical and social properties of the place and an intervention in the place that could change the place and the people in it.

Paris

Tanaka was invited to Paris in 1978 for the MA Exhibition (along with Ashikawa), but it seems that his invitation was somewhat of a happy accident. Initially the organizer, Isozaki Arata, wanted Hijikata to come, and Tanaka was only invited after Hijikata turned him down (Pagès 2009, 43). His dance was billed as *Hyper Dance*, but the promotional materials also introduced the term "Dance State," and the Drive series was still ongoing, so all three titles are useful for understanding his dance (Pagès 2015, 32, and for photos 33, 66–67 and Figure 7.2). Despite the fact that Tanaka did not profess to practice butô, he was understood by contemporary reviewers as belonging within that realm and immediately compared and contrasted with Ôno, Kasai, and Sankai Juku (Michel 1978; Michel 1980; Godard 1980a). His association with butô helped him, but he helped butô as well. His austere dance attracted the attention of prominent intellectuals, in a way that Murobushi, Ikeda, and Ashikawa had not. Soon the likes of Roger Callois and Foucault were opening their homes for improvisations, and Roland Barthes and Felix Guatarri were singing his praises. This gave butô an air of respectability that it had not acquired through the dances of Murobushi and Ikeda (Pagès 2015, 33). Moreover, it opened up avenues for Tanaka to be welcomed around the world.

Body Weather Laboratory

In 1978, Tanaka also began a series of important workshops for his career arc: the "Body Weather Workshops" (Fuller 2016, 117). The initial workshops were attended by Dairakudakan dancers, as well as musicians and other dancers. The participants explored "manipulations" which were "partnered exercises combining yoga, shiatsu, and physical therapy" (117). The workshops evolved into the Body Weather Laboratory, in which Tanaka assembled experts in various fields (including Yoga, acupuncture and sports medicine) and assigned groups of people to explore the body, sound, visual arts, and language (118).

Initially, Tanaka actively promoted Body Weather Laboratories and assisted others in setting up their own laboratories. The longtime Tanaka dancer Frank Van de Ven describes a Body Weather Laboratory in 1982 consisting of 12 to 15 people living in the south of France:

> One person would not talk for twenty-four hours, one person was blindfolded for twenty-four hours, one person didn't use [their] arms for twenty-four hours, one person didn't eat for twenty-four hours, one person didn't drink for twenty-four hours, two people were connected as [conjoined] twins for twenty-four hours, and then on top of that we did our daily program. . . . Body Weather workshops. So in the cottage there was a stretcher for the guy who didn't use [his] legs and was carried by the blind [guy]. The person who could not use [their] arms had to be brought to the toilet, had to be fed by the one who didn't drink. It was all really really intense. And then at night after a full day program and then eating, at night there would be discussions about the work going on. (Quoted in Fuller 2016, 121)

The idea of Body Weather was to continue to grow, spread, and gain importance in Tanaka's practice. One outgrowth of the Body Weather Laboratory was the formation in 1981 of the group Maijuku (Dance School). Tanaka had primarily been focused on solo dances and research, but with the constitution of a dance group, he began to communicate his ideas to dancers in a way that enabled them to realize his vision on stage.

MMD and Polyrhythm

In 1979, Tanaka met Milford Graves (an improvisational percussionist), and then in 1980, he met Derek Bailey (an improvisational guitarist), both from the free jazz movement. In 1981, the three embarked on a tour of Japan called MMD Project 81 Improvization (MMD=Milford, Min, Derek). Graves was deeply involved in polyrhythmic exploration, and Fuller observes that after the encounter with Graves and

Bailey, Tanaka's predominantly birhythmical movements became more polyrhythmical so that different parts of Tanaka's body would move at different speeds (Fuller 2016, 91–93).[2] It would be an overstatement to say that Tanaka was merely transposing free jazz improvisation into a bodily form, because Tanaka had already been experimenting with improvisation. But the two became valuable lifelong collaborators in pushing the boundaries of improvisation.

Harada argues that Tanaka was pivotal in introducing to Japan many of the experiments of Judson Dance Theater (Harada 2004, 321). These included the use of minimalism or stillness, pedestrian or quotidian movements, nudity, the incorporation of chance procedures into dance, and a reconfiguration of the relationship between the performer and audience.[3] Similarly, the reviewer Byron Brown compared Tanaka and the micromovements of Continuum and the cellular movements of Margaret Fisher (Brown 1981, 8).[4] Fuller demonstrates that Tanaka went beyond his Judson counterparts, particularly in exploring techniques for moving different parts of his body at different tempos and to different rhythms. According to Fuller, Tanaka was particularly interested in developing "an inner and outer speed" in his body (Fuller 2016, 70). In his memoirs, Tanaka wrote, "I began to pay attention to the various speeds within my body. The body is created of various complicated speeds (some of which I am not conscious of) such as breathing, blood flow, heartbeat, consumption, perspiration, and evacuation." He continues, "I love the image of all the body's speeds responding to the slightest of breezes" (Tanaka and Okada 2011, 13).

Emotion

In the *Emotion* (Kanjô, 1982–1983) series, Tanaka turned from the movement-centered dances, Hyperdance, and MMD, to everyday life and also to an exploration of the emotion of the title. He wore athletic clothes or a raincoat, and in his own words, "I scream . . . pound the floor with my feet repeatedly, and cry to the distance "Not yet? Not yet? . . . I stare at my body as though looking might bore through it. I touch, lick, bite, pinch, beat, tear, and rub my body. . . . I feel sad not knowing why" (Tanaka 1987 [1983], 65). Fuller writes, "Emotion was a striking return to the emotional expression that postmodern dance rejected, presented in a raw, visceral mode with no narrative framework. It was as if all the feelings and impulses restrained in Hyperdance were allowed full range in Emotion" (see Figure 13.2 and Fuller 2016, 97; for photos, 98–101).

The year 1982 was also important for Tanaka because he cofounded the Plan B performance space. As with other artists such as Hijikata, Maro, and Kasai, Tanaka understood the importance of having a venue in which to present his works. Plan B gave him that venue, but also the ability to exert an influence on the world of dance by who was booked in the space.

Figure 13.2 Tanaka Min in *Emotion*, La Mama, 1983. Copyright by and courtesy of Charles Steiner.

Work with Hijikata

Tanaka had actually admired Hijikata for a long time before he began to work with him. He attended *Hijikata Tatsumi and Japanese People*, and approximately twenty nights of *Twenty-Seven Nights for Four Seasons* (Fuller 2016, 60). One senses that Tanaka was initially wary of Hijikata because he feared Hijikata would dominate him (Tanaka and Okada 2011, 24, 40, 60; Tanaka and Stein 1986, 144). Finally, in 1982, he wrote an homage, proclaiming himself a true heir of Hijikata. Hijikata apparently then went unannounced to Plan B to see Tanaka perform. Tanaka then asked Hijikata to choreograph on him. This is admirable. Tanaka was already an established performer with a worldwide following. He did not need to become a student again. That he did so demonstrates his dedication to continually renewing his dance.

Tanaka spent at least two months working with Ashikawa learning Hijikata's evocation and imagery work (Fuller 2016, 105–106). Apparently, he learned one thousand images. These were assigned to different parts of his body so that he had to be able to "perform four separate movement/image combinations at once: one for each section of the body, as well as remember the specific order of the combinations" (Fuller 2016, 105). This work resulted in two dances. The first was the 1983 duet of Tanaka and Ashikawa entitled *Extremely Quick Respiratory Bromide*. In it, Hijikata toyed with the conventions of pornographic movies.

Around this time, Tanaka also started a series, *Form of the Sky* (Sora no kata). In one solo, he wore a black suit coat, his face was painted white, and he had black circles around his eyes. He enacted a seemingly enfeebled and demented old man with Parkinson's disease, to the sounds of Baccara's "Roses in the Snow."[5] The music switches to Simon and Garfunkel's "The Boxer," and Tanaka's movements become more animated and even frenzied. Tanaka identifies the black suit as having belonged to his father (Tanaka and Okada 2011, 30–31). A photo of another dance in the series performed in Kanda three years later shows the same black-clad character dancing with a white leghorn chicken. Tanaka writes that his father used to wring the heads of chickens to kill them. It is as if Tanaka channeled Hijikata and made his own version of *Forbidden Colors*, but also as if he had learned from watching Hijikata and Ôno that one way into dance creation is through the use of characters. This black-suited character was to become a staple for Tanaka over the years (see Figure 13.3).

At this time Tanaka began choreographing dances for Maijuku. One early dance was *Kandinsky: Sonorite de Violette* (1983). In it, a robotic Tanaka, seemingly equipped with vampire teeth, looks as though he is about to be ripped to shreds by two naked women, who ham it up for the audience like delighted strippers air-kissing and embracing in a male fantasy of lesbian sex (Hoffman and Holborn 1987, 104–111). As with *Form of the Sky*, this dance seems to have Hijikata and butô written all over it.

Figure 13.3 Tanaka Min as black-suited character in *The Rite of Spring*, 1990. Courtesy of Fonds Jean-Marie Gourreau-Médiathèque du Centre national de la danse.

The second dance with Hijikata was the 1984 *Performance to Commemorate the 1501st Solo Dance of Tanaka Min: The Foundation of the Pure Love-Dance School* (Tanaka Min 1501 kai dokubu kinen kôen: Ren'ai butô-ha teiso).[6] The Pure Love-Dance School (or possibly Pure Love-Butô School) was a company of just two people: Hijikata and Tanaka (Tanaka 2009, 42). In this dance, Tanaka embodied a series of characters including a bald man wrapped in several different shawls, a man in a dark gray robe, a nearly naked character wrapped in tape and cords, and a character in a sheer white robe biting a stick. Beyond transmitting imagery techniques, Fuller observes that Hijikata conceived of the costume. He "tied up [Tanaka's] body with rubber, tape, and cord. These provided physical sensations or stimulations to Tanaka, as well as limit[ed] his range of movement" (Fuller 2016, 104; for photos see Hoffman and Holborn 1987, 67–75). Tanaka seems to have learned from Hijikata a new focus on props, costumes, physical actions, distinct characters, and emotional display. His dances began to seem more surreal, grotesque, and filled with eroticism. What is more, he seems to have taken from Hijikata a clue for how to communicate with other dancers using imagery work.

Farming

Ever looking to challenge himself, in 1985, Tanaka expanded upon the Body Weather work by creating the Body Weather Farm in Hakushu, Yamanashi prefecture. Tanaka used farming as bodily training for the next twelve years. Fuller argues that "the ultimate goal of this training was an ideal non-hierarchic body, to be pursued through exposure to a wide variety of physical stimulations and through an egalitarian mimesis that inverts traditional pedagogical models" (Fuller 2016, 113).

Farming attracted Tanaka, because it "provided a means of subsistence income (and food) for Maijuku and Tokason members, alleviating the need to rely entirely on outside funding sources" (Fuller 2016, 17). In contrast to butô companies that used the cabaret as a source of funding, Tanaka chose a different funding mechanism.

Beyond brute economics, farming was important philosophically. It forces you to recognize and accommodate yourself to something other than your own self. Fuller puts it this way, "Rather than a training environment where the place is subservient to the needs of the people, the place functions as a teacher" (Fuller 2016, 132). Paraphrasing Sherwood Chen: You have to feed the goats even when it's cold or rainy (Chen, pers. communication August 27, 2014). You also have to change the position of your body to optimize your task. Fuller writes, "Harvesting potatoes, for example, required a very different use of the body than harvesting peppers. Weeding a carrot patch involved a very different use of the body than weeding a rice field" (Fuller 2016, 131–132). Chen concurred (again paraphrasing): You must change your body position to get the right angle to pick the fruit (Chen, pers. communication August 27, 2014).

Tanaka sometimes talks dismissively of people who use the environmental movement purely for making money (Tanaka and Okada 2011, 129), but a strong ecological critique pervades his practice and writing that is partly a result of farming. Tanaka mentions that a horse used to live in their farmhouse where the bathroom is. Then he writes (somewhat awkwardly), "Our rented house still has the smell of human dwellings that have a place set aside indoors for domestic animals and, the feeling that there is relationship with an animal as a member of the workforce, as is common throughout the world" (Tanaka and Okada 2011, 126–127). Here Tanaka raises the issue of the proximity of humans and animals, and its connection to their labor relationship.

Humans use several kinds of animal labor, including draft labor (moving loads), and energy-conversion labor (as animals such as chickens and cows convert plants into food that some humans consume). In the United States, we often confine animals that labor *for us* in crowded disgusting living conditions far from where we live, so we cannot smell them. Smelling animals entails being close enough to them that some part of them can enter your body through your nostrils. Tanaka's embodied ecology suggests altering the labor- and proximity-relations with animals from "for us" to "with us." The proximity of "with us" would enable us to understand the conditions of the animals more fully. This, in turn, might make us ensure that such conditions do not get too bad (smelly), because the animals' living conditions are our own living conditions.[7] Implicit in Tanaka's concern with being able to smell the animals that labor with us is a mandate to be aware of and concerned with the living conditions of all the entities that labor and live with us.

Body Weather as a Philosophy

More than the name of the farm, Fuller argues that Body Weather "envisions the body as a force of nature: ever-changing, omni-centered, and completely open to external stimuli" (2016, 128). Let's unpack this. As already noted, this is a demand to be in the weather and attuned to the world, the weather, and its minute changes. It is an indication that performing in the weather will cause the nature of the light on the body to change, and thus that the performance will change (like a bodily version of *plein air* painting) (see Figure 13.4). Moreover, paraphrasing Chen, the dancer should be as malleable and mercurial as the weather, able to change and transform as quickly as the weather can. It is a directive to be as polyrhythmic as the weather (for example, the speed of rainfall versus the speed of mist particles almost lingering in the air). Finally, Body Weather seeks to understand what kinds of prehistoric markings, abilities, or aspects are on (or in) our body due to weather. In this, Body Weather is the relative of other butô techniques that seek to understand basic fundamentals of the body-mind.

Figure 13.4 Tanaka Min dancing on the edge of a pond in Pushkin State University, Pushkin, Russia, 1996. Copyright by and courtesy of Charles Steiner.

Specific Training Exercises of Body Weather

MB

One part of Body Weather is called MB. This is both a philosophy and an open-ended set of accumulative training movements. The letters stand for muscle/bone, mind/body, music/body, movement/balance, and for Tanaka, "myself as a boy" (Fuller 2016, 123, fn 35). Finally, a blank m____ and b____ are implied, which serve as a constant invitation to let the letters open out into something new (Chen, pers. conversation April 2014). The philosophy seeks to understand the relationships between these pairs, while at the same time, undoing those same relationships in order to find new possibilities. Physically, MB is an ever-shifting rhythmic and aerobic floor exercise in which dancers move across the rehearsal space in rows, doing progressively harder movements in time to music. These exercises develop endurance, strength, flexibility, and coordination. Longtime Body Weather practitioner Sherwood Chen cautions,

> [MB] resists being defined as a "technique" in the traditional sense of developing specific vocabulary to apprehend and lock down. Rather, the movements . . . serve to decontextualize the dancer's known/mastered body, demanding individual observation of habits/tendencies, acute observation and drawing upon group energy, and refusing to settle in a single point of movement reference. As such this

training engages the interplay of physical and mental speed, and strives to surface for each participant the individual borderline of limits in balance, endurance, awareness and speed. (Chen 2013)

As with many of the other activities of Body Weather, MB was not the goal, but rather a means to move the body-mind into an unknown beyond.

Manipulations

MB was often coupled with the aforementioned Manipulations. They were based on shiatsu massage and physical therapy. One practitioner describes them as a "series of compressions, pulls, and range of motion exercises done on a mostly passive" recipient (Jarrett n.d.). Partners alternate back and forth using their hands to focus their body weight on the other person to compress and stretch parts of the receiver's body. The combination of MB and Manipulations exercises, stretches, and relaxes the body so as to ensure that the participants are always increasing their abilities and flexibility.[8]

Exercises or Studies

After MB and manipulations, participants engaged in exercises or studies. These changed constantly but often entailed pair or trio work in which one person gives directives or stimuli to another person (Fuller 2016, 136–137). The receiver begins in a relaxed state and then tries to carry out the directive as fully as possible before returning to the base state. At this point they can receive another stimulus, or they might be interrupted during the process by a fresh stimulus. The giver might alter the base position, the speed of movement, the direction of the movement, or the part of the body or joint to be moved. It was even possible to alter the physical place of the exercise. Fuller writes of depositing a blindfolded partner atop a pile of donkey dung and observing them as they experienced the feeling of insects crawling all over themself (139). After the exercises, there was always a chance to talk about what the participants had experienced, learned, and observed. These exercises can be compared to the imagery work of other butô dancers, such as Kasai's commands to perform a movement in a noun way while internally voicing a set vowel to change the tone and quality of the movement.

Antihierarchy

Fuller notes one important ideal in Body Weather was to achieve nonhierarchical relationships (2016, 120). Of course, there was no escaping the fact that Tanaka was fully in charge, but in principle, no one was supposed to be any more important than anyone else, and no part of the body was supposed to be any more important than any other part. In workshops, Tanaka would not demonstrate movement for students to copy, but rather encouraged participants to observe each other's bodies (140). Writes Fuller, "The ideal was to observe closely and imitate the movement of a wide range of different individual bodies, even those made by people one might consider oneself to be a 'better' dancer than" (136). Fuller relates a moment in which one participant was having trouble doing an exercise. Tanaka praised her for trying hard and scolded other more technically skilled dancers for not trying as hard as she was. Then Tanaka demanded that the skilled dancers execute her movements exactly as she was dancing them (135). Fuller refers to them "develop[ing] the capacity to imitate the personal idiosyncrasies of a variety of individuals with the same degree of competence that a technical dancer would display in learning a new [form] or repertory piece . . . as if each individual body were a new form to be studied" (141). This is powerful. Tanaka was suggesting that rather than spend your effort to approximate an ideal that was created long before you, such as ballet movements, you should use your time learning how to imitate idiosyncratic individuals near at hand.

Transforming Hijikata's Methods

With the creation of Maijuku, Tanaka "began to devote significant energy to the development of a group dedicated to collaboratively creating dance performances while training, rehearsing, laboring, and living collectively" (Fuller 2016, 162). As part of that creative process, Tanaka used Hijikata's imagery work in his exercises (138). In one session, dancers were required to maintain four different images in four different parts of their bodies: head, torso, arms, legs. Fuller gives the following example: "a noisy fly lands on your forehead, your hands float up a waterfall, your feet become worms, a fishhook is pulling your chest" (138). They could choose how they responded to the images, but ideally each participant should keep all the images in mind simultaneously. It is a testament to how thoroughly Tanaka absorbed Hijikata's evocative experiments that he used this imagery work extensively in his group choreography.

Overtime, Tanaka developed his own way of using images, which moved away from Hijikata. He progressed from using Hijikata's prompts, to using his own prompts, to having the dancers create their own prompts. The arc is important for what it says about Tanaka, but also about the evolution of the world of performance.

In one early Maijuku dance, *Moon at Noon* (1985), Hijikata supplied the images and choreography for the group dance (Fuller 2016, 168). This is the most Maroesque of all Tanaka's dances. The choreography is vigorous and muscly. In one scene, one of a pair of dancers carries the other, ramrod straight, on his shoulder, creating a T-body. In another scene, five people are bent over in a line with their heads on the buttocks of the person in front of them and two or three people are sitting on the group. One person is positioned out front, looking like the centaur-head of a strange beast. Tanaka moves through them improvising, seemingly unaware of them. He walks in a way that makes it seem as if he is suspended. His feet are not fully in contact with the ground, and he does not appear to be subject to gravity. In another scene, Graves drums very fast and Tanaka matches the drumming with twitches in his body, and then shakes his knees as fast as the drumming.

Later, Tanaka used the Hijikata's images in his group choreography, but let the dancers come up with their own responses to the images. In an interview, Tanaka claimed that it was "fascistic" to supply both the images and the expected response to the images (Fuller 2016, 138). In *Rite of Spring* (Haru no saiten, 1989/1990), Tanaka gave the men the following images from Hijikata: "human characters ('foolish boy' 'hot lady'), animals ('flat fish' 'spider'), gestures ('crossing arms' 'looking through the hands'), sequential series of images of an animal underwater, and a sequence about a monkey subjected to various experiences" (Fuller 2016, 147, 168).[9] Tanaka added some images and themes of his own, such as "ant becomes elephant," "children and old people; a woman being bathed in light; insects gradually emerging out of the ground into the sunlight," and "pregnant woman giving birth, becoming a baby, a wet heavy hammer in the rain, becoming small because the environment becomes big, becoming absent" (Fuller 2016, 169–170). He had the women

> make a study of five animals: dog, cat, goat, insect, and chicken. For each animal they were to come up with five "situations and movement." The "situations" translated into physical actions ... includ[ing], for example, dog "spinning, try to catch his tail," chicken "plays with sand," "shitting cat/makes a hole," goat "fighting/hitting goat from forehead," "fly washing face and arms." (Fuller 2016, 170)

Tanaka would pick and choose from among the movements created by the dancers and "would then modify these, altering or developing rhythm, effort, shape, and movement quality" (Fuller 2016, 168).

Still later Tanaka gave general movement directives and used images, but had the dancers create their own images rather than him supplying them. For *Romance: Love in Fluxus* (1999), Fuller writes, "Dancers were repeatedly told to use as little muscular effort as possible: to move from the bones and initiate movement from the joints. Tanaka emphasized fragility, delicacy, the use of micro movements, and an asymmetrical omni-centered body involving the segmentation of body parts" (Fuller 2016, 190). Within those confines, Fuller writes, "Different dancers at different times performed multiple characters simultaneously, or transformed from one character to the next" (197). One was "a woman losing her leg, a woman who wants to become a scarecrow, an old woman, and an infant who wants to drink sap from the tree." Another was "a (male) pilot, a girl waiting for the pilot, and the pilot's mother" and Onoda Hirô (a Japanese intelligence officer who refused to believe that the war was over and hid in the jungle in the Philippines for 30 years) (198). A third was a "skeleton, a puppet, an 'unborn baby', ... a young girl" and a high-class prostitute (198). Fuller concludes, "performers in *Romance* developed composite personae.... Rather than

representing individuated characters, the character studies and the transitions between these multiple identities, engaged in incomplete, broken or blurred actions,
constituted the movement score for each individual dancer" (203). Fuller then observes, "The vast majority of the images used in making the dance came from the
dancers themselves. He often *did not even ask* what individual images the dancers
were using. There was no common pool of images, as there was in Maijuku" (202, my
emphasis). This is an important moment within the butô world, but also within the
world of performing arts.[10]

Fuller focuses on the disparity between what the audience knows, what goes on inside the mind of the dancer, and how much control the choreographer has. He situates
this moment of Tanaka's practice within two simultaneous evolutions in the world of
performing arts. One is the transformation in which the audience is accorded the
power to imagine for themselves and (borrowing the words of Duchamp) "complete
the work of art" (Fuller 2016, 175). The other is an evolution in which the choreographer exercises less control over the dancers and treats them more as coequals.
Quoting Susan Leigh Foster, Fuller observes that the "understanding of the role of
the choreographer shifted from being someone who develops dance movements and
teaches them to other dancers to being a 'manager, facilitator, or director' of those
involved in a dance project, including the other dancers" (156). Tanaka does both.
He was not just empowering the audience; he was empowering the dancer as well.
Hijikata had done half of this in saying that "interpretation is the right of the viewer."
But he controlled the body and mind of the dancer by dictating to them what to think
(imagine) and how to move. Tanaka demanded the same level of mental engagement
as Hijikata but allowed the dancers to imagine for themselves their own internal mo-
tivation for their actions.

Later Performances

Two later performances have stayed with me (both choreographed under the banner
of Tanaka and Hijikata's private company *Pure Love-Dance School*, even though
Hijikata was long since dead). In 2002, I saw Tanaka perform *Dislocated Child's Body*
(Dakkyû dôtai, 2002). In one scene, naked, Tanaka runs clockwise in a large circle
around the stage. At first the stage is bare and his running unimpeded, but gradually
stagehands throw angular rocks onto the stage. Some hit Tanaka. Others fall harmlessly to the floor. Harmlessly, that is, until Tanaka circles around the stage again.
Without so much as a wince, and without ever hesitating or altering the placement of
his feet to avoid rocks, he runs on and on. Each time his bare feet hit a rock, or each
time a rock hit him, I winced. On he went—the stage growing more covered with
rocks by the minute. My stomach tightened each time he stepped on a rock. Round
by round, there were fewer times when his foot hit bare ground and more times when
it hit a rock. Fewer moments when I could breathe easily because his foot had not hit
a rock, and more moments when my stomach tightened. This scene was centered on

Tanaka's ability to tread on sharp rocks without betraying the slightest manifestation of pain, and on the involuntary response in the pit of my stomach.

In *Passing through the Body and Sloughing It Off* (Tôtai datsuraku, November 6, 2005, and November 12, 2006, Setagaya Public Theater), Tanaka makes his way on stage from the audience, dressed in a black jacket and pants. There is a circle of sand on stage and behind it some orangish dirt and rocks.[11] At the back of the stage, there is a curtain of tattered clothes. Tanaka ducks under the curtain and then pulls the curtain down just far enough to look over it. He has donned a samurai helmet made out of newspaper. He seems to be punching at the curtain from the back side. A stagehand holds up the curtain and we can see Tanaka now sitting in the dirt behind the curtain wearing a khaki-colored shirt and shorts. The newspaper helmet has a sun on it with rays that radiate out somewhat like the Japanese naval flag. He crawls out in front of the curtain and then stands and vaguely looks like he is sword fighting with a bamboo stick. The light goes down and then comes up on Tanaka (with no shirt on) hanging from a pull-up bar. He crawls into the audience and up the aisle and then stands and totters back down and onto the stage, where he sprawls in the sand. The ambient noise sounds like cicadas and crashing waves. He wanders back into the darkness at the back of the stage and then curls around to a dog house at the right of the stage. He climbs inside and then pokes his nose out. Then he comes out and makes his way to the middle of the stage where he takes off his short pants and sits with his back to the audience. He is lit from above so that we can see the skin between his ribs suck in and out with each breath. He goes to the back of the stage and puts on the black pants, white shirt, black jacket, and a black overcoat. He goes behind the stalks of pampas grass at the back of the stage and then curls around to stage right, always just on the edge of the light, flapping his arms ethereally. He walks pigeon-toed into the dirt pile, waves his jacket around, and then goes over and drapes it over the doghouse. He goes back to the sand, takes off his shirt and then pants, and stands naked in the sand. At some moments he looks cold, and at other moments he looks embarrassed, but then he just stares straight forward. He gradually leans back with the light shining directly down on him. There are tiny tremors in his hands and head. He lays down and rolls in the sand and rocks, and then backs into the darkness at the back of the stage, turning to give us a profile from time to time of him on his hands and knees looking quite animalistic. He turns to face the audience and gradually comes to standing as the lights go down.

From these two performances, we can see that Tanaka was still very much interested in the abstract limit-conditions of the body from early in his career, but that he also seems to have fully absorbed one aspect of Hijikata: portraying a strange story or character in the dance that only the choreographer knows about, but giving hints to the audience as to possible avenues into the dance. The title of the second dance, *Passing through the Body and Sloughing It Off* (tôtai datsuraku) is a term from the Buddhist monk Dôgen. It essentially means, if you have truly liberated yourself from illusions and desires, in a Buddhist sense, then you become one with everything and slough off the body (Bielefeldt 2009). It is not clear what Tanaka would have intended by sloughing off the body, but we know two things about Tanaka that *might* be pertinent to this dance. First, he suggested to Dana Iovacchini that she explore Onoda Hirô as a character in one of her dances (Fuller 2016, 198). Second, he has a soft spot for Don Quixote and for people who do quixotic things (Fuller 2016, 160). Given the sand, the sound of the waves, the dirt and pampas grass behind, and the samurai helmet folded out of newspaper, the dance might concern a Japanese holdout after World War II, possibly Onoda. But that is pure conjecture on my part. For my concerns, the dance is important only in that it demonstrates how much some of Tanaka's dances came to resemble the dances of Hijikata and Ôno.

Relationship to Butô

Recently, Tanaka has strenuously distanced himself from the term "butô." But he used the term for himself between 1983, when he danced Hijikata's choreography, and 2000. There are a couple of problems with taking at face value Tanaka's repudiation of butô. Tanaka was watching Hijikata's dances from at least 1968. There is no telling how much of Hijikata he absorbed in those years. He and Goi Teru were collaborating from 1972, and Goi was also to become a self-proclaimed butô artist. Moreover, he and some Dairakudakan dancers were working together for some time in 1978. Tanaka had possibly already absorbed some aspects of butô before 1983, and the community of butô may have also absorbed a significant amount from Tanaka as it took shape. Whatever the case, by 1983, Tanaka then studied with Hijikata extensively and used Hijikata's imagery work for the rest of his career. The upshot is that quite simply many of Tanaka's dances, including both solos and group choreography, *look* like butô. Whether it is the porn video tone of *Sonorite de Violette*, which looks for all the world like a Dairakudakan performance, or the black suit–clad character of *Form of the Sky*, which looks like a Hijikata- or Ôno-inspired character, or the doghouse character in *Passing through the Body and Sloughing It Off*, many of Tanaka's dances look and feel like butô.

In part, Tanaka was drawn to Hijikata out of a desire to continually improve his dance abilities. One of the difficulties of improvisation is that it is easy to fall into a rut, and the challenge is to find a way to get out and do something new. Fuller argues that over time Tanaka accumulated a massive store of movements that he could use in improvisation. The fact that some of his dances look so much like the dances of other heirs of Hijikata is a testimony to the strength of his engagement with Hijikata's dance as part of his own quest to keep exploring the wider world of dance.

Conclusion

Tanaka has had a long and varied career which continues to this day. He still dances and still strives to remake his dance at every turn. He broke new ground in improvisation in dance. He benefited from butô, because his early association with butô opened doors that might have otherwise remained closed. But butô benefited from him as well when French intellectuals gravitated to him rather than to other dancers who were more interested in contesting specifics of Japanese life onstage. And then the benefit came full circle as he studied with Hijikata and invigorated his own dance. His focus on farming and nature contributed to the side of butô invested in dancing in nature. Much as with his repudiation of the term "butô," he has frequently moved on from parts of his own past, such as Tokason or Body Weather Laboratories and Farm, but he has just as quickly started new projects, such as the Locus Focus series in 2006–2007 and the Ba-Odori series (literally Place-Dance—2008–present). He has also taken up film and television acting (for which he won a Japanese Academy award).

However, the people who participated in prior projects have also gone on to carve out important spots for themselves in the performing arts landscape. One such Body Weather–inspired project was Oguri's *Height of Sky* (2001–2002), a two-year, multifaceted investigation into the desert after Oguri relocated to Los Angeles.[12] The initially cocky Oguri, who imagines that he can hike for two straight days in the heat, quickly comes to appreciate the power and danger of the desert. Over the course of sixty-five days in the desert, he encounters abandoned mines and mills and waxes indignant at the former occupants who left them there, learns about the way that salt left its mark on the animals (including humans) that passed through, observes the aqueduct that channels water through the desert to elsewhere while seeking to let not a drop spill out to the parched land. Sometimes he blends into the land and sometimes dances seemingly to confront it, and on one occasion severely lacerates his back when he accidentally slides down a hill on his back. It is the kind of performance that nicely melds Hijikata's concern for how places imprint themselves on bodies and how people imprint themselves on places with Tanaka's concern for how bodies can be minutely responsive to nature. Moreover, Oguri's dance exploration brings butô into dialogue with modern western American nature writing such as Edward Abbey's *Desert Solitaire* and Terry Tempest Williams's *Refuge*, and land art such as Robert Smithson's *Spiral Jetty*. Whether Tanaka accepts or rejects the label "butô," the aftereffects of his remarkable career (including the interaction between Tanaka and butô) continue to unfold.

14
Conclusion

It's been a wild ride, but let's take stock. Genres are inherently fuzzy beasts. They are partly created by artists working together, but they are also created by the way people talk and write about art, and the way that archivists group artistic activities (Nowak and Whelan 2018, 452). I hope it does not happen, but even this book may contribute to the solidification of the idea of a butô genre, despite my efforts to indicate the varied activities of the artists featured here. Each of the ten people in this book have worked with many other people to make some dances that have similarities, but other radically different kinds of dance. One of them even repudiates the word "butô," thinking that it has now become a hindrance to further creativity. And maybe it was, for him. But, butô did not stop with those ten. Butô has been many things to many people, and it continues to explode.

In *Flash* (2015), Michael Sakamoto teamed with the hip-hop dancer Rennie Harris to do a butô-hip-hop examination of themselves and their mutual fascination with each other's cultures. Sakamoto explored his fascination with African American West Coast funk culture in East LA, and Harris looked into his infatuation with Japanese robot cartoons and Hong Kong martial arts films in West Philadelphia. Hata Kanoko, picked up Hijikata's hints about Hansen's disease and performed five "butoh-actions" in a leprosaria in Taiwan to protest plans to relocate the leprosaria to make way for a train station (Seetoo 2018). Shakina Nayfack clung to butô through gender confirmation surgery (Shannon 2018). Australian performer Jeremy Neideck and Korean p'ansori singers Park Younghee, and Tak Hoyoung mixed butô with the Korean musical storytelling form p'ansori (Niedeck 2018). Anmar Taha only saw butô in images and read Hijikata's writings but was moved to use those images as the basis for a dance about the discrimination Iraqis faced after 9/11 (Dellcave 2018). jackï job used butô to explore race in South Africa (job 2018), and then used it again to contest the boundaries between humans, animals, vegetation, and minerals (job 2021). Carla Melo and Joe Talkington used the "dead body" of butô to create "moving mass graves" in an antiwar protest (Melo 2018). I could go on and on, and I could expand into fashion, music, and art (for more, see Baird and Candelario 2018, 11–12). As I was in the final stages of writing this book, my kids came running in to tell me that Kumiko on *Cobra Kai* told Daniel that she had gone all over the world dancing for the "Hijikata Tatsumi Dance Company" (Cobra Kai, Season 3, "The Right Path"). There is no such thing as the Hijikata Tatsumi Dance Company. He called his group many things, but never that. What is more, his dancers only went to four cities outside of Japan, so it is a stretch to say that a Hijikata dancer "traveled all around the

A History of Butô. Bruce Baird, Oxford University Press. © Oxford University Press 2022.
DOI: 10.1093/oso/9780197630273.003.0014

world." But there it was, Hijikata creeping into one more place, as the ultimate in-the-know reference.

Is there anything that holds this fuzzy genre together? Probably not. And were I to venture such a connection, someone would come along and dance a butô that did not belong. But threads crisscross this burgeoning form and connect everyone. Three entwined threads are databases of movement, minute sensation, and granularity of movement. Hijikata and Ashikawa created tons of new steps, poses, and movements, and then created thousands of new imagery exercises that can be combined and used as tools to create new kinds of affect and performance. The audience only sees the surface performance, but underneath is a veritable maelstrom of mental activity—the biting bugs, artists living behind kneecaps, that produce the exact performance we see. Maro's "flavored ma" functions in a similar way as do the directives in Tanaka's exercises.

Kasai's systemic use of a database works in a different way: It starts with a massive research project to understand every possible mode of being, the noun way of being, the properties and power of voicing an "ah," and the hermaphrodite way of being. Then, he assumes that in order to work against something (monolithic gender norms, monolithic languages, or any monolithic structure), first you have to practice inhabiting each option of these from the inside. You have to have an underlying mental and bodily grasp of all the modes of the world. Then, in a manner highly reminiscent of Hijikata and Ashikawa, you can mix these building blocks in novel ways in order to find new modes of movement and being. Tanaka goes to a veritable database of places—garbage dumps, forests, parking lots, farms, and fields—and tries to sense and respond to everything about them—shivers of wind, rays of sunlight, rocks biting into his skin, ferns prickling his body. Amagatsu and his dancers practice on a stage until they can sense if another stage is slightly different sized, and they train themselves to hold their internal stream unbroken for long stretches.

Another tangled pair of threads are nature and universals. Hijikata seeks to know how nature, culture, and history inscribe themselves on body-minds. Tanaka and his students dance in nature, work in nature, and interact directly with animals. Hijikata, Ashikawa, Maro, and Ikeda study animals carefully and seek to take from animals cues for new ways of moving. Amagatsu imagines a time either before or after civilization and brings nature (in the shape of rippling water and falling sand) to his audiences. Ōno imagines correspondences between natural activities such as the birth of a star and giving birth to new life.

To these we could add other threads. Amagatsu's absolute minimum effort necessary is linked to Tanaka's idea of using as little muscular effort as possible in dancing from the bones. And both are related to but on the opposite end from Maro's use of imagery work to enable the body to do something for much longer than it could do with only a direct signal from the mind. Amagatsu's stacking of the bones along the gravitational radius is related to but opposite Hijikata and Maro, who purposely used twisted, contorted movements that were intentionally out of balance and tensed. They both might have been more interested in seeking out the maximum effort necessary (and in enabling their dancers to actually achieve that impossible goal). Ôno's survival guilt and gratitude are allied with Maro's "Thanks to you." And his self-dispossession is similarly related to Maro's space body, which can be filled by something, and to his interval (ma). Ôno's assumptions that any movement in either side of the body-mind will ripple through the whole and that we are connected to the entire universe is the sibling of Kasai's assumption that every particle of the chaos-mathematics universe is connected to every other particle, so we can speak across the universe, and both are in turn related to Yoshioka's idea that humans and the environment affect each other mutually and to Ikeda's attempt to let the body read texts. Kobayashi and Amagatsu both understand the human to pass through evolutionary states in its embryonic development and think that the human body holds species memory. Kobayashi, Kasai, and Ôno assume the existence of unseen powers in the universe, whereas Tanaka seems much more skeptical of such things. Kasai's revolutionary moment when the first amphibian crawled up on land is paralleled in Amagatsu's dialogue with gravity when horizontal creatures first stood up vertically. Hijikata, Ashikawa, Ikeda, and Amagatsu demand intense concentration and precise control. Hijikata, Ashikawa, Maro, and Ikeda feature ethnically Japanese elements and characters (which they are invariably citing and distancing themselves from at the same time). Tanaka, Ôno, and Amagatsu have fewer such characters (although Amagatsu is never far from an association with shaven-headed Zen monks and rock gardens). Everyone implicitly treats political themes (whether Hijikata's shaven-headed dancers as a symbol of Japanese or US power, or Tanaka's hint at a solder who battles on long after the war is over). Some choreographers, however, bury their themes more deeply than others. Tanaka, Amagatsu, and Yoshito (when he danced opposite his father, Ôno) are more like deodorized Sony Walkman culture and international style architecture. Tanaka and Ashikawa both collaborated with free jazz musicians and took hints from free jazz into their improvisations. In general, the people closer to the improvisation side (such as Tanaka, Ôno, Kasai, and Yoshioka) often use imagery work or structures to guide their improvisations. All but Amagatsu and Ôno insist on fragmentation and compartmentalization of the body. The grotesque and marginal are never far from anyone's mind. Gender bending and variation within gender are also spread across the genre (although as noted, the men get to do more gender-bending than the women). Surrealist juxtaposition abounds. But no one just rearranges elements that were given to them. They all create new bodily vocabulary.

No single strand holds all these artists together, but that is one helluva set of threads criss-crossing the group.

I end by returning to the idea that butô is closely related to aspects of contemporary (Japanese) life. To consider butô in relation to cyborgs/otaku/unassisted speed runners is to say several important things. One is that many people thought they saw in butô a kind of privileged access point to the real, because it was concerned with the weighty matters of the universe. They were right. Butô is indeed such an access point to the real. In part, it accesses the real when it concerns itself with life, death, disease, madness, suffering, and peripheral members of society. But in part it accesses the real because the butô dancer, in physical and mental ways, tries to capture fully what it means to live in a world in which bodies are bent and contorted, but also minds are taxed like never before.

Otaku and speed runners are not important for this comparison solely because of their ability to cope with the information world, although that is no small feat. They can and must be attentive to the minutia of an increasingly complex world, but at the same time, they have the extra ability to access and manipulate the underlying codes of the world. Azuma's work is most hopeful when he refers to the ability of otaku to manipulate the world at the underlying level, the level of the code. Otaku and speedrunners use the setting and characters to write a derivative work, or hack into the game and recreate an entirely new game, or figure out how to walk through videogame walls. We might characterize butô artists as body-mind hackers, who do the work of understanding all the visible and invisible ways that bodies and minds are connected, and then work to find new ways of thinking and moving.

Bear in mind that butô shares the rule of thumb of the otaku world: Participate yourself. Butô is not just for professional dancers. Butô says to everyone: Make yourself more perceptive and nuanced about your world. Exercise your imagination. Not just in imagining hundreds of bugs crawling over your body, but in imagining yourself outside the confines of your society. Or imagining yourself in the geta of the person who is marginalized by society. The idea of butô is that everyone can and should use their imagination and dance. Of course, it will take work. Do not make the mistake of those people in the early 1980s who thought that butô takes no effort. Whether you come from the inside or attempt to make your own butô from the outside, whether you perform on stage or by yourself in nature or in your room, it will not be easy. The promise of butô is not the promise of easy, but the promise that anyone can and should(!) do the work to find new ways to think, to do, to change themselves and their world.

Notes

Acknowledgments

* In acknowledging "narrowly defined rationalities," I do not mean to give a pass to irrational things and ideas. As we see all around us, irrationality is a huge problem and this book is not a defense or praise of it in any way. I only mean to indicate that there are things and ideas whose sense takes time and hard work to understand.

Chapter 1

1. Yoshioka, interview with the author, May 5, 2014.
2. For photos, see the Murobushi Kô Archive, https://ko-murobushi.com/eng/works/view/38; the Jean-Marie Gourreau Archive, CND, http://mediatheque.cnd.fr/spip.php?page=mediatheque-numerique-rechercher (search for "dernier eden"); and Pagès 2015, 29, 60, 62, 115, 130, 151, 236.
3. Attendance figures from the Murobushi Kô Archive.
4. That said, butô is already bigger than any book. I have excluded some dancers based on the amount of available information. For example, Furukawa Anzu was important to the establishment of butô in Germany, but there is little information available about her. On the other end, Murobushi Kô is already the subject of a book by Katja Centonze (2018a).
5. Julie Dind notes that Hijikata's disability is "disability danced by a non-disabled dancer—or at the very least, an attempt at dancing someone else's disability." As such, "In a sense, he exploits disability for its foreignness and shock-value rather than exploring it as a fully embodied experience" (Dind 2019, unpublished ms.).
6. See Wurmli 2008, 179, 245, and 258, and Baird 2012, 203–204.
7. Saulnier et al. 1978. https://www.ina.fr/video/CAA7801575201/la-danseuse-japonaise-video.html.
8. See Fraleigh 2010, 158 and "Part Two."
9. Centonze has written prolifically on the *nikutai* (carnal body) and the *shintai* (social body) (Centonze 2009, 170–172, esp. fn. 7 and 9; and Centonze 2010). Slaymaker argues that the *nikutai* was gendered as male (Slaymaker 2004, Introduction).
10. To recognize the butô dancer as a quasi-cyborg is not unambiguously positive, as with Haraway's idea that the cyborg is post gender (Haraway 1991, 150). In fact, many otaku fictional fantasies double down on gender, with woman as maids, sex slaves, and weapons for men (Daly 2019, 104). However radical butô's gender experimentation may have felt for the men, it was much less radical for women.
11. Other scholars generally agree with Azuma. For example, Okada Toshio asserts that otaku have three kinds of visual acuity (Saito 2011, 13) and Keith Vincent claims that otaku are "better equipped to cope in a media-saturated postmodern society" (Vincent 2011, xix).

12. Saito Tamaki writes that otaku are "SS (short or side) story writers who borrow the setting and characters from [prior] works, [and] write novels and scenarios in different versions" (Saito 2011, 20).

13. Body-mind hacking differs from the body hacking movement in which people surgically implant technologies into their bodies. I am more interested in how people change their bodies (most often without surgical procedures) when exposed to new technologies. For body-hacking, see Duarte 2014.

Chapter 2

1. For more on blackness and its erasure from butô, see Arimitsu 2015 and 2018.

2. For Yoneyama, see Huston 1976, 354–362.

3. According to contemporary accounts, the chicken did not die.

4. For a full reconstruction and detailed analysis, see Baird 2012, 15–31. See also Shiga 2005, and Kuniyoshi 2006.

5. Yoshito says that the dance was inspired by a Terayama Shûji poem about Algeria. I have not been able to locate such a poem.

6. See Iimura 2005; and for more about these two dances, see Baird 2012, 67–99.

7. For more on Hosoe and *Kamaitachi*, see Baird 2012, 106–111.

8. I have added a few details (about *Metemotionalphysics*, Noziere, and the Shibusawa essay in *Notice from a Telescope*), but nearly all this discussion comes from Marotti 2019.

9. For more on Hijikata's treatment of Heliogabalus, see Baird 2012, 123–125, 134–135.

10. For more on Hijikata's treatment of the back, see Baird 2012, 39, 50, 54, 86–88.

11. Scholarship on shôjo is proliferating; see Shamoon 2012; Prough 2011; Toku 2015. For disposable income, see Tanaka Yukiko 1995, 78–80. For Japanese women and travel, see Ivy 1995, 29–41; and Kelsky 2001, 2, 5, 135.

12. The movie by Sano Toshifumi is undated, but the lighting does not match the January, 21, 1972 performance photographed by Onozuka Makoto, so it is likely the November 1970 performance. The movie appears to collate two different performances, one in a dark theater, and one that is extremely washed out.

13. This section is based on Yoshida 2018, 138–140, and Marenzi 2018, 143. For the triangles, see Barrault 1951, 58.

14. This section adapted and shortened from Baird 2016.

15. I am dubious that the *namba* gait really was the basis for all Japanese performing arts, but for a discussion of *namba*, see Isaka 2018; and Takechi and Tomioka 2018, 91, fn. 1.

16. For the parallel process in which a small group of songs became standardized as Japanese *min'yô* "folk songs" with one correct way of singing, see Hughes 2008, 283, 286, 291.

17. For more on Japan's "internal" or "domestic colonies," see Hopson 2013, 5–6.

18. For the photograph (also available online), see Smith and Smith 1975, 138–139. For congenital Minamata disease, see Walker 2010, ch. 5, esp. 168.

19. See Arai 2003. The video contains heavy editorializing that was not part of the original dance.

20. For the original Latin, see http://runeberg.org/olmagnus/0857.html. For English, see https://mythicalcreatures.edwardworthlibrary.ie/dragons/sea-serpent-of-norway/. My thanks to Karsten Theis for transcribing the German and locating the English and Latin versions.

21. Footage is preserved as part of a documentary by NHK, *Hijikata Tatsumi to butô*. The dance was restaged for the documentary. There are only about eleven minutes of the dance, sometimes with voice-overs from talking heads. The date of the performance is unclear.
22. Gagaku is imperial court music and haniwa are clay figures that were interred with the dead during the third to sixth centuries. One theory is that haniwa were receptacles for the soul. There are also haniwa dancers and drummers, so it is thought that they are related to early theatrical forms. For haniwa, see Miki 1974; and for gagaku, see Ortolani 1995, 39–53.
23. For legendary Japanese people flying on kites, see Streeter 1974, 160–161. For kabuki characters sticking out their tongues, see Brandon and Leiter 2002a, 50–53, 56; and Brandon and Leiter 2002b, 238.
24. Here we could consider Heidegger's treatment of tools, and Graham Harman's provocative one-upping of Heidegger to propose "'tool being' or an 'object oriented philosophy' in which humans . . . are on precisely the same footing as glass bottles, pitchforks, windmills, comments, ice cubes, magnets, and atoms" (Harman 2002, 2).
25. Sakurai Keisuke alerted me to the possible connection between Hijikata's cabaret acts and fashion show aesthetics.

Chapter 3

1. Public lecture, Keio University, December 7, 2000.
2. One piece of evidence for her role in the choreography turns out to be a mistake. In a pamphlet prepared for Kasai Akira's US tour in 2004, it says that Hijikata's "techniques were developed mainly by women" (Kuniyoshi 2004, 2), but this is a mistranslation of the original essay by Kuniyoshi. The translation should read, "techniques were mainly brought to perfection on women['s bodies]" (email from Kuniyoshi Kazuko, January 11, 2021).
3. For a video, see Amano 2015, Ch. 2, where the dance is misidentified as co-choreographed by Ashikawa and Tomoe Shizune. https://www.tomoe.com/text/tree_story_2.html.
4. William Marotti made this archival letter available to me.
5. For the original title, see the Toga Festival program: https://ko-murobushi.com/eng/works/view/197.
6. For the clips of this dance, see the Tomoe Shizune & Hakutôbô Vimeo Channel: https://vimeo.com/93726375, https://vimeo.com/93721199, https://vimeo.com/93718308, https://vimeo.com/308780663.
7. The video is available on the Tomoe Shizune and Hakutôbô webpage: https://www.tomoe.com/item/movie2020_tree.html.
8. Ashikawa reports that this happened a year after Hijikata's death (Ashikawa 2018, Section 3).
9. My thinking is based on interviews with Nakajima Natsu (December 14, 2013), SU-EN (December 18, 2013), Joan Laage (September 29, 2015, and January 9, 2021), Rob Schwartz (July 14, 2015), and Seisaku (January 29, 2021).
10. Both Nakajima Natsu and SU-EN have told me that Ashikawa was quite devastated by Hijikata's death, and also that she had no ambition to become the leading choreographer of her own company.
11. Observations based on the San Francisco Butoh Festival (2002), but see SU-EN 2001: https://www.suenbutohcompany.net/past-projects/headless/.

Chapter 4

1. In this evolution, he matches practitioners including Abe Kôbô and Ôta Shôgô, who evolved over time to theater of fewer and fewer words. For Abe, see Keene 1993, xi–xii; and for Ôta, see Boyd 2006, 104–107.
2. Centonze traces a set of preoccupations that stretched over 6 years and (at least) 17 dances (Centonze 2018, 228–231).
3. The extant recording is an experimental film, with music/soundscape persisting seamlessly across cuts. Thus, the temporal progression and spatial layout likely differ from the stage performance (Susumura 1973a).
4. Maro, email to the author via manager Shinfune Yoko, February 13, 2017. Lyrics to *Aleutian Ballad* by Takatsuki Kotoba, set to a folk tune collected by Yamada Ei-ichi. See https://iss.ndl.go.jp/books/R100000002-I024584890-00?locale=ja&ar=4e1f.
5. This Horsehead is the counterpart to the possible Oxhead of *Last Eden*.
6. It was not until 1974 that women's surnames were included in promotional materials (Yamada 1992, 211).
7. For the imperial family's roots in Korea, see Ledyard 1975, 234, 247; Ôbayashi 1984, 180; and Ellwood, 1990, 200.
8. Observations based on an experimental film, Susumura 1973b.
9. For the ways that maps influence how we view the world and also reflect and entrench power structures, see Harley 2002.
10. This might be related to the idea of the Global South. See Rigg 2007.
11. Summary from Aihara 2018; Bradley 2017, 87–93; Maro n.d.a, n.d.c, 2004; Maro and Konuma Jun-ichi 2005; Matsuoka et al. 1985; Neideck 2018; and Vessey 2018.
12. We now recognize that "empty" spaces are not empty at all: They contain gravity, air, dark matter, and/or antimatter, and exert various pressures on what we see. Compare with Shibusawa's indestructible nothingness; Ôno's "self-dispossession" (Ch. 8) and relatively recent Buddhist philosophies of the generative nature of emptiness (Nishitani Keiji 1999, 179–217).
13. This is like "stom-paa" in Calamoneri 2018, 420.
14. For the historical inaccuracies of bushido culture, see Hurst 1990.
15. For close-ups of Maro firing his toy gun, see Vélez 1989.

Chapter 5

1. Miki Shigeo was an anatomist and embryologist, who studied Goethe's morphology, Haeckel's recapitulation theory, Karl Gegenbaur's comparative anatomy, and the paleontology of William King Gregory, Alfred Romer, and Edwin H. Colbert. He published a widely selling book *The World of the Fetus: The Life Memory of Humanity* (Miki 1983), in which he argues that "life memory" is "the history of evolution that is etched in the human body and heart" (Gotô 1994, 45).
2. Kobayashi first used the word "Aura" in a dance title in 1988, and then she started a "Butô Aura" series. She first used the word "hysterica" in a dance title in 2004.
3. Of course, we know she cannot see us, but performance often depends on the fiction that the dancer can see the people in the audience.

4. See: http://kobayashi-saga.holy.jp/words.html. Compare with Didi-Huberman's original: "An aura is air, air blowing across a face or through a body, the air of pathos, the event it imposes. It is the proof and its breath, that is, its imminence, a slight breeze before the storm. *Aura*, a Greek word, was an attested medical formula since Galen, a breath that 'traverses the body' the very moment the body finds itself plunged into pain and crisis" (Didi-Huberman 2004, 100).

Chapter 6

1. It is difficult to compare values over time and across currencies, but the figures are calculated based on Williamson and Cain 2020. They explain that different valuations will produce different approximations: www.measuringworth.com/defining_measures_of_worth.php
2. For the 500 yen wage (and other information about the communal lifestyle), see Coker 2018, 410–411. Also pers. conversation with Waguri Yukio, July 21, 2013, and interview with Maro Akaji, January 21, 2014.
3. See photos 4 and 5 in https://ko-murobushi.com/jpn/works/view/10.
4. All the information for this section is from Maro 2011, 220–231.
5. In an interview, Maro defended Hijikata and Motofuji's use (and implicitly his use) of the cabaret, because they were not getting rich either and the dancers could quit any time they liked (January 21, 2014). This defense overlooks the power dynamic between the head of the troupe and the dancers. Although dancers complain about not getting enough to eat and being forced to steal daikon radishes, it does not appear that Hijikata and Motofuji suffered the same level of privation. Moreover, the dancers tell stories of being too scared to leave and sneaking away in the night (Pers. conversation, Waguri, July 21, 2013).
6. Suzuki Tadashi similarly relocated to a rural village. In that case, Toga-village was happy to house a famous theater company on the assumption of increased tourism (Alain 2002, 21 and passim). The early butô dancers simply took a subsidiary show to the rural areas in order to funnel cash back to their main pursuit. Compare with Tanaka's work in rural areas in Chapter 13.
7. For the *iemoto* system, see Sellers-Young 1992, 71–84; Nomura 2008; and Moeran 1987, 27–50.

Chapter 7

1. See Pagès 2015, 37. I draw heavily from Pagès throughout this section.
2. Koseki had studied *shintaido* (New Way of the Body), which is a movement form based on martial arts.
3. For photos and materials, see Pagès 2015, 29, 60, 62, 115, 130, 151, 236; and https://www.ko-murobushi.com/jpn/works/view/38.
4. Centonze 2018b, 228–230. For *sokushinbutsu*, see Jeremiah 2010.
5. An English translation of the text is readily available online.
6. For photos, see the Jean-Marie Gourreau Archive, CND, http://mediatheque.cnd.fr/spip.php?page=mediatheque-numerique-rechercher (search for "Tanaka"), and www.festival-automne.com/en/edition-1978/japon-tanaka-min-danseur-nu.
7. For cultural deodorization, see Allison 2006, 116–117; Iwabuchi 2002, 27–28.

8. Murobushi Kô Memorial Archive material.

9. Amagatsu, interview with author May 18, 2014, and email exchange with Amagatsu's agent, Pierre Barnier, May 20 and 21, 2014.

10. See Lambourne 2005; Duncan 1994; Zatlin 1997; Wood 2000.

11. See Alter 1968; Cooke 1998; Albright 1985; Gillespie 1982–1983; Barthes 1982; and Patterson 2002.

12. Performers can make money if they gross more in ticket sales than the cost of the theater rental.

13. Murobushi, pers. conversation, January 29, 2014; Yoshioka, pers. conversation, May 4, 2014.

Chapter 8

1. Information comes from four slightly contradictory biographies on the Japanese and English Ôno Kazuo Dance Studio webpages. See "Ôno Kazuo ni tsuite, gaiyô," http://www.kazuoohnodancestudio.com/japanese/kazuo/; "Ôno Kazuo ni tsuite, nenpyô," http://www.kazuoohnodancestudio.com/japanese/kazuo/chro.html; "Kazuo Ohno: Short Biography," http://www.kazuoohnodancestudio.com/english/kazuo/; "Kazuo Ohno: Full Biography," http://www.kazuoohnodancestudio.com/english/kazuo/chro.html.

2. For Uchimura, see Howes 2010; Miura 1996; and Karatani 1993, 84–96. Yoshito and Harada make it seem as if Ôno's choice of faith was rather haphazard (Ohno and Ohno 2004, 114; Harada 2004, 91).

3. For undôkai (sports day), see Guttmann and Thompson 2002, 92.

4. Ôno would have been aware of cannibalism, because the Japanese military specifically prohibited the consumption of Japanese flesh on the penalty of death (Doglia 2011). See also Rees 2001, and Yuki Tanaka 2010 and 2019.

5. I can find no information about Matsuzumi or the source material.

6. The costumes were shabbier in the original performance (Schwellinger 2018, 117, paraphrasing Goda 1994, 21), but the costumes were to grow increasingly flashy.

7. Maria Pia D'Orazi wryly observes that Ôno danced flamenco to tango music (D'Orazi 2018, 262).

8. Charlotte Marr, lighting designer for the Munich Kamerspiele, explained the changes in lighting (email exchange February/March 2010). Sawa Reiko is credited with the lighting design in some promotional materials, but Mizohata Toshio says that Hijikata dictated the original lighting (email to the author July 21, 2014).

9. For a dramatic demonstration of the changes in lighting, see the respective "Bird" scenes from 1977 and 1994 in Ôno Kazuo Kenkyûjo, dir. 2000.

10. This passage is specifically directed to the "way Ohno works with and against the music," but it also nicely describes his relationship to Mercé.

11. He postulated that "species be understood as the substratum of human [Existence] itself" (Tanabe 1990, xvi).

12. This review was actually for Ôno's *The Dead Sea* (1986), but it likely captures how audiences negotiated the relationship between the program notes and the dances.

13. This version cuts out before the ending and any curtain calls.

14. This is what made a twitter stream challenge "describe yourself like a male author would" so heart-breaking. Many responses presumed that men would see women in a sexual way, but the most poignant responses were from women who assumed that men would not see

them at all because they were old and/or frumpy. A user named GLynny writes, "Over 50 and invisible." Kathleen writes, "Let's be realistic, as a middle-aged woman in tech, no male author would describe me ever." Katie: "Rotund and dowdy, she enjoyed the company of men more than they enjoyed hers."
      https://twitter.com/whitneyarner/status/980330317247545349.

15. Supree comments on Bausch's presentation of ugliness on stage in "Hit Me with Your Best Shot" (Supree 1985a).
16. Ôno performed in *Isshin* (One Mind) with Yoshito in December 2005, but 2003 was really his last year of performing, with six performances throughout Japan. See: http://www.kazuoohnodancestudio.com/english/kazuo/chro.html. Compare Ôno with the depiction of puppeteer Yoshida Tamao, and chanter Takemoto Sumitayu, aged 84 and 79 respectively (Ueno and Miura 2003).
17. Schwellinger observed that the "the torso follows suit" but did not connect it to Ôno's age (Schwellinger 2018, 123).
18. I inadvertently mistranslated this passage in the English version of Kuniyoshi's essay, making it mean the *opposite* of what Kuniyoshi intended. The correct translation should read, "Ohno felt that [Ishii's] exalted dramatic dance is rather unnaturally forced, and he could *not* get used to such lofty spheres and a universality that surpasses everyday human emotion" (Kuniyoshi 2018, 27).
19. For Japanese typeset transcriptions of Ôno's notes, see Ôno 1998: *Admiring La Argentina*, 106–109; *My Mother*, 124–128; *Dead Sea* (two different versions presumably for different performances), 167–173; *Waterlilies*, 180–181.

Chapter 9

1. See the explanation by Y.O. concerning "Female Volcano": https://ko-murobushi.com/eng/works/view/17.
2. See "Document" at https://ko-murobushi.com/eng/works/view/17, nos. 2 and 3.
3. See respectively, "Kansai" 1975; *Nikkan supôtsu* 1975a, 1975b; "Scrap" at https://ko-murobushi.com/eng/works/view/17, nos. 5, 6, and 10.
4. See "Zarathoustra de Carlotta Ikeda," Orange Videos https://video-streaming.orange.fr/actu-politique/zarathoustra-de-carlotta-ikeda-CNT000001e9Q7i.html.
5. The documentary version differs from the staged versions in the setting but resembles them in the narrative arc (Arvers 1993, 47; Willems 1993).
6. To get a sense of the dance, see Ikeda 2002b and Ikeda and Spina 2002.
7. See http://web.archive.org/web/20151126002334/http://ariadone.fr/eng/workshop/.

Chapter 10

1. All information taken from an interview with the author, May 4, 2014.
2. For videos and programs of tatoeba TDG, see http://www.tatoeba.de/html/d-performances.html.
3. See http://www.tatoeba.de/html/e-media.html.
4. See a digest at http://youtu.be/r1sAAb2RfJc.
5. See a digest at http://youtu.be/BDvHFHT8aBk.
6. See a digest at https://www.youtube.com/watch?v=WLQQrShQF1s.

7. See https://www.youtube.com/watch?v=MmXKLYENunc.
8. See a short digest at http://www.yumiko-yoshioka.com/100lightyears/.
9. Houwer and Teers 1995. https://www.youtube.com/watch?v=Eka3ruG6DD0&feature=youtu.be.
10. Loh 2007. https://www.youtube.com/watch?v=HEpPGGpeiCo&feature=youtu.be

Chapter 11

1. The exchange was in Japanese between Oguri (of the Tanaka lineage) and Kasai. See Flournoy 2018, 317, and Nicely 2018, 193 (quoting Flournoy remembering different words, "How dare you say that. This is my dance. This is my life").
2. For specific festivals, see Flournoy 2018 and Garnica 2018.
3. Kasai speaks approvingly of what he terms an "atheistic, material esoterics," which he attributes to Kawamura Satoru (Kasai and Kawamura 1992, I. 19).
4. Observations from archival video.
5. For Kasai's eurythmy choreography, see Ito 2013, approximately 35:00.
6. Observations based on training with Kasai geared to professional dancers. See also Nicely's account of training for *Exusiai* in 1998 (Nicely 2012, 224–228).
7. This sentence—presented out of context as if universally true—is a fragment of a sentence from Tacitus's *Histories*, 4:17, in which the Batavian leader Gaius Julius Civilis seeks to stir up rebellion against Rome. "At the same time [Civilis] reminded them in confidential conversations of the wrongs which they had endured for so many years, while they *falsely gave to a wretched slavery the name of peace*" (Tacitus 1942, 604, my emphasis).
8. Nicely analyzes these grammatical person categories with reference to Deleuze's notion of the "impersonal pronoun" (Nicely 2012, 194).
9. This point is debatable, but there are movements in noh, kabuki, and sumo that resemble the plié. See the discussion in Morinaga 2018, 91.
10. All vowels could be combined with all directions, but Kasai showed a marked preference for voicing A coupled with moving forward and voicing U while moving backward.
11. Compare with Kasai and Ishii, 2013, 10, in which Kasai says,

> we practice the enunciation of vowels and consonants. For example, the "ah" sound is pronounced from deep in the throat, the "oo" sound is made by shaping the lips in a "u" shape, and for the "eh" sound the tongue is used. Each sound is pronounced precisely, one by one, and then repeated. Using the Eurythmy method, the reverberation of the sound of the words is listened to with the whole body as you move.

12. Many of these categories are from the previously described training. The terms are usually mine, to describe something Kasai talks about, but some are taken from other sources.
13. Kasai's categorization parallels Tanaka Min's avowal to "Dance the Place/Space" rather than dancing in the place.
14. Presumably this category could open out into all musical modes.
15. Kasai might be seen to follow Nietzsche, who wrote that the "seduction of language" caused people to think that there are "deeds," which are separate from "subjects," when "in fact there is nothing but [. . .] driving, willing and acting" (Nietzsche 1994, 1: 13 [p. 26]).
16. To be more accurate, the categories articulate $3 \times 12 \times 4 \times 3 \times 3 \times 3 \times 3 \times 3 \times 2 \times 4 \times 2 \times 5 \times 3 \times 3 \times 5 \times 5 = 629,856,000$ different ways of combining these orientations.
17. Megan Nicely analyzes the dance more extensively (Nicely 2012, 233–235; 2018, 192–196).

18. Kasai uses uchu (literally "universe-al") rather than the usual word for universal (fuhen, 普遍) to emphasize the fact that the ideals span the entire cosmos, not just that they apply everywhere.

19. The Wikipedia page for the Japanese constitution has a section on the proposed changes, including deleting mentions of "human rights" and increasing the power of the emperor. https://en.wikipedia.org/wiki/Constitution_of_Japan#Amendment_Drafts_by_the_LDP (accessed, August 14, 2018).

20. For Steiner's poetry see, Steiner 2012. For Yosano's antiwar poem, see Rimer and Gessel 2005, 333–334. For the constitution see, https://japan.kantei.go.jp/constitution_and_gove rnment_of_japan/constitution_e.html.

Chapter 12

1. Similar accounts proliferate. Tom Mococci, executive director of City Center, gushed that seeing Sankai Juku was one of the "top five theatrical experiences of his life" (Perron 1999).

2. The following history is taken from Amagatsu 2015, 1–15.

3. Amagatsu can seem tone deaf on why there are no women in his troupe. On one occasion he said, "At first the composition of the group was random, and now I do not want to change it" (Hassiotis 2014, 8). Amagatsu added that he enjoys choreographing women on other occasions, but in this day and age, his answer seems wrongheaded. His refusal to change deprives women of the opportunity to learn from (and network through) him, but also deprives him of the opportunity to learn from them. If his dances are indeed concerned with evolution, you might think that females are necessary to evolution, so it should be necessary to include females in the exploration of evolution.

4. Analysis based on the restaged version, September 8–9, 2009 (Tokyo Geijutsu Theater). According to reports, there are significant variations from the original in 1978.

5. According to William Marotti, in the original version, Amagatsu mimed humping the peacock, but this does not occur in the archival version (Pers. conversation, June 30, 2020).

6. Michel mentions that the aesthetics of Sankai Juku have a "pronounced homosexual character" (Michel 1982).

7. The Issun Bôshi folk tales originated during a time (1336–1573) when the power of religion waned and people increasingly relied on their own wits (see Skord 1989 and Lafleur 1983, esp. 133–148). Such tales must have struck a chord in postwar Japan as well.

8. See "Sankai Juku en suspension," https://fresques.ina.fr/en-scenes/liste/recherche/Theme. id/29/df/#sort/DateAffichage/direction/DESC/page/1/size/10

9. Nihon Seinenkan Performance, March 3, 1984.

10. Godard's 1982 comparison of Sankai Juku with bande dessinée is not, I think, intended as a compliment.

11. Observations taken from the Oya Stone Quarry performance, August 29–31, 1986 (Amagatsu 2006d).

12. See Dent 2004, 175. Dent vents righteous anger at Amagatsu for being more concerned with striking images than with the safety of his own dancers.

13. Amagatsu does not use this term, but his idea may be related to the martial arts idea of "seiryoku saiyûkô" (most effective use of body and mind) developed by the founder of judo, Kano Jigoro (Hamaguchi 2006, 12).

14. See Repke 2018, "Nature exposure and human health" and "Possible mechanisms" for a succinct overview of research. There is considerable debate within the scientific community about the extent to which such reactions are primal responses or socialized responses stemming from urbanization. See Joye and de Block 2011, for a counter argument that evolutionary biology cannot explain the effects attributed to nature, but rather that these are culturally determined.

Chapter 13

1. This has also been translated as "space." See Shannon 2018, 397, fn 4.
2. For a later collaboration, see Sandrin and Hillaire 1988. https://www.youtube.com/watch?v=8N4P6tz0PRo&list=PLuTPacq5B6EtJCm5HibVn-WIga1sRjfWe&index=50.
3. Fuller compares Tanaka with American postmodern and Judson Dance dancers, including Anna Halprin, John Cage, Steve Paxton, Yvonne Rainer, Carolee Schneeman, Trisha Brown, Grand Union, Simone Forti, and Meredith Monk (Fuller 2016, 68–69).
4. For cellular movement, see Fisher 2006, 21–26.
5. See https://www.youtube.com/watch?v=MFAqJ0XF3b8.
6. For the posters and programs, see http://www.art-c.keio.ac.jp/old-website/archive/hijikata/portas/performance/RCA_TH_EP51.html.
7. Of course, the forces of industrialization and urbanization are so powerful that it is no longer possible for everyone to maintain this kind of contact with the food/labor chain.
8. For a video of two Manipulations, see Hug 2013. https://www.youtube.com/watch?v=Ff3aDNuvZUo.
9. Premiered in Hakushu; for the Paris version, see Sandrin 1990.
10. Others were moving in this direction, but Tanaka provides a particularly clear example in the evolution from *Rite of Spring* to *Romance*. Amagatsu was splitting the difference by assigning some mental imagery but expecting the dancers to supplement such imagery with their own internal stream. Other choreographers such as Kobayashi Saga and Omori Masahide also asked their dancers to come up with their own internal imagery.
11. My account is from the revised version, Iribe 2006. https://www.youtube.com/watch?v=sdiw6gCb0pQ.
12. See Steiner and Steinberg 2007, and Oguri 2019.

References

Note: Japanese names are given in Japanese order without a comma separating the surname and given name. Japanese language sources without a specific place of publication were published in Tokyo.

Aihara Tomoe. 2018. "Open Butoh: Dairakudakan and Maro Akaji." Translated by Robert Ono. In *The Routledge Companion to Butoh Performance*, edited by Bruce Baird and Rosemary Candelario, 181–190. New York: Routledge.

Alain, Paul. 2002. *The Art of Stillness: The Theater Practice of Tadashi Suzuki*. New York: Palgrave MacMillan.

Albright, Daniel. 1985. "Pound, Yeats, and the Noh Theater." *Iowa Review* 15, no. 2: 34–50. http://www.jstor.org/stable/20156175.

Allison, Anne. 2006. *Millennial Monsters: Japanese Toys and the Global Imagination*, Berkeley: University of California Press.

Alter, Maria P. 1968. "Bertolt Brecht and the Noh Drama." *Modern Drama* 11, no. 2 (Summer): 122–131. doi: https://doi.org/10.1353/mdr.1968.0008.

Aloff, Mindy. 1982. "Reviews VII." *Dance Magazine* 63, no. 1 (January): 45–50.

Altice, Nathan. 2015. *I Am Error: The Nintendo Family Computer/Entertainment System Platform*. Cambridge: MIT University Press.

Amagatsu Ushio. 2006a. "A Conversation with Ushio Amagatsu, Artistic Director of Sankai Juku: Interview." Interviewed and translated by Kyoko Yoshida. *Walker Reader, Fourth Wall*. Walker Art Center, November 1, 2006. http://www.walkerart.org/magazine/2006/a-conve rsation-with-ushio-amagatsu-artistic-d.

Amagatsu Ushio. 2006b. "Interview with Ushio Amagatsu." By Choi Su-ling. *Break-a-Leg*. November 25, 2006. http://break-a-leg.blogspot.fr/2006/11/d-interview-with-ushio-amaga tsu-nov-22.html.

Amagatsu Ushio and Senda Akihiko. 2006. "Interview." In *Unetsu: The Egg Stands out of Curiosity*. Amagatsu Ushio, choreog. and dir. IO Factory. DVD.

Amano Uzumi. 2015. "Ippon no ki no Monogatari." Tomoe Shizune and Hakutobo. http://www.tomoe.com/text/treestory1.html.

Arai Misao, dir. 2003. *Hijikata Tatsumi, Natsu no Arashi, Hangidaitôkan 2003–1973*. Daguerro Press/Image Forum.

Ariall, Kate Dobbs. 2008. "Japanese Mini-Fest at ADF—Kochuten and Dairakudakan." *CVNC* (Classical Voice of North Carolina), July 16, 2008. https://cvnc.org/article.cfm?articl eId=1911.

Arimitsu Michio. 2015. "From Voodoo to Butoh: Katherine Dunham, Hijikata Tatsumi, and Trajal Harrell's Transcultural Refashioning of 'Blackness.'" MoMA-Museum of Modern Art, October 2015. https://www.moma.org/d/pdfs/W1siZiIsIjIwMTUvMTAvMzAvdTJ5djQ3 MmpuX1RyYWphbF9IYXJlbGxfTWljaGlvX0FyaW1pdHN1Xy5wZGYiXV0/TrajalHarel lMichioArimitsu.pdf?sha=166dd6cb0fa189b9.

Arimitsu Michio. 2018. "From Vodou to Butoh: Hijikata Tatsumi, Katherine Dunham, and the Trans-Pacific Remaking of Blackness." In *The Routledge Companion to Butoh Performance*, edited by Bruce Baird and Rosemary Candelario, 37–51. New York: Routledge.

Artaud, Antonin. 1958. *The Theater and its Double*. Translated by Mary Caroline Richards. New York: Grove Press.

Arvers, Fabienne. 1993. "Le buto est repassé par là." *Liberation*, June 16, 1993, 47.

Ashikawa Yôko. 1978. "Rûburu kyu no tame no jûyonban—Pari 'Nihon-ten' de no ankoku butô." *Shingeki* 25 no. 12 (December): 96–101.

Ashikawa Yôko. 2018. "Owarinaki butô mesoddo sôzô e no tabi." Tomoe Shizune & Hakutobo, https://www.tomoe.com/text/never-ending1.html. [This essay has taken many forms and been gradually expanded over time. This version first appears on the webpage on December 31, 2018. https://web.archive.org/web/20190306025633/https://www.tomoe.com/text/men u050101.html.

Aslan, Odette. 2002a. "Ikeda Carlotta." In *Buto(s)*, edited by Odette Aslan and Beatrice Picon-Vallin, 149–155. Paris: CNRS Editions.

Aslan, Odette. 2002b. "Introduction." In *Butô(s)*, edited by Odette Aslan and Beatrice Picon-Vallin. Paris: CNRS Editions.

Atkins, Paul S. 2008. "Chigo in the Medieval Japanese Imagination." *Journal of Asian Studies* 67, no. 3 (August): 947–970. doi:10.1017/S0021911808001216.

Aubry, Chantal. 1986. "Kazuo Oono: Naissance, Mort et Resurrection." *Pour la Danse* 127 (July/August). Dossier special Biennale international de la danse de Lyon. Special Suite 4. Np.

Azuma Hiroki. 2009. *Otaku: Japan's Database Animals*. Translated by Jonathan E. Abel and Shion Kono. Minneapolis: University of Minnesota Press.

Baird, Bruce. 2012. *Hijikata Tatsumi and Butoh: Dancing in a Pool of Gray Grits*. New York: Palgrave Macmillan Press.

Baird, Bruce. 2016. "Dancing in an Archive of (Digital) Evocation." *Teatro e Storia* (Nuova Serie) 37: 69–86.

Baird, Bruce, and Rosemary Candelario. 2018. "Introduction: Dance Experience, Dance of Darkness, Global Butoh: the Evolution of a New Dance Form." In *The Routledge Companion to Butoh Performance*, edited by Bruce Baird and Rosemary Candelario, 1–22. New York: Routledge.

Baird, Bruce, and Rosemary Candelario, eds. 2018. *Routledge Companion to Butoh Performance*. New York: Routledge.

BankArt 1929. 2013. "Ôno Kazuo fesutibaru 2013." BankArt 1929. http://www.bankart1929.com/news/pdf/ohnofes2013s.jpg.

Barber, Stephen. 2005. *Hijikata: Revolt of the Body*. London: Creation Books.

Barrault, Jean-Louis. 1951. *Reflections on the Theater*. Translated by Barbara Wall. Westport, CT: Hyperion.

Barthes, Roland. 1982. *Empire of Signs*. Translated by Richard Howard. New York: Farrar, Straus and Giroux.

Basting, Anne Davis. 1998. *The Stages of Age: Performing Age in Contemporary American Culture*. Ann Arbor: University of Michigan Press.

Berman, Leslie. 1988. "New Age Music?" In *Not Necessarily the New Age*, edited by Robert Basil, 250–268. Buffalo, NY: Prometheus Books.

Boisseau, Rosita. 2004. "Carlotta Ikeda: L'intimité brute du butô." *Le Monde*, January 14, 2004.

Boyd, Mari. 2006. *The Aesthetics of Quietude: Ôta Shôgo and the Theatre of Divestiture*. Tokyo: Sophia University Press.

Bradley, Lynne M. 2017. "Found in Translation: Transcultural Performance Practice in the 21st Century." PhD dissertation, Queensland University of Technology.

Brandon, James R., and Samuel L. Leiter, eds. 2002a. *Kabuki Plays on Stage. Volume 3: Darkness and Desire, 1804–1864*. University of Hawaii Press.

Brandon, James R., and Samuel L. Leiter, eds. 2002b. *Kabuki Plays on Stage. Volume 2: Villainy and Vengeance, 1773–1799*. Honolulu: University of Hawaii Press.

Broinowski, Adam. 2016. *Cultural Responses to Occupation in Japan: The Performing Body during and after the Cold War*. London: Bloomsbury.

Brown, Byron. 1981. "Review Notes: Min Tanaka, Pier 3, Fort Mason, San Francisco, December 11, 1980." *Contact Quarterly* 6, no. 3/4 (Spring/Summer): 8–9.

Calamoneri, Tanya. 2012. "Becoming Nothing to Become Something: Methods of Performer Training in Hijikata Tatsumi's Butô Dance." PhD dissertation, Temple University.

Calamoneri, Tanya. 2018. "Butoh Pedagogy in Historical and Contemporary Practice." In *The Routledge Companion to Butoh Performance*, edited by Bruce Baird and Rosemary Candelario, 418–425. New York: Routledge.

Candelario, Rosemary. 2018. "'Now We Have a Passport': Global and Local Butô." In *The Routledge Companion to Butoh Performance*, edited by Bruce Baird and Rosemary Candelario, 245–253. New York: Routledge .

Centonze, Katja. 2009. "Resistance to the Society of the Spectacle: the '*nikutai*' in Murobushi Kô." In *Danza e ricerca. Laboratorio di studi, scritture, visioni* 1, no. 0 (October): 163–186. http://danzaericerca.cib.unibo.it/article/view/1624 (accessed February 2, 2015).

Centonze, Katja. 2010. "Bodies Shifting from Hijikata's Nikutai to Contemporary Shintai: New Generation Facing Corporeality." In *Avant-Gardes in Japan. Anniversary of Futurism and Butō: Performing Arts and Cultural Practices between Contemporariness and Tradition*, edited by Katja Centonze, 111–141. Venezia: Cafoscarina.

Centonze, Katja. 2018a. *Aesthetics of Impossibility: Murobushi Kō on Hijikata Tatsumi*. Venice, Italy: Cafoscarina.

Centonze, Katja. 2018b. "Murobushi Kô and His Challenge to Butoh." In *The Routledge Companion to Butoh Performance*, edited by Bruce Baird and Rosemary Candelario, 226–236. New York: Routledge.

Chen, Sherwood. 2013. "Body Weather/MB Training." IDOCDE (International Documentation of Contemporary Dance Education). June 17, 2013. http://www.idocde.net/idocs/562.

Chong, Doryun, et al. 2012. *Tokyo, 1955–1970: A New Avant-Garde*. New York: Museum of Modern Art.

Coker, Caitlin. 2018. "The Daily Practice of Hijikata Tatsumi's Apprentices from 1969 to 1978." In *The Routledge Companion to Butoh Performance*, edited by Bruce Baird and Rosemary Candelario, 409–417. New York: Routledge.

Cooke, Mervyn. 1998. *Britten and the Far East: Asian Influences in the Music of Benjamin Britten*. United Kingdom: Boydell Press.

Dalmau, Yves. 1991. *Une journée blanche*. Choreography Carlotta Ikeda and Hervé Diasnas. https://vimeo.com/69123304.

Daly, Ryan. 2019. "Everything Feels like the Future but Us: The Posthuman Master–Slave Dynamic in Japanese Science Fiction Anime." Masters thesis. University of Massachusetts Amherst 766. https://doi.org/10.7275/14280113.

Deleuze, Gilles. 1988. *Spinoza: Practical Philosophy*. Translated by Robert Hurley. San Francisco: City Lights Publishers.

Dent, Michelle. 2016. "Review: Hijikata Tatsumi and Butoh: Dancing in a Pool of Gray Grits." *Journal of Asian Studies* 75, no. 1 (February): 246–247. doi:10.1017/S0021911815001874.

Didi-Huberman, Georges. 2004. *Invention of Hysteria: Charcot and the Photographic Iconography of the Salpêtrière*. Cambridge: MIT Press.

Dind, Julia. 2019. "'When I Begin to Wish I Were Crippled': Exploring Ideas and Images of Disability in Tatsumi Hijikata's Work." *Butoh Next Symposium*, October 31–November 3. CUNY Graduate Center.

Doglia, Arnaud. 2011. "Japanese Mass Violence and Its Victims in the 'Fifteen Years' War (1931–45)." SciencesPo, Mass Violence and Resistance—Research Network, October 7, 2011. https://www.sciencespo.fr/mass-violence-war-massacre-resistance/en/document/japanese-mass-violence-and-its-victims-fifteen-years-war-1931-45.html.

D'Orazi, Maria Pia. 2018. "The Concept of Butoh in Italy: From Ohno Kazuo to Kasai Akira." In *The Routledge Companion to Butoh Performance*, edited by Bruce Baird and Rosemary Candelario, 262–275. New York: Routledge.

D'Orazi, Maria Pia. 2019. "Butoh Training and the Quantum Body." Butoh Next: A Symposium to Celebrate and Expand upon the Routledge Companion to Butoh Performance. October 31, 2019.

Dower, John. 1999. *Embracing Defeat: Japan in the Wake of World War II*. New York: W.W. Norton/The New Press.

Druet, Lucille. [2017]. "Carlotta Ikeda: Butô from a Free Spirit." Unpublished manuscript.

Duarte, B. N. 2014. "Entangled Agencies: New Individual Practices of Human-Technology Hybridism through Body Hacking." *Nanoethics* 8: 275–285. https://doi.org/10.1007/s11 569-014-0204-z.

Duncan, Allistair. 1994. *Art Nouveau*. London: Thames and Hudson.

Dunning, Jennifer. 1981. "The Dance: Kazuo Ohno." *New York Times*, July 31, 1981. https://www.nytimes.com/1981/07/31/arts/the-dance-kazuo-ohno.html.

Eckersall, Peter. 2018. "Butoh's Remediation and the Anarchic Transforming Politics of the Body in the 1960s." In *The Routledge Companion to Butoh Performance*, edited by Bruce Baird and Rosemary Candelario, 150–157. New York: Routledge .

Ellwood, Robert S. 1990. "The Sujin Religious Revolution." *Japanese Journal of Religious Studies* 17, no. 2/3: 199–217. http://www.jstor.org/stable/30234018.

Fisher, Margaret. 2006. "Directing the Light Flux Scripts for Cellular Movement." *Performance Research* 11, no. 1 (April): 21–26.

Flournoy, Brechin. 2018. "Global Butoh as Experienced in San Francisco." In *The Routledge Companion to Butoh Performance*, edited by Bruce Baird and Rosemary Candelario, 313–322. New York: Routledge .

Fraleigh, Sondra Horton. 2010. *Butoh: Metamorphic Dance and Global Alchemy*. Urbana, IL: University of Illinois Press.

François, Patrice. 1990. "Carlotta Ikeda à Pully: Danse butoh: L'appel de la danse primale." *Tanz und Gymnastik* 46, no. 1: 22.

Franklin, Eric N. 1996. *Dynamic Alignment Through Imagery*. Champaign, IL: Human Kinetics.

Franko, Mark. 1992. "Where He Danced: Cocteau's Barbette and Ohno's *Water Lilies*." *PMLA* 107, no. 3 (May): 594–607.

Franko, Mark. 2011. "The Dancing Gaze across Cultures: Kazuo Ohno's *Admiring La Argentina*." *Dance Chronicle* 34, no. 1: 106–131. doi: 10.1080/01472526.2011.549404.

Fuller, John (Zack). 2016. "On Endless Dance: Tanaka Min's Experimental Practice." PhD dissertation. The City University of New York.

Fuller, Zack. 2018. "Tanaka Min: The Dance of Life." In *The Routledge Companion to Butoh Performance*, edited by Bruce Baird and Rosemary Candelario, 483–490. New York: Routledge.

G (Goda Nario?). 1977. "Ikkan shita genzai taigen: Ôno Kazuo butô kôen." *On Sutêji shinbun*, October 28, 1977, 5.

Genet, Jean. 1963. *Our Lady of the Flowers*. New York: Grove Press.

Geoffroy, Camila, and Eduardo Oliveira. 2017. *Dancing in Between: A Portrait of Butô with Tadashi Endo*. Bauhaus-Universität Weimar. https://www.youtube.com/watch?v=yla-ZhPEByo.

Gillespie, John K. 1982–1983. "Interior Action: The Impact of Noh on Jean-Louis Barrault." *Comparative Drama* 16, no. 4 (Winter): 325–344. https://www.jstor.org/stable/41153035.

Gôda Nario. 1987. "'Hijikata butô': Sakuhin nôto." Pt. 2. *Asubesutokan tsûshin* 5 (October 5): 38–43.

Gôda Nario. 1994. "'Okâsan' to yobikakeru tachisugata no utsukushii Ôno Kazuo no butô." *Weekly Asahigraph* 3746 (March 4): 19–21.

Gôda Nario. 2004. "Gyôkô wo taigen shita nikutai." In *Hijikata Tatsumi no butô: Nikutai no shururearisumu, shintai no ontorojî*, edited by Morishita Takashi et al., 148. Keio University Press.

Godard, Colette. 1980a. "À Nancy la mort complice." *Le Monde* May 21, 1980.

Godard, Colette. 1980b. "Sankai Juku." *Le Monde*, May 30, 1980.

Godard, Colette. 1982. "'Jomon sho' par les Sankai Juku au Théâtre de Paris: Les métamorphoses." *Le Monde*, April 24, 1982.

Gotô Masatoshi. 1994. "Miki Shigeo no shôgai to gyôseki." *Moruforogia: Geete to shizenkagaku* 16 (November): 30–51. https://doi.org/10.11460/morpho1979.1994.30.

Guttmann, Allen, and Lee Austin Thompson. 2002. *Japanese Sports: A History.* Honolulu: University of Hawai'i Press.

Hall, Dennis. 1994. "New Age Music: A Voice of Liminality in Postmodern Popular Culture." *Popular Music and Society* 18, no. 2: 13–21. doi: 10.1080/03007769408591551.

Hamaguchi Yoshinobu. 2006. "Innovation in Martial Arts." In *Japan, Sport and Society: Tradition and Change in a Globalizing World,* edited by Joseph A. Maguire and Masayoshi Nakayama, 7–18. New York: Routledge.

Hara, Kazuya. 2001. "The Word "Is" the Thing: The "Kotodama" Belief in Japanese Communication: Part II." *ETC: A Review of General Semantics* 58, no. 4: 408–419.

Harada Hiromi. 2004. *Butô taizen: Ankoku to hikari no ôkoku.* Gendai shokan.

Haraway, Donna. 1991. *Simians, Cyborgs and Women: The Reinvention of Nature.* New York: Routledge.

Harley, J. B. 2002. *The New Nature of Maps: Essays in the History of Cartography.* Edited by Paul Laxton, with an introduction by J. H. Andrews. Baltimore: John Hopkins University Press.

Harman, Graham. 2002. *Tool-Being: Heidegger and the Metaphysics of Objects.* Chicago, IL: Open Court.

Hassiotis, Natasha. 2014. *Great Choreographers: Interviews.* Bloomington, IN: Authorhouse.

Hawkins, Richard. 2015. "A Talk as part of Theory of Achievement." Yale Union, Portland Oregon.

Hijikata Tatsumi. 1998. *Hijikata Tatsumi Zenshû.* 2 Vols. Edited by Tanemura Suehiro et al. Tokyo: Kawade Shobô.

Hijikata Tatsumi. 2000a. "Inner Material/Material." Translated by Nanako Kurihara. *TDR* 44, no. 1 (Spring): 36–42.

Hijikata, Tatsumi. 2000b. "To Prison." Translated by Nanako Kurihara. *TDR* 44, no. 1: 43–48.

Hirata, Hosea. 2005. *Discourses of Seduction: History, Evil, Desire, and Modern Japanese Literature.* Cambridge, MA: Harvard University Asia Center.

Hoffman, Ethan, and Mark Holborn. 1987. *Butoh: Dance of the Dark Soul.* New York: Aperture Foundation.

Hopson Nathan. 2013. "Systems of Irresponsibility and Japan's Internal Colony." *Asia-Pacific Journal* 11, no. 52 (December 30). Article ID 4053. https://apjjf.org/2013/11/52/Nathan-Hopson/4053/article.html.

Hosoe Eikô. 1969. *Kamaitachi.* Gendai Shichôsha.

Hosoe, Eikoh, and Ronald Hill. 1986. *Eikoh Hosoe.* Carmel, CA: Friends of Photography.

Houwer, Bibiena, and Steve Teers. *Ex … IT 1995.* Schloss Bröllen/Dive Pictures. https://www.youtube.com/watch?v=Eka3ruG6DD0&feature=youtu.be.

Howes, John F. 2010. *Japan's Modern Prophet: Uchimura Kanzô, 1861–1930.* Vancouver: UBC Press.

Hughes, David. 2008. "Folk Music: from Local to National to Global." In *Ashgate Research Companion to Japanese Music,* edited by Alison McQueen Tokita and David W. Hughes, 281–302. Burlington, VT: Ashgate.

Hurst, G. Cameron. 1982. "Samurai on Wall Street: Miyamoto Musashi and the Search for Success." *USFI (Universities Field Staff International) Reports,* no. 44. Reprinted in *InYo: The Journal of Alternative Perspectives on the Martial Arts and Sciences,* January 2001. https://ejmas.com/jalt/jaltartHurst0101.htm.

Hurst, G. Cameron. 1990. "Death, Honor, and Loyality: The Bushidô Ideal." *Philosophy East and West* 40, no. 4: 511–527. doi:10.2307/1399355.

Huston, Hollis. 1976. "The Zen Mime of Mamako." *Educational Theatre Journal* 28, no. 3 (October): 354–362.

Huysmans, Joris-Karl. 2003. *Against Nature*. Translated by Robert Baldick and Patrick McGuinness. Penguin Classics.

Iimura Takahiko, dir. 2005. *Cine Dance: The Butoh of Tatsumi Hijikata: Anma (The Masseur) + Rose Color Dance*. Takahiko Iimura Media Art Institute. DVD.

Ikeda, Carlotta. 2002a. "Interview: Carlotta Ikeda, butô mobile." *Libération* (online), July 20, 2002. https://www.liberation.fr/culture/2002/07/20/carlotta-ikeda-buto-mobile_410738/.

Ikeda Carlotta. 2002b. *Togué*. La Belle Ouvrage. https://vimeo.com/252342324.

Ikeda, Carlotta, and Jette Bastien. 2001. "Words of Bone and Muscle." *The Open Page* no. 6 (March): 63–65.

Ikeda, Carlotta, and Kamal Musale. 1994. *Ai-Amour, Carlotta Ikeda and Her Butoh*. Dance in Video/Artworks Video. https://search.alexanderstreet.com/view/work/bibliographicent ity%7Cvideowork%7C1773881/ai-amour-carlotta-ikeda-and-her-butoh.

Ikeda, Carlotta, and Spina. 2002. "Spectacle 'TOGUE' Par ARIADONE." Youtube. https://www.youtube.com/watch?v=kvQakqnHnio.

Imura Tôru. n.d. "Tanaka Min: Kôdai ryokuchi." Video (approximately 1977).

Inata Naomi. 2008. *Hijikata Tatsumi: Zetsugo no shintai*. Nihon Hoso.

Inata Naomi. 2018. "Rethinking the 'Indigeneity' of Hijikata Tatsumi in the 1960s as a Photographic Negative Image of Japanese Dance History." Translated by Bruce Baird and the author. In *The Routledge Companion to Butoh Performance*, edited by Bruce Baird and Rosemary Candelario, 56–70. New York: Routledge .

Iribe Shin, dir. 2006. *Tôtai datsuraku, saien*. 6 pts. Noguchi Minoru. Youtube. https://www.yout ube.com/watch?v=sdiw6gCb0pQ.

Isaka, Maki. 2018. "Takechi Tetsuji, the *nanba* Gait, and Japanese Performing Arts." In *The Routledge Companion to Butoh Performance*, edited by Bruce Baird and Rosemary Candelario, 88–91. New York: Routledge.

Itô Takashi. 2014. "Kasai Akira "Nihon kenpô o odoru' dai 2 suteeji o kankô." *Sesshon hausu sutaffu burogu* (blog), May 3, 2014. https://fromstaff.exblog.jp/20670774/.

Iwabuchi, Koichi. 2002. *Recentering Globalization: Popular Culture and Japanese Transnationalism*. Durham, NC: Duke University Press.

Ivy, Marilyn. 1995. *Discourses of the Vanishing: Modernity, Phantasm, Japan*. Chicago: University of Chicago Press.

Jansen, Sara. 2018. "Returns and Repetitions: Hijikata Tatsumi's Choreographic Practice as a Critical Gesture of Temporalization." In *The Routledge Companion to Butoh Performance*, edited by Bruce Baird and Rosemary Candelario, 99–112. New York: Routledge.

Jarrett, Benjamin. n.d. "Body Weather Manipulations." *Body Therapie*. https://bodytherapie. wordpress.com.

Jays, David. 1995. "Dance Umbrella '95: Hervé Robbe, Siobhan Davies Dance Company, Matthew Hawkins and Carlotta Ikeda." *Dancing Times* 86, no. 1023 (December): 271–273.

Jeremiah, Ken. 2010. *Living Buddhas: The Self-Mummified Monks of Yamagata, Japan*. Jefferson, NC: McFarland.

job, jackï. 2018. "Butoh as an Approach to Performance in South Africa." In *The Routledge Companion to Butoh Performance*, edited by Bruce Baird and Rosemary Candelario, 456–463. New York: Routledge.

job, jackï. 2021. "Re-Imagining Race through *Daai za Lady* and Butoh." In *African Somaesthetics: Cultures, Feminisms, Politics*, edited by Catherine F. Botha, 60–78. Leiden, The Netherlands: Brill, doi: https://doi.org/10.1163/9789004442962_006.

Joye, Yannick, and Andreas de Block. 2011. "'Nature and I Are Two': A Critical Examination of the Biophilia Hypothesis." *Environmental Values* 20, no. 2: 189–215. www.jstor.org/stable/23048439.

Kamiyama Teijirô. 2014. *Kamiyama Teijirô shashinshû: I Love Butoh*. Gendai shokan.

Kanazawa Makoto. 1994. "Actors Cut: Maro Akaji." *Kinema Jumpo*, no. 1143 (October): 124–127.

Karatani, Kôjin. 1993. *Origins of Modern Japanese Literature*. Durham, NC: Duke University Press.

Kasai Akira. 2004a. "Hijikata Tatsumi wo kataru: Ishiki no henkaku wo mezashita butôka." In *Hijikata Tatsumi no butô: Nikutai no shururearisumu, shintai no ontorojî*, edited by Morishita Takashi et al., 55–63. Keio University Press.

Kasai Akira. 2004b. "Interview with Akira Kasai." Translated by Haruko Nishimura. *Blog the Boards*. September 27, 2004. https://web.archive.org/web/20050515053853/http://www.ontheboards.org/interview%20translation.pdf.

Kasai Akira. 2004c. *Mirai no buyô*. Dansu waaku.

Kasai Akira. 2013. "Kyô wa ichinichi, kenpô nitsuite omoi o megurashite orimashita." Kasai Akira Blog, September 23, 2013: http://www.akirakasai.com/jp/2013/09/?cat=4.

Kasai Akira and Ishii Tatsurô. 2013. "Artist Interview: A Look into the Choreographic Art of Akira Kasai Fifty Years after Entering the World of Butoh." Japan Foundation Performing Arts Network, February 26, 2013.https://performingarts.jp/E/artinterview/1301/artinterview1301e.pdf.

Kasai Akira, Ishii Tatsuro, and Nomura Kiwao. 2005. "Hatsuwa suru shintai, ugokidasu kotoba." *Bijutsu Techo* 48, no. 3 (March): 54–72.

Kasai Akira and Kawamura Satoru. 1992. *Angelic Conversation*. 2 Vols. Edited by Oda Kaname and translated by Richard Hart. Tokyo: The Hallelujah Series.

Keene, Donald. 1993. "The Plays of Kôbô Abe: An Introduction." In *Three Plays by Kôbô Abe*, translated by Donald Keene, ix–xiii. New York: Columbia University Press.

Kelsky, Karen. 2001. *Women on the Verge: Japanese Women, Western Dreams*. Durham, NC: Duke University Press.

Kimu Yonsu (possibly Kim Yongsu or Yoengsu). 1976. *Shashin: Tanaka Min*. Dansu Waaku.

Kimura Satoshi. 2012. "Shisho to isshô ni odoru shintai: *Ra Aruhenchina shô* no bunseki." In *Ôno Kazuo: Butô to seimei*. Edited by Okamoto Akira, 95–110. Shichôsha, 2012.

Kisselgoff, Anna. 1984. "Dance: Sankai Juku, Japanese Troupe in Debut." *New York Times*, October 31, 1984, C17.

Kisselgoff, Anna. 1985. "The Dance: Kazuo Ohno's 'Dead Sea.'" *New York Times*, November 21, 1985, C19.

Kitano Ryuichi. 2002. "The End of Isolation: Hansen's Disease in Japan." *Harvard Asia Quarterly* 6, no. 3 (Summer): 39–44.

Kleeman, Faye Yuan. 2015. "Body (Language) across the Sea." In *Comparatizing Taiwan*, edited by Shu-mei Shih and Pin-hui Liao, 217–244. New York: Routledge.

"Kansai sutorippu mo bikkuri." 1975. [Title not visible] November 9, 1975. ("Scrap" #5, https://ko-murobushi.com/eng/works/view/17).

Kobayashi Saga. 2005. *Ume no Sunakusa: Butô no kotoba*. Atorie Saado.

Kosuge Hayato. 2018. "The Expanding Universe of Butoh: The Challenge of Bishop Yamada in Hoppo Butoh-ha and *Shiokubi* (1975)." In *The Routledge Companion to Butoh Performance*, edited by Bruce Baird and Rosemary Candelario, 214–225. New York: Routledge.

Kunimoto Namiko. 2018. "Olympic Dissent: Art, Politics, and the Tokyo Olympic Games of 1964 and 2020." *Asia Pacific Journal: Japan Focus* 16, no.15 (August 1): Article ID 5180. https://apjjf.org/2018/15/Kunimoto.html.

Kuniyoshi Kazuko. 1989. "Shômetsu suru kôzô" [Perishing Structure] *Kikan shichô* 4 (April): 81.

Kuniyoshi, Kazuko. 1990. "Butoh in the Late 1980s," transcribed lecture from Orientation Seminars on Japan #19, translated by Richard Hart. Japan Foundation Amsterdam.

Kuniyoshi Kazuko. 2002. *Yume no ishô; Kioku no tsubo*. Shinshôkan.

Kuniyoshi Kasuko. 2004. "Contemporary Dance in Japan: New Wave in Dance and Butoh after the 1990s." Translated by Kyoko Yoshida and edited by Autumn Patterson, 1–10. Walker Arts Center. http://media.walkerart.org/pdf/akira.pdf.

Kuniyoshi Kazuko. 2006. "Two Kinjiki: Diametrical Oppositions." *TDR: The Drama Review* 50, no. 2 (T190, Summer): 154–158.

Kuniyoshi Kazuko. 2008. "Ankoku butô tôjô zenya: Ôno Kazuo sakuhin 'Rôjin to umi' kara mita 1959 nen." *Buyôgaku* 31: 23–33.

Kuniyoshi Kazuko. 2012. "Ankoku butô tôjô zenya: Sengo Nihon no modan dansu to Ôno Kazuo." In *Ôno Kazuo butô to seimei*, edited by Okamoto Akira, 43–94. Shishôsha.

Kuniyoshi Kazuko. 2014. "Chotto okurete, sukoshi hayasugite: Kamiyama-teki shunkan 40 nen." Translated by Kawaguchi Takao as "A Little Too Late, a Bit Too Early: 40 Years of Moments Captured by Kamiyama Teijiro." In *I Love Butoh!: Kamiyama Teijirô Shashinshû*, edited by Minami Shokichi, 476–489. Gendai Shokan.

Kuniyoshi Kazuko. 2018. "On the Eve of the Birth of Ankoku Butoh: Postwar Japanese Modern Dance and Ohno Kazuo." In *The Routledge Companion to Butoh Performance*, edited by Bruce Baird and Rosemary Candelario, 25–36. New York: Routledge .

Kurihara, Nanako. 1996. "The Most Remote Thing in the Universe: A Critical Analysis of Hijikata Tatsumi's Butoh Dance." PhD dissertation, New York University.

Kurihara Nanako. 2000. "Hijikata Tatsumi: The Words of Butoh." *TDR: The Drama Review* 44, no. 1 (Spring): 18–28.

Kuroki Hiroshi. 1990. "Intabyuu: Shintai no naka no "tasha" o sagasu: Ashikawa Yôko to Hakutôbô no genzai." *Kikan shichô* 7 (January): 160–171.

LaFleur, William. 1983. *The Karma of Words: Buddhism and the Literary Arts in Medieval Japan*. Berkeley: University of California Press.

Lamarre, Thomas. 2013. "Cool, Creepy, Moé: Otaku Fictions, Discourses, and Policies." *Diversité urbaine* 13, no. 1: 131–152. https://doi.org/10.7202/1024714ar.

Lambourne, Lionel. 2005. *Japonisme: Cultural Crossings between Japan and the West*. New York: Phidon Press.

Lamolière, Maëva. 2020. "Carlotta Ikeda: Entre exotisme et érotisme, construction d'une figure trouble et subversive." *Loxias-Colloques, 16. Représentations littéraires et artistiques de la femme japonaise depuis le milieu du XIXe siècle*, April 21, 2020. http://revel.unice.fr/sympo sia/actel/index.html?id=1556.

Lawler, Dwayne. 2021. "De-Domesticating the Actor: Applying Ankoku Butoh's Training Process of De-domestication to Develop Presence in Western Actor Training through Experiences of Awareness, Discipline and Energy." PhD diss., Griffith University. https:// doi.org/10.25904/1912/4194.

Le Monde. 1998. "Paris." *Le Monde*, June 18, 1998.

Ledyard, Gari. 1975. "Galloping along with the Horseriders: Looking for the Founders of Japan." *Journal of Japanese Studies* 1, no. 2: 217–254. doi:10.2307/132125.

Loh, Jan Van, dir. 2007. "Ex … it '07." Cuyuyo Films. https://www.youtube.com/watch?v= HEpPGGpeiCo&feature=youtu.be.

Marenzi, Samatha. 2018. "Foundations and Filiations: The Legacy of Artaud in Hijikata Tatsumi." In *The Routledge Companion to Butoh Performance*, edited by Bruce Baird and Rosemary Candelario, 142–149. New York: Routledge.

Maro Akaji. 1994. "Butôka Maro Akaji: Seishun shashinkan Look Back." *Sandê Mainichi* 73, no. 35, August 14, 1994.

Maro Akaji. 1999. "Uzu no Shirushi: Taizôkai mandara kô." *Kyû purasu* [*Cue+*] no. 3, 24–27.

Maro Akaji. 2004. "Shadan to zôshoko: Hijikata Tatsumi no modaniti." *Butai geijutsu* no. 6 (July): 138–143.

Maro Akaji. 2011. *Kaidanji: Maro Akaji ga yuku: Ukiyo tawamuretesôrô*. Asahi Shinbun shuppansha.

Maro Akaji. 2018. "Maro Akaji: Me no hikikata, kinpunshô de hakken." *Asahi Shinbun*, March 15, 2018. https://www.asahi.com/articles/DA3S13402868.html.

Maro Akaji. n.d.a. "Creating Butoh Drama." Unpublished Dairakudakan pamphlet.

Maro Akaji. n.d.b. "Interviews: 1) Maro." Translator unknown. "Edin Vélez Papers and Videos, 1970–1994." Stanford University Libraries. https://searchworks.stanford.edu/view/4084 451, http://www.oac.cdlib.org/findaid/ark:/13030/kt867nb2t9/entiretext/.

Maro Akaji. n.d.c. "Kyôkaisenjô no aato." http://gotoh.com/hanada/syorinji/maro.htm (accessed July 19, 2021).

Maro Akaji and Konuma Jun-ichi. 2005. "Artist Interview." Japan Foundation Performing Arts Network. https://performingarts.jp/E/artinterview/0506/artinterview0506e.pdf.

Marotti, William. 2009. "Japan 1968: The Performance of Violence and the Theater of Protest." *American Historical Review* 114, no. 1 (February): 97–135. https://doi.org/10.1086/ahr.114.1.97.

Marotti, William. 2013a. "Creative Destruction." *Artforum International* no. 51 (February): 192–201.

Marotti, William. 2013b. "The Lives and Afterlives of Art and Politics in the 1960s, from Anpo/Anpan to Bigakkô." In *Anti-Academy* by Alice Maude-Roxby. Edited by Joan Giroux, 27–37. Southhampton, UK: John Hansard Gallery.

Marotti, William. 2015. "The Art of the Everyday as Crisis: Objets, Installations, Weapons, and the Origin of Politics." *boundary 2* 42, no. 3 (August): 79–96. doi: https://doi.org/10.1215/01903659-2919513.

Marotti, William. 2018. "The Problematics of Butoh and the Essentialist Trap." In *The Routledge Companion to Butoh Performance*, edited by Bruce Baird and Rosemary Candelario, 92–98. New York: Routledge.

Marotti, William. 2019. "Hijikata Tatsumi and the Revolution: Revolt of the Flesh in 1968." Butoh Next symposium, CUNY, November 2019. Forthcoming in *The Art of Revolution: Politics and Aesthetic Dissent in Japan's 1968*. Durham, NC: Duke University Press.

Marotti, William. 2020. "The Perception of Violence, the Violence of Perception, and the Origins of Japan's 1968." In *The Red Years: Theory, Politics, and Aesthetics in the Japanese '68*, edited by Gavin Walker, 57–76. London: Verso.

Martin, Ian. 2011. "Cruel to be Kind: Does *Noruma* Work in Bands' Favor?" *Japan Times*, October 27, 2011. japantimes.co.jp/culture/2011/10/27/music/cruel-to-be-kind-does-noruma-work-in-bands-favor/.

Matsuoka Seigô, Tanaka Min, and Maro Akaji. 1985. "Butoh '85: Butô no kokoro to katachi o kataru." *Asahi Jaanaru* 27, no. 7 (February 22): 94–100.

Maza, Sarah. 2012. *Violette Nozière: A Story of Murder in 1930s Paris*. Berkeley: University of California Press.

McLelland, Mark J. 2000. *Male Homosexuality in Modern Japan: Cultural Myths and Social Realities*. Richmond: Curzon.

Melton, J. Gordon. 1988. "A History of the New Age Movement." In *Not Necessarily the New Age*, edited by Robert Basil, 35–53. Buffalo, NY: Prometheus Books.

Michel, Marcelle. 1977. "Le Festival de Nancy—à la Recherche du Geste." *Le Monde*, May 6, 1977.

Michel, Marcelle. 1978. "L'énergie dansée." *Le Monde*, October 12, 1978.

Michel, Marcelle. 1980. "Et toujours Pina Bausch." *Le Monde*, May 27, 1980.

Michel, Marcelle. 1982a. "Carlotta Ikeda, l'embellie." *Le Monde*, January 28, 1982.

Michel, Marcelle. 1982b. "Sankai Juku au Théâtre de Paris: La nudité d'avant l'enfance." *Le Monde*, April 16, 1982.

Michel, Marcelle. 1984. "Rencontre Carlotta Ikeda, la star du buto." *Le Monde*, January 6, 1984.

Michel, Marcelle. 1986. "Métaphores et métamorphoses de la danse buto." *Le Monde*, April 3, 1986.

Miki Shigeo. 1983. *Taiji no sekai: jinrui no seimei kioku*. Chûô kôronsha.

Mezur Katherine. 2014. "Stranger Communities: Art Labour and Berliner Butoh." *Theatre Research International* 39, no. 3 (October): 217–232. doi:10.1017/S0307883314000480.

Mezur, Katherine. 2018. "Butoh's Genders: Men in Dresses and Girl-Like Women." In *The Routledge Companion to Butoh Performance*, edited by Bruce Baird and Rosemary Candelario, 361–370. New York: Routledge.

Mezur, Katherine. 2020. "Cracking History's Codes in Crocodile Time: The Sweat, Powder, and Glitter of Women Butoh Artists." In *Corporeal Politics: Dancing East Asia*, edited by Katherine Mezur and Emily Wilcox, 241–260. Ann Arbor: University of Michigan Press.

Mikami Kayo. 1993. *Utsuwa toshite no Shintai: Ankoku butô gihô e no apurôchi*. ANZ-Do, 1993. Translated by Rosa van Hensbergen as *The Body as a Vessel*. Birchington, UK: Ozaru Books.

Mikhaila. 2004. "Reader Comment: Review of 'Pollen Revolution' by Akira Kasai." Blog the Boards, September 28, 2004. http://www.artsjournal.com/blogs1/otb/akira.shtml.

Miki, Fumio. 1974. *Haniwa*. Translated by Gina Lee Barnes. New York: Weatherhill.

Mikka. 2013. "Kasai Akira oiryutomii koza 2013 in Biwa-kô vol. 2." MA=Ma Blog: https://ame blo.jp/studio-ma/.

Millett, Kate. 2000. *Sexual Politics*. Champaign Urbana: University of Illinois Press.

Mishima Yukio. 1953. *Higyô: Kinjiki daini bu*. Shinchosha.

Mishima Yukio. 1968. *Forbidden Colors*. Translated by Alfred H. Marks. New York: Knopf.

Miura, Hiroshi. 1996. *The Life and Thought of Kanzo Uchimura, 1861–1930*. Grand Rapids, MI: W.B. Eerdmans.

Miyamoto Musashi. 2021. *The Complete Musashi: The Book of Five Rings and Other Works*. Translated by Alexander Bennett. North Clarendon, VT: Tuttle Publishing.

Moeran, Brian. 1987. "The Art World of Contemporary Japanese Ceramics." *Journal of Japanese Studies* 13, no. 1 (Winter): 27–50.

Morishita Takashi. 2000a. "Hijikata Tatsumi no butô to *Barairo dansu*." Translated by Bruce Baird. In *Barairo dansu no ikonorojî: Hijikata Tatsumi wo saikôchiku suru*, edited by Sumi Yôichi et al., 6–8. Tokyo: Keio University Center for the Arts.

Morishita Takashi. 2000b. "Yokô Tadanori *Barairo dansu* postâ wo bunkai suru." Translated by Bruce Baird. In *Barairo dansu no ikonorojî: Hijikata Tatsumi wo saikôchiku suru*, edited by Sumi Yôichi et al., 32–33. Tokyo: Keio University Center for the Arts.

Morishita Takashi and Yamazaki Yôko, eds. 1997. *Bijutsu to butô no Hijikata Tatsumi ten*. Ito, Shizuoka: Ikeda Museum of 20th Century Art.

Morishita Takashi, et al., eds. 2004. *Hijikata Tatsumi no butô: Nikutai no shururearisumu, shintai no ontorojî*. Keio University Press.

Motofuji Akiko. 1990. *Hijikata Tatsumi to tomo ni*. Chikuma Shobô.

Muramatsu, Naoko, and Hiroko Akiyama. 2011. "Japan: Super-Aging Society Preparing for the Future." *The Gerontologist* 51, no. 4 (August): 425–432. doi.org/10.1093/geront/gnr067.

Murobushi Kô and Ishii Tatsurô. 2011. "A Body at Its Physical Edge." Japan Foundation Performing Arts Network. https://www.performingarts.jp/E/artinterview/1109/artintervi ew1109e.pdf.

Nagao Kazuo. 1998 (1978). "Ôno Kazuo no fukokuga." In Ôno Kazuo, *Ôno Kazuo butôfu: Goten, sora wo tobu*, 269–271. Shinchôsha.

Napier, Susan. 1989. "Death and the Emperor: Mishima, Ôe, and the Politics of Betrayal." *Journal of Asian Studies* 48, no. 1 (February): 71–89. doi:10.2307/2057665.

Niedeck, Jeremy. 2018. "'We Need to Keep One Eye Open . . .': Approaching Butoh at Sites of Personal and Cultural Resistance." In *The Routledge Companion to Butoh Performance*, edited by Bruce Baird and Rosemary Candelario, 343–356. New York: Routledge.

Nicely, Megan. 2012. "Choreography from the Outside: Dance Experiments in Thinking, Perception, and Language after 1960." Dissertation. New York University.

Nicely, Megan. 2018. "Growing New Life: Kasai Akira's butô." In *The Routledge Companion to Butoh Performance*, edited by Bruce Baird and Rosemary Candelario, 192–202. New York: Routledge.

Nietzsche, Friedrich. 1994. *On the Genealogy of Morality*. Cambridge: Cambridge University Press.

Nikkan supôtsu. 1975a. "Geijutsu? Tokushutsu shi? Tonikaku hadaka hadaka hadaka." *Nikkan supôtsu*, July 9, 1975, 14. ("Scrap" #10, https://ko-murobushi.com/eng/works/view/17).

Nikkan supôtsu. 1975b. "Nani! Kyôdai de nûdo dato?" *Nikkan supôtsu*, November 9, 1975. ("Scrap" #6, https://ko-murobushi.com/eng/works/view/17).

Nishi Tetsuo. 1960. "Kore ga makoto no 'geijutsu' da: Gaitô ni odori deta ankoku buyô." *Kokusai Shashin Jôhô* 34, no. 10 (October): 61–65.

Nishitani, Keiji. 1982. *Religion and Nothingness*. Translated by Jan Van Bragt. Berkeley: University of California Press.

Nishitani Keiji. 1999. "Emptiness and Sameness." In *Modern Japanese Aesthetics: A Reader*, edited by Michele Marra, 179–217. Honolulu: University of Hawai'i Press.

Nomura, Nao. 2008. "The *Iemoto* System and the Development of Contemporary Quiltmaking in Japan." *Textile Society of America Symposium Proceedings*, 2008. Paper 119. http://digital commons.unl.edu/tsaconf/119.

Nugent, Ann. 1995. "The Paradox of Ariadone." *Dance Theatre Journal* 12, no. 3: 14–17.

Ôbayashi, Taryô. 1984. "Japanese Myths of Descent from Heaven and Their Korean Parallels." *Asian Folklore Studies* 43, no 2: 171–184.

Oe, Kenzaburo. 1977. *Teach Us to Outgrow Our Madness: 4 Short Novels*. Translated by John Nathan. New York: Grove Press.

Oguri. 2019. "Height of Sky: A Dance Exploration Project by Oguri." Body Weather Laboratory Los Angeles, January 8, 2019. https://www.bodyweather.org/projects/2019/1/8/height-of-sky-a-dance-exploration-project-by-oguri.

Ohno Kazuo and Ohno Yoshito. 2004. *Kazuo Ohno's World: From Without and Within*. Translated by John Barrett. Middletown, CT: Wesleyan University Press.

Ôno Kazuo. 1998. *Ôno Kazuo butôfu: goten, sora wo tobu*. Shinchôsha.

Ôno Kazuo Kenkyûjo, dir. 2000. *Bi to chikara* [Beauty and Strength]. NHK Sofutowea. DVD.

Ortolani, Benito. 1995. *The Japanese Theatre: From Shamanistic Ritual to Contemporary Pluralism*. Princeton, NJ: Princeton University Press.

Pagès, Sylviane. 2009. "La réception des butô(s) en France: Représentations, malentendus, et désirs." PhD dissertation, Université Paris 8—Vincennes—Saint Denis.

Pagès, Sylviane. 2010. "Résurgence, transfert et voyages d'un geste expressionniste en France: Une historiographie discontinue et transnationale. Le butô entre le Japon, la France et l'Allemagne." In *Mémoires et histoire en danse*, edited by Isabelle Launay and Sylviane Pagès, 373–384. Paris: L'Harmattan.

Pagès, Sylviane. 2015. *Le butô en France: Malentendus et fascination*. Pantin: CND.

Pagès, Sylviane. 2018. "A History of French Fascination with Butoh." In *The Routledge Companion to Butoh Performance*, edited by Bruce Baird and Rosemary Candelario, 254–261. New York: Routledge.

Patterson, David. 2002. "Cage and Asia: History and Sources." In *The Cambridge Companion to John Cage*, edited by David Nicholls, 41–60. Cambridge: Cambridge University Press. doi:10.1017/CCOL9780521783484.004.

Pears, Pamela A. 2018. "From Alienation to Activism: Richard Wright, Jean Genet and the Black Panthers." In *Paris and the Marginalized Author: Treachery, Alienation, Queerness, and Exile*, edited by Valérie K. Orlando and Pamela A. Pears, 11–26. Lanham, MD: Lexington.

Perron, Wendy. 1999. "The Power of Stripping Down to Nothingness." *New York Times*, November 7.

Poulton, M. Cody. 2014. "The 1960s and Underground Theater [Introduction]." In *The Columbia Anthology of Modern Japanese Drama*, edited by J. Thomas Rimer, Mitsuya Mori, and M. Cody Poulton, 315–325. New York: Columbia University Press.

Prough, Jennifer S. 2011. *Straight from the Heart: Gender, Intimacy, and the Cultural Production of Shojo Manga*. Honolulu: University of Hawaii Press.

Repke, Meredith A., et al. 2018. "How Does Nature Exposure Make People Healthier? Evidence for the Role of Impulsivity and Expanded Space Perception." *PloS One* 13, no. 8 (August 22): e0202246. https://doi:10.1371/journal.pone.0202246.

Rees, Laurence. 2001. *Horror in the East: Japan and the Atrocities of World War II*. Cambridge: Da Capo Press.

Regensburger, Karl, and Ismael Ivo. 2014. "'Life Is Training for Death'—In Memoriam Carlotta Ikeda." ImPulsTanz, https://www.impulstanz.com/en/news/aid2655/.

Rigg, Jonathan. 2007. *An Everyday Geography of the Global South*. London: Routledge.

Rimer, J. Thomas, and Van C. Gessel. 2005. *Modern Japanese Literature*. New York: Columbia University Press.

Sade, Marquis de. 1958. *Hisan monogatari, aruiwa yûgenia do furanvaru*. Translated by Shibusawa Tatsuhiko. Gendaishichosha.

Saitô, Tamaki. 2011. *Beautiful Fighting Girl*. Translated by J. Keith Vincent and Dawn Larson. Minneapolis: University of Minnesota Press.

Sakai, Naoki. 2000. "Subject and Substratum on Japanese Imperial Nationalism." *Cultural Studies* 14, nos. 3–4: 462–530. doi: 10.1080/09502380050130428.

Sandrin, Eric. 1990. "Min Tanaka—The Rite of Spring." *MySandertube*. https://www.youtube.com/watch?v=E9QrTA-Q4Xg.

Sandrin, Eric, and Patricia Hillaire. 1988. "Milford Graves and Tanaka Min Performance—Hakushu." *MySandertube*. https://www.youtube.com/watch?v=8N4P6tz0PRo&list=PLuTPacq5B6EtJCm5HibVn-WIga1sRjfWe&index=50.

Saulnier, Adam, and Serge Aokea; filmography, Phillippe Maillard. 1978. "La danseuse japonaise." *TF1 Actualités 20H*, Television Francaise 1, October 19, 1978. https://www.ina.fr/video/CAA7801575201/la-danseuse-japonaise-video.html.

Schwellinger, Lucia. 1998. *Die Entstehung des Butoh: Voraussetzungen und Techniken der Bewegungsgestaltung bei Hijikata Tatsumi und Ono Kazuo*. Munchen: Iudicium Verlag.

Schwellinger, Lucia. 2018. "Ohno Kazuo: Biography and Methods of Movement Creation." Translated by Charlotte Marr and Rosemary Candelario. In *The Routledge Companion to Butoh Performance*, edited by Bruce Baird and Rosemary Candelario, 113–125. New York: Routledge.

Sellers-Young, Barbara. 1992. "Kanriye Fujima's Adaptation of the Iemoto System." *Asian Theatre Journal* 9, no. 1 (Spring): 71–84.

Senda Akihiko. 1970. "Situation Theater: Red Tent South." Translated by Eric Gangloff. *Concerned Theatre Japan* 1, no. 1 (Spring): 18–25.

Senda Akihiko. 1988. "Kara Jurô, Maro Akaji, Jûnananenburi no kyôen." *Asahi Graph*, May 27, 1988, 24–27.

Senda Akihiko. 1997. *The Voyage of Contemporary Japanese Theatre*. Translated by J. Thomas Rimer. Honolulu: University of Hawai'i Press.

Shamoon, Deborah Michelle. 2012. *Passionate Friendship: The Aesthetics of Girls' Culture in Japan*. Honolulu: University of Hawai'i Press.

Shannon, Jacquelyn Marie. 2018. "Butoh beyond the Body: An Interview with Shakina Nayfack on Transition, Evolution, and the Spirit at War." In *The Routledge Companion to Butoh Performance*, edited by Bruce Baird and Rosemary Candelario, 388–398. New York: Routledge.

Shibusawa Tatsuhiko. 1986. *Kenrô toshi (Kyunoporisu)*. Fukubu Shoten.

Shiga Nobuo. 2005. "Hijikata Tatsumi no *Kinjiki*: Shôgensha Ôno Yoshito, Gôda Nario." *Bakkasu* [Bacchus] 3 (Summer): 74–79.

Siegel, Marcia B. 1981. "Cultural Exchange: Kazuo Ohno's Admiring La Argentina." *The Soho News*, August 11, 34.

Skord, Virginia. 1989. "Monogusa Tarō: From Rags to Riches and Beyond." *Monumenta Nipponica* 44, no. 2: 171–198. doi:10.2307/2384967.

Slater, Emi. 1997. "Compagnie Ariadone, Le Langage du Sphinx/Le Souffle de la vie." *Total Theatre Magazine* 9, no. 3 (Autumn): 24. http://totaltheatre.org.uk/archive/reviews/compag nie-ariadone-le-langage-du-sphinxle-souffle-de-la-vie.

Slaymaker, Douglas. 2004. *The Body in Postwar Japanese Fiction*. London: RoutledgeCourzon.

Smith, W. Eugene, and Aileen Mioko Smith. 1975. *Minamata*. New York: Holt, Rinehart, and Winston.

Steiner, Charles, and Morleigh Steinberg, dir. 2007. *Height of Sky*. Dance Heritage Video Archive. http://digitallibrary.usc.edu/digital/collection/p15799coll105/id/1513.

Steiner, Rudolf. *An Introduction to Eurythmy*. Translated by Gladys Hahn. Steiner Books.

Steiner, Rudolf. 2012. "Prayers for Mothers and Children." Translated by Harry Collison. Rudolf Steiner Archive and e.Lib. https://wn.rsarchive.org/Articles/Prayers/Prayrsindex.html.

Strassberg, Richard E. 2018. *A Chinese Bestiary: Strange Creatures from the Guideways through Mountains and Seas*. Berkeley: University of California Press.

Streeter, Tal. 1974. *The Art of the Japanese Kite*. New York: Weatherhill.

SU-EN. 2001. *Headless*. Mon no kai/SU-EN Butoh Company. https://www.suenbutohcomp any.net/past-projects/headless/.

SU-EN. 2018. Light as Dust, Hard as Steel, Fluid as Snake Saliva: the Butoh Body of Ashikawa Yôko." In *The Routledge Companion to Butoh Performance*, edited by Bruce Baird and Rosemary Candelario, 203–213. New York: Routledge.

Supree, Burt. 1985a. "Hit Me with Your Best Shot." *Village Voice*, October 29, 1985.

Supree, Burt. 1985b. "Tokyo Trio." *Village Voice*, August 13, 1985, 78.

Susumura Yasuji, dir. 1973a. *Batôki*. Ijoka.

Susumura Yasuji, dir. 1973b. *Yôbutsu shintan*, Ijoka.

Sykes, Jill. 1986. "Bizarre but Very Credible." *The Advertiser*, March 19, 1986, 30.

Tacitus, Cornelius. 1942. *The Complete Works of Tacitus*. Translated by Alfred John Church and William Jackson Brodribb. New York: Modern Library.

Takahashi Kazuko. 2011. "Ōno Kazuo no dansu kyôiku ni kansuru kôsatsu." *Nihon joshi taiiku renmei gakujutsu kenkyû* 27: 1–20. Translated by John Barrett as "Ohno Kazuo's Dance Training and Pedagogical Methods at Soshin Girls' School." Ono Kazuo Dance Studio, 2012. http://www.kazuoohnodancestudio.com/english/archives/analysis/analysis_001.html.

Takechi Tetsuji, and Tomioka Taeko. 2018. "'Inserting the Hip/s' and 'Lowering the Hip/ s': Except from Chapter 1, 'That which is Namba-like' from *What are Traditional Arts? A Dialogue for Criticism and Creation*." Translated by Maki Isaka. In *The Routledge Companion to Butoh Performance*, edited by Bruce Baird and Rosemary Candelario, 85–88. New York: Routledge.

Takeda Kenichi. 1985. "Yôzumi to natta nikutai to shintai no rika." *Gendaishi Teichô* 28, no. 6 (May): 106–108.

Tanabe Hajime. 1990. *Philosophy as Metanoetics*. Translated by Takeuchi Yoshinori. Berkeley: University of California Press.

Tanaka Kôji. 2011. "Kamigata no Omosa." In *Hijikata Tatsumi: Kotoba to shintai o megutte*. Edited by Yamada Setsuko, et al., 30–42. Kyoto: Kyoto Performing Arts Center, Kyoto University of Art and Design.

Tanaka Min (text) and Okada Masato (photos). 2011. *Boku wa zutto hadaka datta: Zen'ei dansā no shintairon*. Kōsakusha.

Tanaka Min. 1987. "I Am an Avant-Garde Who Crawls the Earth: Homage to Tatsumi Hijikata." Translated by Kobata Kazue. In *Butoh: Dance of the Dark Soul*, edited by Ethan Hoffman et al., 65. New York: Aperture Foundation.

Tanaka Min and Bonnie Sue Stein. 1986. "Min Tanaka: Farmer/Dancer or Dancer/Farmer: An Interview." *The Drama Review: TDR* 30, no. 2: 142–151. doi:10.2307/1145733.

Tanaka, Yuki. 2010. "War and Peace in the Art of Tezuka Osamu: The Humanism of His Epic Manga." *Asia-Pacific Journal* 8, no. 38 (September 20): Article ID 3412. https://apjjf.org/-Yuki-Tanaka/3412/article.html.

Tanaka, Yuki. 2019. "'Yamazaki, Shoot Emperor Hirohito!' Okuzaki Kenzo's Legal Action to Abolish Chapter One (The Emperor) of Japan's Constitution." *Japan Focus: The Asian Pacific Journal* 17, no. 20 (October 15): Article ID 5318. https://apjjf.org/2019/20/Tanaka.html.

Tanaka, Yukiko. 1995. *Contemporary Portraits of Japanese Women*. Westport, CT: Praeger.

Temin, Christine. 1986. "Butoh Founder Ohno Rare, Inspiring Performer." *Boston Globe*, July 2, 1986.

Ténenbaum, Yvonne. 1989. "Carlotta Ikeda Corps et Masques." *Pour la Danse* 154 (January): 26–27.

Ténenbaum, Yvonne. 2002. "Ikeda Carlotta, un art de la presence." In *Buto(s)*, edited by Odette Aslan and Beatrice Picon-Vallin, 199–217. Paris: CNRS.

Toku, Masami, ed. 2015. *International Perspectives on Shojo and Shojo Manga: The Influence of Girl Culture*. New York: Taylor & Francis.

Treat, John Whittier. 1994. "Beheaded Emperors and the Absent Figure in Contemporary Japanese Literature." *PMLA* 109, no. 1: 100–115. doi:10.2307/463014.

Ueno, Sako. 1992. "Conflict Arises over Hijikata Legacy." *Dance Magazine* 66, no. 8 (August): 21–22.

Ueno, Tomoo, and Hisashi Miura, dir. 2003. *Bunraku*. Films for the Humanities & Sciences.

UMS Fall 2004 Event Programing Book. 2004. (Interleaved into the *UMS Fall 2004 Season* booklet between pp. 24 and 25). "Kasai Akira in Pollen Revolution," 29–30. https://aadl.org/sites/default/files/docfiles/programs20041002b.pdf.

Uno Kuniichi. 1999. *Shi to kenryoku no aida*. Gendai shichosha.

Uno Kuniichi. 2012. *The Genesis of an Unknown Body*. Translated by Melissa McMahon. São Paulo: N-1 Publications.

Uno Kuniichi. 2013. "Some Episodes through Questions of Media and Body." Unpublished presentation given at the UC Berkeley Media Histories / Media Theories & East Asia Conference.

Uno Kuniichi. 2018. "The Book of Butoh; The Book of the Dead." In *The Routledge Companion to Butoh Performance*, edited by Bruce Baird and Rosemary Candelario, 171–178. New York: Routledge.

Vandenbroucke, Aynsley. "Pretty Girls Devour Akira Kasai" *Reflections on Dance*, October 27, 2007. https://reflectionsondance.blogspot.com/2007/10/pretty-girls-devour-akira-kasai.html.

Vangeline. 2020. *Butoh: Cradling Empty Space*. New York: Butoh Institute.

Van Hensbergen, Rosa. 2018a. "German Butoh since the Late 1980s: Tadashi Endo, Yumiko Yoshioka, and Minako Seki." In *The Routledge Companion to Butoh Performance*, edited by Bruce Baird and Rosemary Candelario, 276–284. New York: Routledge.

Van Hensbergen, Rosa. 2018b. "Waguri Yukio's *Butoh Kaden*: Taking Stock of Hijikata's Butoh Notation." In *The Routledge Companion to Butoh Performance*, edited by Bruce Baird and Rosemary Candelario, 426–436. New York: Routledge.

Vélez, Edin. 1989. *Dance of Darkness*. Electronic Arts Intermix. http://www.eai.org/titles/2337.

Vessey, Julie A. 2018. "My Dairakudakan Experience." In *The Routledge Companion to Butoh Performance*, edited by Bruce Baird and Rosemary Candelario, 451–455. New York: Routledge.

Vincent, J. Keith. 2011. "Translators Introduction: Making It Real: Fiction, Desire, and the Queerness of the Beautiful Fighting Girl." In *Beautiful Fighting Girl*, edited by Tamaki Saitô, ix–xxv. Minneapolis: University of Minnesota Press.

Walker, Brett L. 2010. *Toxic Archipelago: A History of Industrial Disease in Japan*. Seattle: University of Washington Press.

Willems, Caroline. 1993. "Geladen duo-voorstelling van Ikeda en Murobushi in Juli-danspro-gramma; Dans der duisternis van geestverwanten." *NRC Digital Newspaper*, July 14, 1993. https://www.nrc.nl/nieuws/1993/07/14/geladen-duo-voorstelling-van-ikeda-en-murobu shi-in-7189313-a183348.

Williamson, Samuel H., and Louis P. Cain. 2020. "Measures of Worth." *MeasuringWorth*. www. measuringworth.com/definingmeasuresofworth.php.

Winther-Tamaki, Bert. 2001. *Art in the Encounter of Nations: Japanese and American Artists in the Early Postwar Years*. Honolulu: University of Hawai'i Press.

Wood, Ghislaine. 2000. *Art Nouveau and the Erotic*. New York: Harry N. Abrams.

Woodward, Kathleen. 2006. "Performing Age, Performing Gender." *NWSA Journal* 18, no. 1: 162–189. http://www.jstor.org/stable/4317191.

Wurmli, Kurt. 2008. "The Power of Image: Hijikata Tatsumi's Scrapbooks and the Art of Butoh." PhD dissertation. University of Hawai'i at Manoa.

Yamada Ippei. 1992. *Dansâ*. Ota Shuppan.

Yanai Yasuhiro. 2000. "Sakuhin kaisetsu." Translated by Bruce Baird. In *Barairo dansu no iko-noroji: Hijikata Tatsumi wo saikôchiku suru*, edited by Sumi Yôichi et al., 25–31. Tokyo: Keio University Center for the Arts.

Yoshida, Yukihiko. 2008. "Tsuda Nobutoshi to monkaseitachi" *Korupusu* [Corpus] 4 (March): 27–32.

Yoshida, Yukihiko. 2018. "Oikawa Hironobu: Bringing Decroux and Artaud into Japanese Dance Practices." Translated by Bruce Baird. In *The Routledge Companion to Butoh Performance*, edited by Bruce Baird and Rosemary Candelario, 137–141. New York: Routledge.

Zatlin, Linda G. 1997. *Beardsley, Japonisme, and the Perversion of the Victorian Ideal*. Cambridge: Cambridge University Press.

Zrzavy, Helfried C. 1990. "Issues of Incoherence and Cohesion in New Age Music." *Journal of Popular Culture* 24, no. 2 (Fall): 33–53.

Index

For the benefit of digital users, indexed terms that span two pages (e.g., 52–53) may, on occasion, appear on only one of those pages.

Note: Japanese names are given in Japanese name order with the surname first and without a comma between the surname and given name. Dance titles are italicized and followed by the choreographer, a transliteration of the title (where applicable), and the year of the first performance. Scene names and technique names or original dancer concepts are given in quotation marks.

Figures are indicated by *f* following the page number